Militarizing the Border

Militarizing the Border
When Mexicans Became the Enemy

Miguel Antonio Levario

Texas A&M University Press
College Station

This paper meets the requirements of
ANSI / NISO z39.48-1992
(Permanence of Paper).
Binding materials
have been chosen
for durability.
∞ ♻

Library of Congress
Cataloging-in-Publication Data

Levario, Miguel Antonio, 1977–
Militarizing the border : when Mexicans became the enemy /
Miguel Antonio Levario. — 1st ed.
p. cm.
Includes bibliographical references and index.
ISBN-13: 978-1-60344-758-4 (cloth : alk. paper)
ISBN-13: 978-1-62349-302-8 (paperback)
ISBN-13: 978-1-60344-779-9 (e-book)
1. Mexican American Border Region—Ethnic relations—
History—20th century. 2. El Paso (Tex.)—Ethnic
relations—History—20th century. 3. Texas, West—Ethnic
relations—History—20th century. 4. United States—
Foreign relations—Mexico—History—20th century.
5. Mexico—Foreign relations—United States—History—20th
century. 6. Violence—Texas, West—History—20th century.
7. Mexican Americans—Texas—Ethnic identity. I. Title.
F786.L66   2012
972'.1—DC23
2011050642

For my wife, Susie

Contents

List of Illustrations   ix

Acknowledgments   xi

Introduction   1

1. Cowboys and Bandidos:
    A Reexamination of the Texas Rangers   17

2. ¡Muerte a los gringos!:
    The Santa Ysabel Massacre and the El Paso Race Riot of 1916   38

3. "How Mexicans Die":
    The El Paso City Jailhouse Holocaust   53

4. ¡Viva Villa!:
    The Columbus Raid and the Rise of the Mexican Enemy   67

5. "Agents under Fire":
    Prohibition, Immigration, and Border Law Enforcement   88

    Conclusion   110

    Epilogue: "Where the Bad Guys Are"   120

    APPENDIX 1.
    Post Returns for Fort Bliss, 1910–16   127

    APPENDIX 2.
    Demographic Growth
    in El Paso County and City, 1880–1930   134

    APPENDIX 3.
    Special Census of the Population of El Paso, Texas, 1916   136

    Notes   137

    Bibliography   175

    Index   187

Illustrations

1. Brite Ranch after raid   30
2. Sam Neill at the Brite Ranch after raid   30
3. Maurice Anderson and other American victims in Santa Ysabel massacre   46
4. American killed in Santa Ysabel massacre   46
5. American shot near water source in Santa Ysabel massacre   47
6. American shot dead in the back in Santa Ysabel massacre   47
7. Columbus, New Mexico, Home Guard   75
8. Citizens Home Guard, Columbus, New Mexico   76

Acknowledgments

"NO HAY QUE LLEGAR PRIMERO, PERO HAY QUE SABER LLEGAR." THE immortal words sung by Mexican vocalist José Alfredo Jiménez could not be truer for the development of this project. It is because of the generosity and support from many scholars, writers, friends, and family that I was able to conduct research and write this historical narrative. In order for me to do my best to thank everyone it is important that I start from the beginning. The academic genesis of this book began in Enrique R. Lamadrid's Mexican culture and history class at the University of New Mexico one spring semester in 1997. I realized and learned a history unknown to this *fronterizo*. Since that fateful trip through Chihuahua, I have owed a debt of gratitude to *el Profe* for not only opening my eyes to the hallowed stories of *la frontera* but also to the joys of teaching in higher education.

Since my days in Albuquerque and several stops in South Bend, Palo Alto, Austin, and now Lubbock, I benefited greatly from the assistance and guidance of numerous people and institutions. My journey through this intellectual and personal odyssey began in El Paso, Texas, in the C. L. Sonnichsen Special Collections Department of the University of Texas at El Paso. Claudia A. Rivers, head librarian of special collections, was especially generous with her time and expertise regarding the Mexican Revolution and the various archives. Their extensive oral history collection was especially valuable. Also, I would like to thank Thomas F. Burdett, curator of the military history collection at the University of Texas at El Paso. His kindness and direction were valuable to this project.

El Paso's military tradition is rich and extensive. I am thankful to the staff and archivists at the Fort Bliss Museum and Study Center. Jennifer Nielsen and Floyd M. "Twister" Geery were extremely gracious and open to not only share with me some of the invaluable materials located in their fine archive but also to educate me on the vast military tradition right on the Río Bravo/Rio Grande. Moreover, I am indebted to Ms. Nielsen and Ms. Angie Chávez for their work on the Fort Bliss post returns listed in the appendix. I would like to thank the staff of the El Paso Public Library for their assistance in navigating numerous vertical files and their rich photograph collections, especially the Otis Aultman Collection.

A research project positioned within the storm that swept Mexico in 1910 would not be complete without a trip to the Columbus, New Mexico, Historical Society and Museum. Richard R. "Dick" Dean was especially gracious to guide me through their various files and his personal collection. The opportunity provided invaluable insight into a major crux in the project, the role of vigilante justice following the raid.

In no way can I forget the hospitality and generous support I received from the staff of the Archives of the Big Bend at Sul Ross State University. I am especially grateful to the conversations and extensive research material presented to me by B. J. Gallego, field representative for the Archives of the Big Bend at Sul Ross State University. The topic of racialized violence and Big Bend history discussed in this project was largely shaped by the numerous hours spent in their extensive archive. In addition, I would like to thank Melleta Bell, senior archivist at the Archives of the Big Bend, who was a tremendous help and supporter.

In Austin, Texas, I had the great fortune of having access to extensive resource material at various institutions throughout the city and university. Brian Schenik of the Texas Military Forces Museum and Library at Camp Mabry in Austin was an invaluable source of knowledge regarding Texas's National Guard and military history. His expertise and passion regarding military forces in Texas was a tremendous asset in my research regarding the Guard in El Paso and South Texas. I am especially grateful for his sharing of personal mementos from guardsmen that included poems, pictures, and song lyrics. They made quite an impression on me and the direction of this project.

My research on Anglo and Mexican relations in Texas developed in the vast holdings at Lorenzo De Zavala State Archives and Library on the Texas state capitol grounds and the Dolph Briscoe Center for American History at the University of Texas at Austin. I would like to thank the staff and librarians for their patience and care. Their attention to detail and dedication to patrons was exhibited each day I spent sifting through boxes and microfilm. Also, I am indebted to the librarians and staff of the Nettie Lee Benson Library, especially Margo Gutierrez. Her dedication and support of this project will not be forgotten.

This fascinating intellectual journey led me to northwest Texas. I am thankful for the staff of the Southwest Collection at Texas Tech University. Their genuine enthusiasm and passion for all things West Texas was extended to me with every visit and conversation. I am especially thankful to Daniel Sánchez, Jon Holmes, Patricia Clark, Randy Vance, Monte Monroe, and Tai Kreidler for showering me with files and records that supported this project. In addition, I would like to thank Tom Rohrig and Dulcinea Almager of the University Library at Texas Tech University for their guidance in navigating the extensive government collections housed at the main library and ensuring my interlibrary loan requests and extensions. These materials proved vital to my research.

This project stems from a "bottom-up" perspective and cannot present itself as such without the voices of extraordinary everyday people. Several generous and kind individuals opened their family histories to me, and I am humbled by their trust. More specifically, I am grateful to Tony Cano and Ann Sochat. The story of Chico Cano allowed for two *paisanos* from West Texas to bridge generations and find common ground in their love of history and the human story. David Dorado Romo, with whom I share a love for the El Paso–Ciudad Juárez borderlands and its exquisite stories and nuances, reminded me that it is in the "cracks of the sidewalk" where stories are told. His unique approach to El Paso history allowed me to ask more questions and peer around the corners I never thought to pursue. The insight from these individuals allowed me to understand the human story of this historical narrative.

I owe a tremendous debt, for not only the development of this project but also my own intellectual maturation and evolution, to a wide field of scholars. They come from all walks of life and their various perspectives made an impact on this project. Texas Tech, the University of Texas at Austin, the University of Texas at El Paso, and other university communities that include both staff and faculty offered me great support and encouragement throughout this project. I would like to thank Randy McBee, chairperson of the history department at Texas Tech. His continuing support of my professional development has not gone unnoticed. I am also thankful for my close associations with Professors Paul Carlson, Jorge Iber, Rodolfo Rocha, Jeffrey Sheppard, José G. Pastrano, José Ángel Gutiérrez, Anne Martínez, Emilio Zamora, David Montejano, José Limón, Arnoldo De León, Carlos Blanton, and Roberto Calderón. I would also like to thank my friend and colleague, John Klingemann. His unequivocal passion for la frontera forced me to delve deeper into the nuances of borderland studies, and his friendship is an asset and gift. Lastly, I am eternally grateful to my dear friends and colleagues Aliza Wong and Stefano D'Amico. Their genuine love and friendship has made Lubbock and Texas Tech our home. They not only prove to be amazing colleagues by supporting and editing this work but also have become part of our family.

Teaching in higher education is a true passion of mine largely because of the organic relationships developed in and outside the classroom. I do want to acknowledge my undergraduate and graduate students in my classes on borderlands, Texas, and US history—especially Heather Thomas—who read parts of the manuscript and worked tirelessly researching for this project. Our conversations and her meticulous research allowed me to see my work from many vantage points. Undergraduate and graduate students with whom I have developed professional and personal relationships have been especially helpful with their observations, suggestions, and encouraging words. They include Maggie Elmore, Juan Coronado, Ana Satterfield, Valerie Martínez, Beth Callaway, Laura Dixon, César García III, Tracy Stewart, Guadalupe Encinia, Daniel Carrera, Amy Morales, Larry Gaytán, Omar Alcorte, Diego Vega, and Brent Aldendifer.

Every great journey is supported by the generous financial support of individuals and institutions that believe in research-driven scholarship. Texas Tech and the Department of History have been especially generous in supporting the development of this project. I am grateful for the support offered to me by Juan Muñoz, Jobi Martínez, and the Cross-Cultural Academic Advancement Center at Texas Tech in the form of the Faculty Diversity Development Award. I am also thankful to Lawrence Schovanec, Dean of the College of Arts and Sciences at Texas Tech, for the college's Scholar Incentive Award, which allowed me the gift of time to complete the manuscript in a timely manner. I would also like to thank the Harry Ransom Center at the University of Texas at Austin for awarding me the Marlene Nathan Meyerson

Fellowship Endowment and access into their rich holdings regarding the Big Bend and the Mexican Revolution. Parts of this project were presented in a symposium hosted by the Center for Mexican American Studies at the University of Houston and its director, Tatcho Mindiola. The feedback I received allowed me to strengthen specific parts of the manuscript. Lastly, my sincere thanks to Dr. José Limón and the Center for Mexican American Studies at the University of Texas at Austin. Since the beginning of my studies at the university, Dr. Limón and the center nurtured and cared for my growth as a scholar and as a man. I am eternally indebted to them.

Alas, this book was not only shaped by the institutions and resources I utilized but also by the people directly involved in the manifestation of this idea into a piece of scholarship. First, I would like to thank my mentor Emilio Zamora. He served as a supervisor over this project and was a confidant and close friend. Dr. Zamora possesses a selfless attitude and an intense loyalty to his students that is unparalleled. I owe much to Aliza Wong, whose fine editing skills allowed this project to blossom. A debt of gratitude is owed to Mary Spears for her meticulous editorial eye and enthusiasm for this project. Finally, I would like to thank the staff at Texas A&M University Press for their support of this project, especially Mary Lenn Dixon, Thom Lemmons, and Dawn Hall.

This academic journey that was both professional and personal could not have been completed without the love and support of my family and friends. My friends and colleagues are always there to lend their support or order another round of laughs and spirited conversation. My parents, Daniel P. and Catalina Levario, continue to provide a loving foundation for our immediate and extended families. They remind me that perseverance, dedication, love, faith, and *ganas* are the way to navigate the complex web of life. My brothers, José Daniel and René Levario, are without a doubt the best brothers any person can ask for in a lifetime. Their unconditional love and encouragement has allowed me to live out this wonderful path. Finally, my wife, Susanna Levario, teaches and shows me a profound love and comfort that is unmatched by anything in this world. This book was completed because of her selfless support of my professional endeavors and her endless love for our family, now blessed with our son, Diego Ysidro.

Militarizing the Border

Introduction

> This explains why the character of the movement is both desperate and redemptive . . . they mean that the people refuse all outside help, every imported scheme, every idea lacking some profound relationship to their intimate feelings, and that instead they turn to themselves. This desperation, this refusal to be saved by an alien project, is characteristic of the person who rejects all consolidation and shuts himself up in his private world: he is alone. At the same moment, however, his solitude becomes an effort at communion. Once again, despair and solitude, redemption and communion are equivalent terms.
> —Octavio Paz, *El laberinto de la soledad*

I REMEMBER THE DAILY TWENTY-MILE DRIVE TO SCHOOL from Anthony, Texas, to El Paso. My brothers and I attended a small all-male Catholic high school nestled near the downtown district. One morning, as we approached the stretch of highway that hugs the University of Texas at El Paso, I noticed that the city was preparing for war. Perhaps war, not in the traditional sense, but a war nonetheless as a long line of Border Patrol trucks had positioned themselves side by side along the banks of the Rio Grande to guard against what some people along the border called an "immigrant invasion." It was 1993, the El Paso Border Patrol chief, Silvestre Reyes, had initiated Operation Blockade, later renamed Operation Hold the Line. The strategy called for border agents to stand watch at the boundary line to deter immigrants from crossing illegally into the country.[1] I was confused, incensed, indignant, but I dismissed those feelings as we found our usual parking spot in front of the Stanton Street entrance of Cathedral High School. I have never forgotten the sight of that standoff as we made our daily journey to school that morning.

This project began on that day in 1993. Since then I have tried to discern as much as I could about militarization and migration from Mexico, its causes and explanations. Now that I have the opportunity to systematically expand this understanding, I have chosen to address the history of the West Texas region, in particular its early formative history of racial and international conflict, during the late nineteenth and early twentieth centuries, when US officials sought to pacify the area and incorporate it into the larger national socioeconomic framework. A review of this time period will explain how militarization during the late nineteenth and early twentieth centuries informed enduring relations between Mexicans and Anglos and, to a lesser degree, the relations between the United States and Mexico.[2] A timely study, as twenty-first-century political and social debates once again center on border security and immigration from Mexico. A variety of parallels can be drawn by reviewing early militarization and social relations along the US-Mexico borderlands, which at the turn of the twentieth century reflected broader concerns such as national security, illicit smuggling of goods and people, and citizenship. Militarization in the early twentieth century broadened the scope by which ethnic Mexicans could be categorized and marginalized from the main fabric of the nation.[3]

Militarization and the Mexican Enemy

Border scholar Timothy Dunn broadly defines militarization as the use of military rhetoric and ideology as well as military tactics, strategy, and forces.[4] A more concrete definition of militarization that focuses on the specific US military doctrine of low-intensity conflict will be utilized. According to Dunn, the doctrine orders for integrated and coordinated efforts of police, paramilitary, and military forces to establish and maintain social control over a targeted civilian population.[5] However, a historical overview of militarization along the US-Mexico international boundary line suggests that law enforcement agencies made up only part of the militarization paradigm. Organized and vigilante citizens often partook in low-intensity conflict and responded to perceived threats to their immediate communities and the state as a whole. This expanded prototype of militarization that includes mobilized civilians demonstrates that militarization went far beyond policing and into aggressive acts of war. Militarization at the turn of the twentieth century contributed to a historical construction of ethnic Mexicans as an "enemy other" rather than simply as a racialized other.[6] The introduction of civilian, local, state, and federal authoritative institutions in West Texas was not only a response to regional and international circumstances that called for vigilant policing of the US-Mexico border, it also evolved into protection of the American homogenous society from ethnic Mexicans. Their categorization as interlopers and enemies of the state by the authority structure constituted an act of war on the Mexican community at large.

Resistance to a changing demographic spurred by mass migration from Mexico in the early decades of the twentieth century prompted many in their respective communities to react. The question of "Who is American?" or "Who belongs?" underscored the general sentiment of an anxious society along the US-Mexico border. Borderlands scholar Elizabeth Benton-Cohen, for instance, argues that in 1917 state and private forces in Arizona policed the border in terms that often "invoked race and nation simultaneously."[7] More specifically, racial identities were increasingly tied to national constructs where "American" was "white" and "Mexican" came to mean the opposite of both.[8] Legal scholar Mae Ngai furthers this argument by stating that the "idea of racial 'difference' began to supplant that of racial superiority as the basis for exclusionary policies."[9] As a result of such policies ethnic Mexicans emerged as "alien citizens" who, despite legal residence or formal citizenship, "remain[ed] alien in the eyes of the nation."[10] An extensive authority structure that included both state and private forces enforced the building of these segregated national and racial boundaries. The mere presence of Mexicans threatened the very fabric of American society. Therefore, according to Anglo citizens and the complex authority structure, ethnic Mexicans required vigilant and punitive measures by law enforcement agencies and private organizations. As a result of these organized militarization efforts the ethnic Mexican emerged as an enemy of the state, or "enemy other" and not simply as "non-American" or "nonwhite."

The state plays an active and important role in the formation of the Mexican "enemy other." This study expands Chinese immigration scholar Erika Lee's observations on the role of the state as a system of governmental structures and policies that attempt to organize not only the relationships between people and their government but also relationships and identities among individuals and groups.[11] For ethnic Mexicans in West Texas and along the US-Mexico border, increased policing by state agencies such as the Texas Rangers, National Guard, US Army, and Border Patrol suggested that the state and local communities categorically identified the ethnic Mexican as a threat that required vigilance and punitive action. The state's presence along the border shaped and reinforced the identity of ethnic Mexicans as an "enemy" that must be subdued less their presence undermine the social, political, and cultural fabric of white America.[12] The state viewed ethnic Mexicans as "foreign" and the antithesis of "American" and also used increased militarization efforts to synthesize Mexicans as a threat to American society, its institutions, and Anglo hegemony.

Furthermore, this study demonstrates that militarization complicated social relations and deepened racial and international divisions. "Border troubles" of the early twentieth century gave shape to an authority structure that was composed of border institutions that sought to pacify the region with ever-increasing vigilance and reprisal. The result of such measures was a disciplined society that reinforced racial segregation in towns and regions along the border, especially in El Paso and West Texas, and the vilification of ethnic Mexicans in the region.

The history of border areas cannot be fully understood without examining their early militarization and the relationship of this formative development to social relations in local communities. More specifically, the history of the relationship between law enforcement, military, civil and political institutions, and local communities in the border region around West Texas contributed to the building of two separate, distinct, and racially divided communities. This occurred at two levels—within West Texas and between the United States and Mexico. This study spans the period between 1895 and 1933, during a time when West Texas and El Paso experienced intense militarization efforts by local, state, and federal authorities who were responding to local and international pressures. When under stress, local authorities and Anglos took the opportunity to reinforce their position as the final mediators in cases involving racialized social conflict. Militarization was regarded as a viable and often necessary option. Moreover, the conflict in West Texas demonstrated that the Mexican Revolution, Prohibition, and increased immigration from Mexico figured prominently into relations between Mexico and the United States and into local affairs. On the border, race relations and assimilation were increasingly problematic as Mexicans expressed mixed political allegiances, cultural attachments, and a migratory identity. Anglo conduct during this volatile period validated the long-standing image

3

whites held that Mexicans, regardless of citizenship status, were foreigners and enemies of the state. The special census conducted in January 1916 was designed to identify and "segregate" Mexicans from Anglos, and practically confirmed the Mexicans' position as such.[13]

A case study approach highlights specific events, institutions, and public figures that took part in militarizing the region and in establishing US authority in El Paso. They include the US Army, National Guard, the 1916 El Paso race riot, the Texas Rangers, civilian Home Guards, jailhouse holocaust, and the Border Patrol. Scholars have addressed various aspects of the history of immigration, race, and labor in the border region; however, they have given little attention to militarization and the emergence of authority in the integration of Mexicans and Mexican Americans into American society in the border region.[14] A case study and chronological approach allows for a close examination of both common and unique experiences by each institution in the region. Moreover, a more focused lens aimed at each agency reveals how the community and social relations were affected and varied among authority figures, Anglos, and Mexican residents over time. The complex and varied experiences among authority figures as well as their effects on social relations underlines the tentative nature of this work.

The militarization of the US-Mexico border during the late nineteenth and early twentieth centuries—between 1893 and 1933—helped define social relations in complicated racial terms as Mexicans became increasingly identified as enemies of the state and not just racialized others. Moreover, militarization reveals the extent to which local, state, and federal officials were willing to undertake to bring order to a highly chaotic situation. The violence spilling over from Mexico, especially during the Mexican Revolution of 1910, and unstable relations between Mexico and the United States as well as the increased political and criminal activity on the US side of the border represented a source of major concern among US officials. During this time, West Texas and El Paso witnessed intense militarization efforts by local, state, and federal authorities responding to local and international circumstances.

The dramatic shift in racial demographics and economic hardships that rapid population growth caused affected race relations between Anglos and Mexicans in El Paso. Similar to the "Africanization" in northeast Texas towns in the late nineteenth century, El Paso's "Mexicanization" in the early decades of the twentieth century contributed to strong racial tensions between the region's Anglo population and newly arrived Mexicans.[15] Anglos and Mexicans sometimes resorted to violence as an extremely tense racial situation rapidly spun out of control.

Militarizing the Border: When Mexicans Became the Enemy examines the history of the West Texas region while focusing on the changing relationship between the Mexican-origin community and larger society. This study demonstrates the complex militarization process that occurred in the region and denotes the worsening relations between Anglos and Mexicans and to a lesser extent the United States and Mexico. El Paso and Ciudad Juárez serve as ideal examples of this type of transformation as they fully exemplify the transnational setting of West Texas and its complicated establishment of authority. The isolated nature of the West Texas region hampered the process even more. West Texas existed in the periphery of the United States, and its history was intimately tied to the fortunes of another country. Its peripheral and transnational setting encouraged resistance to authority in two general ways. First of all, isolation and the great distance from seats of power and authority bred a frontier society that became naturally defensive toward policies and institutions that sought to integrate it into the nation-state.[16] Second, the Mexican Revolution, one of the earliest social revolutions of the twentieth century, and Prohibition transcended into the region and created local problems in social relations and law enforcement as well as international misunderstanding, conflict, and distrust. Militarization and its process yielded the emergence of the Mexican "enemy other," reinforced divisions between Anglos and Mexicans, and more specifically, the enforcement of a separate and subordinate place of the Mexican.[17]

Militarization at the turn of the twentieth century affected Mexican racial identity and social position in the United States. Many scholars have delved into the complicated racial questions of Mexican and Mexican American identity that affect its social and political standing in the United States.[18] However, a major gap exists in the role that increased militarization along the US-Mexico divide had on the social, economic, and political position of ethnic Mexicans in the United States. One of the consequences of increased militarization in the early twentieth century was the intensification of local tensions and the categorization of Mexicans as the "enemy other." The application of military rhetoric and strategy in policing the border results in a redefinition of border actors. Mexicans crossing into the United States, once seen as principally laborers or migrants, emerge as a national security threat and thus, the enemy. The convergence of military and border enforcement elevated simple infractions such as crossing through an unmarked port of entry once deemed a common practice, or residing in the United States without proper documentation, to a category of national security concern. Within the context of the Mexican Revolution, mass migration, and Prohibition, the resulting transnational violence during this period subjected ethnic Mexicans as enemies of the state and a threat to the moral fabric of its communities. Crossing between the two cities and social relations within El Paso became more rigid and monitored throughout the early part of the twentieth century as violence escalated and distrust intensified between Anglo and Mexican residents.

The US-Mexico Border Zone

This study acknowledges the transnational character of the history of Mexican Americans. The binational ties that Mexican communities maintained across the border serve as a vantage point from which to study national and regional histories as well as a basis for understanding Mexican identity and Anglo concerns at the turn of the century. As borderland scholars Thomas Wilson and Hastings Donnan argue, "borders are contradictory zones of culture and power, where the twin processes of state centralization and national homogenization are disrupted, precisely because most borders are areas of such cultural diversity."[19] The history of the West Texas region as both a point of convergence and divergence reveals several common and interdependent traits as well as contradictions and instances of resistance against the establishment of authoritarian institutions and the national identity they sought to establish. An emphasis on West Texas as a border region that includes the towns of El Paso and Ciudad Juárez provides a transnational perspective from which to study national and regional histories. The study highlights events and authority figures throughout the late nineteenth and early twentieth century to demonstrate how militarization of the region as a pacification, border security, and institutional building initiative incorporated the region and its people into the political and cultural orbit of the United States. The border was initially militarized in the last half of the nineteenth century to pacify the region and to prepare it for eventual incorporation into the US's social economy. During the late nineteenth century and the early twentieth century US authority was firmly established despite challenges that included a general state of lawlessness, great distance from centers of power in Austin and Washington, DC, and the use of Mexico as a safe haven for clandestine behavior and a staging area for violent depredations into Texas. Establishing authority was not without its problems as many West Texas residents often reacted to the imposition of order. The experiences, policies, and programs that included progressive reform, the Mexican Revolution, racial conflict, and immigration framed and informed this give-and-take process of control.

West Texas and northern Mexico, specifically El Paso and Ciudad Juárez, were an important international commercial and political staging point throughout the late nineteenth and early twentieth centuries. The region boasted a growing population and significant economic development in the late 1880s and 1890s spearheaded by the construction of the railroad connecting the cities to their national centers. The heavy flow of immigrants crossing through El Paso and Ciudad Juárez reflected and reinforced the region's development into a bustling port of trade and commerce between the United States and Mexico.[20] The interdependent characteristic of the border region is woven throughout this study; however, as militarization increased in the region, divisions became increasingly more rigid and reinforced. Local tensions continued to escalate. For example, crossing between the two cities and social relations within El Paso became more rigid and monitored throughout the early part of the twentieth century, as violence escalated and distrust intensified between Anglo and Mexican residents.

During the early 1900s, tensions between Anglos and Mexicans worsened as the policies of prohibition and immigration were enforced in the area. State and federal institutions increased their presence and played a significant role in enforcing laws that locals often disobeyed. A complex struggle developed as American demand for illegal goods and labor escalated and Mexico continued to supply it, thus undermining the integrity and effectiveness of law enforcement agencies such as the United States Border Patrol. Much of the violence that visited the border region involved the smuggling of contraband alcohol as border entrepreneurs sought to avoid the Prohibition law by producing alcohol in Mexico, beyond the view of US officials. Crossing contraband alcohol already involved major investments. As a result, a willingness to import it by any means necessary was ever so present, and violent confrontations on the international line often involved Mexican officials.

Many Mexicans, of course, transported the liquor across the border. Consequently, they were associated with the contraband trade as well as with the related conflict that often occurred in the region. The border resident came to be seen as a person who disregarded the law and was prone to violent measures in pursuing the trade. In this way, the enforcement of prohibition laws in West Texas contributed to the racialization of social relations and the creation of a dual society composed of Mexicans and Anglos.

Tension and conflict represented only part of the story of the development of authoritarian institutions along the border. Rapid social and economic development was also evident. Conflict and development, in fact, emerged together during the turn of the century as El Paso entered its first phase of modernization. The city had a reputation as a haven for undesirables, including tough cowboys, Mexicans evading arrest in Mexico, and criminals. This led to calls for the establishment of authoritarian institutions to ensure the smooth transition into modernity. The establishment of a modern Americanized society was expected in a region that was still being incorporated into the US social economy during the late nineteenth century. The tension and conflict that resulted from the Mexican Revolution and racialized relations on the US side complicated life even more and reinforced the call for stability and order.[21]

The Mexican Revolution of 1910

Francisco Madero's call for uprising in November 1910 and the eventual election of Álvaro Obregón in November 1920 traditionally mark the period of the Mexican Revolution. For this study a narrower lens between 1911 and 1917 of the Mexican Revolution is utilized that focuses primarily in what some American soldiers called the "border trouble days."[22] The successful takeover of Ciudad Juárez by the Madero faction and the exile of dictator Porfirio Díaz in 1911 brought the violence of the revolution to America's doorstep. The series of events that unraveled following that historic event in 1911 not only fractured the revolutionists' dream of a democratic Mexico but also destabilized the fragile relationship between Mexico and the United States.

Following his decisive battle victory in Ciudad Juárez, Madero entered Mexico City in June 1911 and by October was elected president. Soon thereafter Madero's allies splintered into various factions. Southern leader Emiliano Zapata, angry over Madero's ambiguity regarding land reform, broke from him and installed his own initiative. In March 1912 Pascual Orozco went into rebellion and aligned himself with Chihuahua's cattle barons and became leader of a band of counterrevolutionaries defending the big ranchers and their vast land holdings. Madero called on the services of General Victoriano Huerta to defeat Orozco, which he did. However, Huerta set his sights on the presidential chair and led a coup d'état against Madero, eventually executing him and his vice president, José Pino Suárez. Huerta's hold on the presidential seat was shaky at best. He encountered opposition from Francisco Villa in Chihuahua, a former federal senator from the northern state of Coahuila, Venustiano Carranza, as well as the Wilson administration in the United States. President Wilson intervened in the Mexican upheaval and aided Carranza's rise to power in 1915. Carranza troops defeated Villa in two decisive battles at Celaya and Guanajuato, resulting in Villa's sharp decline into mere banditry. The Wilson administration extended Venustiano Carranza de facto recognition in October 1915, consequently initiating a violent reprisal by the defeated Francisco Villa and his supporters against the United States and *carrancistas*.[23] Villa's vindictiveness culminated in his attack on Columbus, New Mexico, in March 1916, killing several American soldiers and civilians. The attack demanded a response from the United States in the form of the Punitive Expedition led by Brigadier General John J. "Black Jack" Pershing. Throughout this violent period, the US-Mexico borderlands region served as center stage for a cycle of political and social unrest.[24]

During the Mexican Revolution, numerous revolutionary factions used West Texas as a staging point to organize, recruit soldiers, and acquire supplies. Ciudad Juárez, in particular, served as a major battleground and a critical link for revolutionaries to ship supplies and men to strategic locales. However, revolutionary activity and violence spilled over into the United States, and some residents along the international boundary line experienced incursions on their property by various revolutionary or independent groups.[25] Many of the residents and authority figures in the region attributed the depredations to Mexicans residing in the United States and the influx of immigrants fleeing the turmoil in Mexico.

The tumultuous state of affairs during the revolution gave rise to massive immigration to the United States beginning in 1910 and continuing through the 1920s. Hundreds of thousands of immigrants flooded the US-Mexico border region. The instability in Mexico coincided with economic growth in the American Southwest, accompanied by a tremendous demand for labor.[26] Increased immigration from Mexico also inspired immigration restrictionists to seek tighter controls of the border. As growers grew increasingly dependent on foreign labor, a system of regulated practices that yielded to ambiguous enforcement between the state and employers affected Mexican incorporation into the American social economy. The authority structure played a critical role in facilitating labor, managing border crises, and defining space for the Mexican in the American cultural enclave. The turn of the century and the early 1900s witnessed the establishment of American rule, although conflict continued largely as a result of efforts to discipline the region's population into an American dominion.

Authority Structures in West Texas

In defining the emergent authority structure in West Texas and northern Mexico, I draw on various works, including Marshall W. Meyer's study of bureaucratic authority. Meyer defines this concept as:

the authorization or legitimation of a particular person to issue commands
or obligations that are binding upon other persons (and himself) in a particular situation . . . authority is an attribute that is attached to specific positions and roles.[27]

His assessment of organization also addresses the circumstance of institutional expansion and the continual need to centralize control for optimal
efficiency.[28] Meyer's definition of centralized organization can be seen in the
establishment of formal state and federal authority, policy, and institutions
along the US-Mexico border. However, under the kind of frontier conditions
evident in West Texas during the late nineteenth century, Anglo and Mexican residents occasionally challenged effective centralized control. In light
of Meyer's assessment of organization that depends on centralized control,
the bureaucratic challenges posed by the frontier, such as distance from the
center, international tensions, conflict, and unreliable communication lines,
often decentralized control. Borderlands scholar Oscar Martínez expounds
on Meyer's take on the inability of traditional institutions to extend their
reach effectively into outlying areas by outlining the unique context the frontier poses.

Martínez contends that those in centralized governments and institutions
view the border as a trouble spot that portrays a breakdown of institutions,
social systems, and legal structures.[29] However, it is within this context that
the border functions normally, according to Martínez. By nature, its distance
from the core spawns independence, rebellion, cultural deviation, and lawlessness. The borderlands, as a peripheral area away from the centers of
power, prevented traditional institutions from taking hold quickly and effectively. Isolation from economic and political centers played a key role in
the fundamental breakdown of the state's influence on the border region.
Martínez further explains that this challenge contributed to ad hoc measures
by authority figures in local border areas:

> Isolation, weak institutions, lax administration, and a different economic
> orientation prompt people on the periphery to develop homemade ap-
> proaches to their problems and unconventional means of carrying on mutu-
> ally beneficial relationships across an international boundary.[30]

The frontier conditions present in West Texas and the distance from centers
of power in Washington, DC; Austin, Texas; and Mexico City prompted local residents and officials to make independent decisions separate from the
state. These unique circumstances gave way to an independent spirit that was
sometimes exercised through acts of resistance, conflict, and vigilantism.

C. Edward Weber brings greater clarity to the development of authority
with his claim that power arises out of certain circumstances relating to person, position, and situation.[31] The peripheral status of the US-Mexico border is reflective of Weber's concept of authority. As events unfolded in West
Texas, power was granted and assumed to address the circumstances that
arose along the region. For example, "self-appointed" authority figures such
as vigilante groups and deputized ranchmen emerged as Home Guards or

Texas Rangers. This falls squarely into the category of situational authority that Weber discusses. The conflict raging in Mexico, the violence associated with Prohibition, and generalized conflict in West Texas provided the context for various authority figures and civilians to assume power along with the traditional institutions in the region. Meyer and Weber provide us with a theoretical snapshot of authority that helps us understand the history of border policing and the disciplining of frontier society in the West Texas region. Ana María Alonso offers a definitive perspective on the development of authority and power in the specific space of the Mexico–United States border region, especially as it relates to Mexican-Anglo relations.[32]

Alonso argues that the subaltern discourse of protest implicitly recognizes that power circulates throughout the social body and is not simply concentrated in government structures. Thus a culture of warfare is bred and maintained within the parameters of the frontier. Alonso also discusses the cycle of violence and how a frontier ethos, military training, and the need for social mobility were perpetuated. Authority structures were maintained by force and were critical to the sustainment of power. Furthermore, space and isolation contributed to the power shifts along the border.[33]

A closer look at Sebastian de Grazia's assessment on the subject of authority is necessary in order to further Alonso's argument concerning power. He situates power and the acceptance of authority within the populace. According to de Grazia, the polis holds certain purposes in common:

> they grant authority to whomever they esteem for being able to guide them to these ends. The holder of authority thus is bound by common goals and by his desire and capacity to move toward them.[34]

If those common goals are compromised, then authority over those people is incomplete. In other words, the leader and the community must have a common understanding, regardless of whether the leader is democratically or undemocratically elected.

Recent scholarship on mob violence in Texas at the turn of the twentieth century sheds light on the complexities of race and culture and their impact on conflict. Although race plays a critical role in such bloody episodes, other variables such as social tolerance and culture act as instigating forces as well. Scholars such as William D. Carrigan try to understand mob activity through the perspective of historical memory. Carrigan's study of the horrific 1916 lynching of seventeen-year-old African American Jesse Washington in Waco, Texas, seeks to understand "how a culture of violence that nourished lynching formed and endured for so long among ordinary people."[35] Carrigan delves into Washington's lynching with at least two purposes: to demonstrate why members of the mob and residents of the community tolerated the lynching and to reveal a deeply disturbing part of American racist culture in the early twentieth century.[36] Carrigan's review of Texas's culture of violence since 1835 allows the reader to grasp how a progressive society in the early twentieth century can accept extralegal activity and brutal acts.

The social setting in the West Texas region was consistent with the Alonso, de Grazia, and Carrigan theses. That is, the Texas Rangers, local law enforcement officials, the US Army, the Mexican Army, and vigilantes assumed authority positions but had to seek the approval of the community. Since they were unable to garner sufficient and consistent support, the resultant violence disrupted authority. This led to efforts at reorganizing authority and centralizing its power, which often aggravated tension and conflict. Martínez's analysis is especially useful in understanding the consequences of this. He uses blunt language to describe them: "if national laws appear unjust or are viewed as impractical in a border context, it becomes culturally acceptable to work around them or ignore them altogether."[37] De Grazia adds an important and relevant point:

> In all cases, without respect for a dedication and a capacity related to the common good, authority does not exist. Those who dominate without esteem may have power, may often have obedience, but authority they have not. They are not rulers; they are tyrants, those who cannot lay down a rule.[38]

The breakdown of a common objective between Mexicans and persons in positions of authority in West Texas and northern Mexico, especially in El Paso and Ciudad Juárez, suggests that various law enforcement agencies exercised tyrannical rule in the late nineteenth and early twentieth centuries and that this undermined their legitimacy and provoked challenges to their authority. Moreover, increased resistance by the target community, in this case ethnic Mexicans, provoked increased participation of white civilians that recognized institutional powerlessness and sought to fill the void.

The conceptual arguments regarding authority and its effect on social relations can be seen in West Texas at the turn of the twentieth century. In addition, the circumstances provided by the industrialization of West Texas, the Mexican Revolution, and Prohibition demonstrate how authority and social relations responded and changed over time. The coupling of intense events and West Texas's location along the international boundary line challenged the effective development of authority and complicated social relations between Anglos and Mexicans. For instance, the violence of the Mexican Revolution exported problems of criminality, radical political activity, displaced workers, and frayed social relations. This hampered the ability of US officials to maintain order and affirm their authority effectively. The conflict that ensued in West Texas thus assumed a binational and racialized nature as Mexicans emerged as a threat to American border communities. This is critical for an understanding of the establishment of authority and racial formation in an unruly frontier society in West Texas and northern Mexico in the late nineteenth century and early twentieth century.

Vigilant measures over Mexican crossings on the border and within Texas became more pronounced at the turn of the century. A number of factors contributed to the resulting conflict. For example, northern Mexico's economic downturn in the early 1900s forced mass migration northward and consequentially saturated labor pools and exhausted civil services. Texas's progressive reform in the late nineteenth century antagonized Mexico as it absorbed much of its vice industry. Moreover, the criminality that ensued with increased ranch incursions, or ranch raids, into Texas made ethnic Mexicans a threat to Anglo settlement and authority in Texas's western frontier.

Militarizing the Border: When Mexicans Became the Enemy contributes to the expanding literature on race relations in Texas by noting that factors similar to ones listed above apply to contexts involving ethnic Mexicans. However, it goes further by explaining how circumstances of a transnational nature reinforced long-standing characterizations of Mexican Americans as being "un-American" or an "enemy other," and by examining the projection of anger through violence upon an innocent group. More importantly, following a militarized trajectory of vigilance and policing of the US-Mexico border resulted in protecting the white American community from the Mexican "enemy." Localized conflict in West Texas was responding to broader international circumstances that consequently delayed ethnic Mexican incorporation into the American social, political, and economic fabric. For most of the twentieth century in the southwest United States, "American" generally meant white, while "Mexican" referred to race and not citizenship.[39]

Changing Demographics at the Turn of the Twentieth Century

The dramatic increase of Mexican immigration, a response to the industrialization of the Southwest, caused problems for places like West Texas. The immediate effect was significant Mexican population growth on both sides of the border. This posed several problems. For instance, the increase in the labor supply complicated social relations as Anglos in urban areas began to complain that the workers recruited for agricultural work were entering the cities and posing problems like labor displacement and depressed wages. Although there is no evidence that immigration depressed wages or displaced US workers, organized labor made the claim. This, in turn, provoked added anti-Mexican feelings that were evident in El Paso and throughout the southwest United States.[40] However, labor and a changing economy at the turn of the century were not the only contributing factors to antagonizing feelings toward Mexicans.

Armed conflict between Anglo authorities and Mexican residents also contributed to the view of the Mexican as a threat. This began during the later decades of the nineteenth century, when gangs of thieves and rustlers flourished in the region.[41] Many Anglo and Mexican criminals saw the region as a safe haven because of its relative isolation and access to the international boundary line. Regardless of the presence of Anglos, criminality became associated with the Mexican community. Their cattle raids and killings, directed from Mexico and often inspired by revolutionary thought, increased significantly during the early twentieth century and reinforced the view of Mexicans as criminals. Moreover, the Mexican Revolution led to violent encounters between law enforcement officials and Mexican residents from both sides of the border. For example, the Plan de San Diego, an irredentist movement of 1915–16 that engulfed Deep South Texas in a race war, drew much inspiration from the Revolution, and its partisans received material support from Mexican revolutionaries along the border.[42] By the late 1910s, Mexican residents on both sides of the border were classified as subject "others" and designated as a threat to Anglo security and national sovereignty.

America's moral code also felt threatened by the changing economy along the international boundary line. As the twentieth century began, Ciudad Juárez's economic base changed from a prospering commercial and agricultural hub to a city focused on tourism.[43] At the same time, Texas's progressive agenda swept across the state and forced much of El Paso's vice industry to shut down, relocate to a regulated sector of the city, or move south of the border. Ciudad Juárez consequently came to be characterized as the progressive's immoral "other," the crude and uncivilized contrast to Texas's and El Paso's modern self. The smuggling of contraband during El Paso's progressive reforms reinforced this view of Ciudad Juárez. It also ushered in a violent era. Increased violence between law enforcement officers and smugglers associated criminality and transgressions with the Mexican community as a whole.

The enforcement of prohibition laws later contributed to transborder conflicts. The Texas Rangers, US customs officials, and the Border Patrol all acknowledged that violence in El Paso during 1918–33 was the most intense and added to the difficulty in enforcing policies. Officials in the United States struggled to curb the alcohol smuggling into the country because of lack of resources, including manpower, technology, and the lack of cooperation by Mexican and American officials. In fact, some officials aided smugglers by serving as scouts and armed guards on the border. At times, Mexican residents living along the river also helped smugglers avoid US law enforcement agents. Suspected smugglers and US law enforcement consistently engaged in gun battles throughout the 1920s. All in all, the El Paso border region provided easy access for smugglers and made it possible for them to avoid prosecution. This constituted a major challenge to state and federal authorities.

Chapter Descriptions

This book addresses a binational experience that sheds light on other border regions of the late nineteenth and early twentieth centuries. Modernization engulfed the socioeconomic systems and produced variations of the same general experience along the US-Mexico border. Border towns witnessed the significant growth and expansion of regional economies and, as a consequence, grew significantly in population. The dramatic economic and demographic growth, as well as the violence that resulted from the Mexican Revolution and Prohibition, overtook the capacity of local authorities to ensure a peaceful transition to a modern state. In numerous cases, ad hoc law enforcement actions as well as the overzealous enforcement of immigration and prohibition laws aggravated matters in local areas and created international conflicts. Militarization, consequently, became an acceptable option as law enforcement agencies also sought greater cooperation and efficiency in disciplining frontier society.

A special framework is established in this book that demonstrates that each institution involved in the militarization process shared similar and unique experiences in West Texas. Each one is affected by larger occurrences and consequently impacts social relations in a particular manner. Local, state, and federal institutions differ in how they adjust to local circumstance and execute their individual agendas. Therefore, the discussion of militarization and development of authority on the border is complicated by focusing on each institution and its unique experience in West Texas from 1893 to 1933. The chapters that follow appear both chronologically and thematically. Themes within each chapter are arranged according to the dominant social, political, and economic issue of the time period.

Chapter 1, "Cowboys and *Bandidos*: A Reexamination of the Texas Rangers," introduces the topic of militarization with a reexamination of the Texas Rangers, who acted as one of the earliest law enforcement entities along the Texas-Mexico border. They addressed social unrest and made significant contributions to socioeconomic change in the region. In the shadow of the Mexican Revolution, a separate battle was raging along the Texas-Mexico borderlands. The Texas Rangers, rancher vigilantes, and Mexican residents along the border were violently engaged in a regionally based struggle that was individualistic and highly racialized. So-called *bandido*/bandit gangs and posses comprised of mostly civilian ranchers and law enforcement officials engaged in a complex cycle of vengeance, distrust, and pride that wounded each side and resulted in a divided community.[44] Many of the ranch raids and violent encounters between *bandidos* and state and local law enforcement addressed local wrongs and sought specific retributive acts that later transcended into full-fledged racial warfare. By utilizing a regional scope into banditry and the execution of justice along the border, a clearer understanding of social relations is revealed. As a result of such conflict, Ranger authority changed over time and consequently affected social relations between Anglos and Mexicans.

Chapter 2, "¡Muerte a los gringos!: The Santa Ysabel Massacre and El Paso Race Riot of 1916," addresses the role of the US Army and vigilantes in racialized conflict in 1916. I argue that military force contributed to the racial divisions that characterized social relations in West Texas, especially in El Paso. The chapter focuses on the race riot of January 1916 in El Paso that resulted in the enforced segregation of the Mexican community from Anglos. The chapter goes further by explaining how circumstances of a transnational nature reinforced long-standing characterizations of Mexicans and Mexican Americans as being "un-American" and by examining the projection of anger through violence upon an innocent population. An evaluation of the Santa Ysabel massacre and El Paso race riot of 1916 demonstrates that international militarization in 1916 contributed to the definition of Mexicans as an "enemy other." For most of the twentieth century in the southwest United States, "American" generally meant white, while "Mexican" referred to race and not citizenship. And, lastly, an assessment of the riot demonstrates in stark fashion that Mexicans, despite their citizenship or long residence in El Paso, could be easily identified as proxies for the Mexican revolutionaries responsible for taking American lives.

Chapter 3, "'How Mexicans Die': The El Paso City Jailhouse Holocaust," examines the aftermath of the El Paso race riot and the simmering racial animosity and violence that persisted, despite heavy vigilance by the US military and local law enforcement.[45] A critical policy of delousing and chemical bathing of immigrants and prisoners added a layer of resentment and suspicion upon the Mexican community in El Paso. A public health review of the Mexican sector in El Paso in 1916 revealed that few typhoid cases existed. However, the bathing practice persisted and developed into a contentious policy that negatively affected both diplomatic and ethnic relations between El Paso and Juárez. The delousing and chemical baths took a violent turn when an explosion occurred in the El Paso city jail and subsequently killed over twenty Mexican prisoners in early March 1916. Although it was officially rendered as an accident, contradictory evidence and eyewitness accounts suggest that the explosion was a retributive act by the El Paso police for the atrocities committed in Santa Ysabel less than two months prior. A review of events between January and March 1916 argues that the militarization of the US-Mexico border by American and Mexican troops triggered the mobilization of civilians and reinforced the categorization of Mexicans as a dissident "enemy other." Suspected banditry and sporadic acts of violence that targeted both Americans and ethnic Mexicans proved that the "undercurrent of tension" expressed by several American officials materialized and created a battle zone drawn along national and ethnic lines. The chemical baths and the city jail holocaust serve as examples of the expanded powers of justice assumed by local authorities and civilians.

In Chapter 4, "¡Viva Villa!: The Columbus Raid and the Rise of the Mexican Enemy," an examination of the National Guard and the civilian Home Guard after the Columbus, New Mexico, raid by Francisco "Pancho" Villa is undertaken. The main contention here is that the National Guard and civilian volunteers bolstered racial and political demarcations along the border between the United States and Mexico. More specifically, I demonstrate that the "border trouble days," meaning the border conflict stemming from the Mexican Revolution, required border institutions to move beyond local vigilance and punitive measures and request that federal institutions assume greater responsibility in securing the border. The federal response to the growing security concerns assumed international importance and reinforced a popular view of the Mexicans as the "enemy." It becomes clear during the occupation by the National Guard along the border that institutions evolved from their localized and state settings into more federalized and concentrated power that extended beyond assuring border security to maintaining social order. As the US-Mexico border witnessed pacification, two distinct and racially divided communities emerged. The US military assumed a major responsibility in this process as its relationship with local Mexicans worsened along the international boundary line. Moreover, the intense militarization of the border by the National Guard complicated intergovernmental relations as Mexico came to see the buildup as a direct threat to its national security.

Chapter 5, "'Agents under Fire': Prohibition, Immigration, and Border Law Enforcement," demonstrates the importance of border security in the region and how it changed over time. Enforcement practices, of course, reflected policy changes in immigration and prohibition laws as well as the accommodated needs of employers, mostly farmers, and an alcohol-thirsty populace willing to pay any price for illegal hooch. Further complicating labor and licentious needs, an increase in the Mexican population created a "race problem" that encouraged restrictionists to call for stricter enforcement in order to preserve the nationalist definition of "American" as white. Mexican immigration increased exponentially since the outbreak of the Mexican Revolution and did not diminish after armed conflict had subsided at the end of the second decade. By the early 1920s, nativist groups identified Mexican immigrants as a threat to the ethnic, economic, cultural, and moral fabric of the United States. Following the repeal of the Eighteenth Amendment and on the eve of World War II, the United States military and Border Patrol reevaluated their roles and priorities as the country entered a new phase of international conflict.

Cowboys and Bandidos
A Reexamination of the Texas Rangers

I have never been known to start a fight . . . but I will finish one if drawn to it.
—Chico Cano

AS THE STATE'S PRIMARY PARAMILITARY POLICE FORCE IN
the nineteenth century, the Texas Rangers had the ostensible responsibility
of maintaining law and order, a duty that meant pacifying Native Americans
and securing the Texas border region from the recurring conflict with Mexicans. For some scholars it also meant the Rangers were extensions of the
state and its political system. They acted as agents of ethnic cleansing and
were the enforcers of "an Anglo-Texas strategy and a policy that gradually
led to the deliberate ethnic cleansing of a host of people, especially people
of color."[1] Borderlands scholar Julian Samora adds that the Rangers were
responsible for "securing the rapidly expanding frontier of the [Texas] Republic, and later the borders of the state of Texas. Their reason for being
was not to arrest drunks and chase bank robbers but to fight 'Injuns' and
'Meskins.'"[2] However, as time and circumstance changed so did their work.
The end of the "Indian Wars" in the 1880s, the expanding frontier, and its
isolated character attracted notorious criminals as well as revolutionary-
minded Mexicans. As a consequence, the Rangers became the state's leading law enforcement body on the border at the turn of the twentieth century.[3]

This chapter is not a comprehensive history of the Texas Rangers nor will
it present overwhelmingly new historical evidence related to the notorious
paramilitary state police force. Rather, this case study is a reexamination, or
reconceptualization, of the Texas Rangers in the late 1800s and early 1900s.
A brief review of the Rangers will offer a lens into its role in establishing authority and how the organization is intimately tied to the development of the
border social economy. The organization commonly used harsh methods
to both pacify the region and usher in a new era of economic development.
Pacification and economic expansion involved racialized conflict, the collapse of a complex Mexican social structure, the isolation of Mexicans in the
bottom segment of the working class, and the Americanization of life along
the US border. Historians differ on the degree to which Ranger violence contributed to this momentous change, but they agree that the state police force
played a crucial role. In the last quarter of the nineteenth century, the Rangers battled with a wide variety of criminals and political misfits that plagued
nearly every county in the state of Texas.[4] This consensus, however, does not
take into account significant differences in the Ranger story, nor does it use
these differences to underscore varying consequences to their law enforcement work.

The West Texas and northern Mexican region that encompasses El Paso and Ciudad Juárez offers an opportunity to reevaluate the role the Rangers played in pacifying the border and in establishing racialized American authority. The region stands apart from the remainder of the state with its largely Mexican demographic and isolated mountainous landscape. The vast space and the long border with Mexico as well as the important point of international exchange at El Paso and Ciudad Juárez presented unique and often insurmountable challenges to effectively pacify and develop the region.[5] Its frontier conditions and sequestration from centralized power inclined the border community to self-sufficiency and fierce resistance to outside interference.[6] As a result of the region's natural and social isolation, the Rangers failed to establish effective authority in West Texas as they did in other parts of the state. In addition, highly racialized conflict appeared frequently, as the opposing factions fought to establish authority in the desolate region. Episodes such as the San Elizario Salt War of 1877 and the illegal prizefight between Bob Fitzsimmons and Peter Maher perpetuated the independent spirit of West Texas as many residents resisted state authority. However, border bandit Chico Cano's feud with Ranger Joe Sitters and the Porvenir Massacre underscored an intensely racialized conflict that transcended personal vendetta and vilified ethnic Mexicans all along the Texas-Mexico border. The final years of the Mexican Revolution and what border scholars Charles Harris III and Louis R. Sadler call "the bloodiest decade" of violence between Rangers and ethnic Mexicans sets up a war zone. Policing of the border by the Texas Rangers evolves into an aggressive act of protecting whites from the enemy, ethnic Mexicans residing along the border.[7]

A review of several events in the closing decades of the nineteenth century and the dawn of the twentieth century will reveal that the Rangers were incapable of successfully asserting their power or permanently subjugating border Mexican residents during this period. West Texas also offers an invaluable opportunity to reevaluate the role the Texas Rangers and Anglo ranchers played in antagonizing border relations and in establishing racialized American authority in the early 1900s. The Ranger force became one of the earliest authoritative institutions to categorize Mexicans as "enemies" of the state and to promote Anglo expansion westward. A study of West Texas highlights the varying ways in which Rangers and Mexicans interacted. Furthermore, it clarifies the complex web of distrust, vengeance, and pride that wounded each community and prompted the use of indiscriminate violence as a principle outlet for their rage. A far more complex network emerged that included individual rivalries, such as that between Texas Ranger Joe Sitters and Chico Cano, that would evolve into full-fledged violence and mass murder based largely on race and the categorization of ethnic Mexicans as the "enemy other."

The Texas Rangers, rancher vigilantes, and Mexican residents along the border were violently engaged in a regionally based struggle that was individualistic and highly racialized. "Bandit" gangs and mixed-company posses comprised of civilian ranchers and law enforcement officials engaged in a complex and volatile cycle of vengeance and distrust that evolved into an intense and divisive antagonistic relationship between Anglos and ethnic Mexicans. Much of the current scholarship regarding banditry along the border during the revolution places the narrative within the larger context of the conflict and/or the political agendas of state and federal governments on both sides of the border.[8] However, many of the ranch raids and violent encounters between alleged *bandidos* and state and local law enforcement addressed local injustices and included specific retributive acts that later transcended into full-fledged racial warfare between Anglo and Mexican communities.

In this reexamination of the Texas Rangers, specific attention is given to the retributive acts between "bandits," the Texas Rangers, and rancher vigilantes, which resulted in the racialized grouping of Mexicans as the "enemy other." A closer review of retaliatory acts committed by both Anglos and Mexicans in West Texas will not only provide a better understanding of social relations in the shadow of the Mexican Revolution, but will also underscore vengeance as a catalyst to the bitter battle between so-called Mexican bandits and Anglo authority figures. Moreover, the cycle of violence transcended the inner sanctum of law enforcement officers and suspected bandits and incorporated civilian posses and innocent victims. The grouping of Mexicans as the common foreign enemy by law enforcement officials and vigilante ranchers alienated the Mexican and Mexican American communities from the main fabric of society. The story of authority in West Texas at the turn of the twentieth century is intimately tied to the development of social relations between the United States and Mexico and, more specifically Anglos and Mexicans.

Brief History of the Texas Rangers: "Texas Frontier Law Was Raw, Rough, and Red with Blood"

Since 1823 the Texas Rangers served primarily as a small volunteer force to protect Anglo settlements from Indian intrusions.[9] However, as the Anglo settlements moved westward, the Rangers served as guardians of this expansion. Samora contends that the Rangers were responsible for "pacification" of Native Americans as well as the removal of Mexicans from their lands. This served as a catalyst for Anglo ranchers and farmers to settle the area and profit from Ranger protection. Cattle barons often funded the Rangers to guarantee their protection and influence. Paired with the responsibility of protecting white property and the "clean up" of undesirables, the force became even more militarized. The Rangers were organized under formal leadership, appointed by the governor, and given specific responsibilities that addressed the western frontier and protection of Texas's southern border.[10]

After Reconstruction, the plans to establish a permanent state force assumed greater importance as Texas resented the presence of federal troops in the state and subsequently became less dependent on the federal government. The planning involved James Davidson, the first adjutant general appointed by the legislature in 1870. One early reform of the Rangers occurred in 1874 when Governor Richard Coke created two separate forces, each with unique responsibilities. The larger of the two forces was the Frontier Battalion. It was commissioned to protect the western settlements from Indian raids and, if necessary, punish the raiders. The group consisted of six companies of seventy-five men each, and Major John B. Jones was entrusted with commanding the battalion. Major Jones described his terrain as the frontier that stretched from the Red River to the Nueces. He relied heavily on his fellow captains to mobilize the various companies and supply them adequately. The Frontier Battalion engaged in approximately fifteen Indian battles in 1874, and by the following year, with the help of the United States Cavalry, forcibly displaced the Comanches and Kiowas from the Texas frontier.[11]

The Frontier Battalion operated until 1881. By that time, the Indian strongholds in West Texas had been destroyed. Cattle and land barons took hold in places like Palo Duro and El Paso. Moreover, by 1882 the Southern Pacific and the Texas Pacific railroads made their way to El Paso, paving the way for Anglo settlement to the West Coast.[12]

Governor Coke's reorganization of the Texas Rangers in 1874 included a smaller Ranger contingent known as the Special Ranger Force. A former Confederate scout and guerilla leader named L. H. McNelly led this group of Rangers. The primary responsibility of the Special Ranger Force was to end what the governor identified as a "state of war" along the Rio Grande between "Mexican banditti" and the people of Texas.[13] For many ranchers and farmers along the Texas-Mexico border, the claims of Mexican banditry had become so acute that in 1875 the governor asked Captain McNelly to "clean up" the Mexican cow thieves from the border and to restore order.[14] For much of the next twenty years, the Special Ranger Force acted as a lawless group of "roughnecks," harassing and tormenting West Texas residents who crossed their path, especially Indians and Mexicans.[15]

The reign of the Frontier Battalion and the Special Ranger Force, as commissioned in 1874 by Governor Coke, ended by 1900. Multiple factors played a role in their dissolution. For one, many Anglo cattle barons, especially in West Texas, resented a centralized police force. For them, such a force represented the arbitrary powers exercised by the state during the Reconstruction era.[16] Also, the Rangers' violent behavior throughout the state led to a popular outcry for their dismissal. Finally, jealousy among local law enforcement officers coupled with corrupt recruits also played a role in the reduction of the force.[17] The Texas Rangers were reorganized on June 1, 1900, into a skeleton crew of four companies of six men each, three officers and three privates. The force continued to be responsible for protecting the frontier against marauding and thieving parties and for the suppression of lawlessness and crime throughout the state.[18]

The San Elizario Salt War of 1877

The "border troubles" of the early twentieth century did not develop in a vacuum. In the late nineteenth century, the region experienced one of the earliest race wars and deployments of Rangers into West Texas. Although numerous confrontations occurred between law enforcement officials and El Paso County residents in the late nineteenth century, none were as significant or as telling as the San Elizario Salt War of 1877.[19] This conflict revealed the growing tension between Anglo entrepreneurs and Mexican residents and highlighted the use of local and state-based authority to impose law that disagreed with the daily and accepted practice of the locals. The ensuing resistance by the residents in turn called for a greater degree of law enforcement and supervision.

The San Elizario Salt War involved a dispute over free access to local salt licks located in El Paso County. American and Mexican citizens from both sides of the river had historically used these; however, local officials privatized the area and denied access. Many Mexican residents continued to frequent the salt licks and eventually decided to challenge the privatization of the land. Louis Cardis, an Italian stagecoach manager and local political boss, and Judge Charles Howard, who had bought the disputed land and declared it off limits to local residents, became embroiled in the early phase of the confrontation.

Two men, Mecedonio Gándara and José María Juárez, challenged Howard's bid to control the salt trade and requested a hearing with the county judge.[20] Their case fell on unsympathetic ears, and Judge Gregorio García ordered the two men to be arrested. The incarceration of Gándara and Juárez incited a mob to seek "justice." According to local newspaper reports, several hundred men, most of whom were Mexican, arrested Judge García and Justice of the Peace Don Porfirio García, the judge's brother, and incarcerated them in the county jail.[21] Sheriff Charles Kerber of El Paso County harbored Judge Howard in his home in Ysleta as Howard awaited transit back to Austin. The next morning a band of armed Mexicans surrounded Kerber's house. The standoff ended with Kerber's arms taken away and Howard held in custody by the mob.[22] In an era when many Anglo Texas farmers and ranchers viewed the Mexican as docile and submissive, the mobilization of a Mexican mob to resist perceived injustices and override traditional authoritative institutions is revealing. A socially conscious community existed despite popular ideas of docility.

The mob detained Howard for three days at San Elizario. He was able to win his freedom by promising to give up his claim to the salt licks and agreeing to be exiled from El Paso. Four Howard allies signed a $12,000 bond guaranteeing that the agreement would be carried out. Howard retreated to Mesilla, New Mexico, to plan his next move. On October 10, 1877, Howard confronted Cardis in a store in El Paso and killed him. Many of Cardis's supporters, most of whom were Mexican, demanded Howard's arrest, and tensions began to hit an all-time high. Solomon Shutz, a prominent El Paso merchant; Joseph Magoffin, customs inspector; and other city elites pleaded with the governor for protection from violence and the angry Mexicans:

> Don Luis Cardis was killed this moment by [Charles] Howard and we are expecting a terrible catastrophe in the county, as threats have been made that every American would be killed if harm came to Cardis. Can you not send us immediate help, for God's sake?[23]

Major John B. Jones of the Frontier Battalion organized a detachment of Rangers under the command of Lieutenant John B. Tays of the Presidio Del

Norte, Company C, Frontier Battalion stationed in Ysleta, El Paso County, Texas. Company C had a notorious reputation of disorderly conduct and a lack of discipline. Among many El Pasoans, the company of Rangers was seen as a joke because of accidents involving the death of rangers, deserters, drunkenness, and prisoners escaping.[24] Howard was arraigned for Cardis's murder and admitted to bail under the supervision of Sheriff Kerber.[25]

Again, a group of armed Mexican militiamen seeking retribution for Cardis's death surrounded Kerber's home and demanded Howard be released into their custody. The sheriff surrendered Howard to the group along with Company C of the Texas Ranger force and many of their coconspirators. A firing squad executed Charles Howard and some of his cohort. The remaining Rangers were then allowed to leave the town without their weapons.

Retaliatory efforts were set in motion almost immediately following the execution and humiliating surrender of the Texas Rangers. Sheriff Kerber appealed to white nationalism and patriotic duty when he desperately sent a telegram to Second Lieutenant Simon Vedder, commander at Mesilla, following Howard's death:

> I am informed that Judge Howard will be shot this evening, I am informed that you are in charge of a detachment of a U.S. cavalry, be so kind as to send us those men, do not depend too much on your regulations when the lives of all the white men of this county are endangered. We are about 25 white men but we cannot fight 300, excuse my remarks but for the honor of the Old Army help me and help your countrymen.[26]

Kerber, Tays's Rangers, and several civilians organized an armed outfit to attack San Elizario and the armed Mexicans. Several innocent Mexican residents served as proxies for the crimes of the Mexican militiamen and were harassed and murdered.[27] Order was not restored until "buffalo soldiers" from Fort Davis and other frontier posts were dispatched to El Paso County and were able to suppress the uprising and forced the leaders of the rebellion to flee into Mexico.[28] Finally in 1878, after a haphazard investigation and the reestablishment of Fort Bliss to suppress future uprisings, El Paso area residents paid to access the salt licks under the watchful eye of the Texas Rangers.[29] The tensions resulting from the Salt War persisted throughout the remainder of the century, and racial tension and strife between Anglos and Mexicans subsequently required a heightened number and greater intensity of law enforcement and supervision.

The Salt War underscored two developments that were to reappear at the turn of the century and during the era of the Mexican Revolution. First, residents were "swept up" by circumstances that quickly took on a life of their own. In the process, residents took the law into their own hands and violently expressed latent racial feelings. Second, the opposing factions generally divided themselves along racial lines that transcended citizenship and class. Rangers roamed the streets of San Elizario and nearby Socorro, harassing and killing Mexicans in the wake of the Salt War.[30] The conflict left a bitter impression on many Mexicans, especially the merchants who were to be excluded from the opportunities of the new developing economy. The Salt

War demonstrated that both sides were willing to use force to impose their will, and many Mexicans were left with the distinct impression that social relations had become even more racialized.

Rangers in West Texas

The Ranger account of West Texas that emerged at the turn of the century differed from other areas of the state, in part because residents resisted outside influence and authority. Much of this defiance was attributed to the great geographic distance between West Texas and Austin, the seat of state authority. It was difficult for supervisors such as the adjutant general, who commanded the Texas Rangers, to manage their work. In addition, the isolation of West Texas encouraged local officials and citizens to seek local justice or retribution. Additionally, the international boundary line was a unique obstacle for the Rangers that made evasion from the law more plausible. The variety of problems presented to the Rangers in West Texas included rebellion, defiance, and general disorder. This was evident in 1896 when locals again tested the authority of the governor and Rangers by hosting an illegal prizefight in the region and across the international boundary line, tauntingly and purposefully beyond the jurisdiction of the state police.

The incident began when a boxing promoter named Dan Stewart offered heavyweights Bob Fitzsimmons and Peter Maher $10,000 to fight in Ciudad Juárez. When news outlets reported that the fight would take part near El Paso, Governor Charles Culberson sent a company of Rangers to the city to enforce the state's antigambling legislation. Civic leaders, of course, had anticipated this and went ahead with their plans for the fight to be held outside of El Paso, on a disputed stretch of land in the middle of the Rio Grande.[31] The intrusion by the state was met with stiff resistance from local politicians and the populace.[32]

In preparation for the Fitzsimmons and Maher fight, El Paso mayor Colonel Bob Campbell and the city council called an emergency session and passed several resolutions denouncing "in strong terms" the governor's actions. The council asserted the city's right to enforce laws without the governor's interference.[33] It became obvious at this point that the issue went beyond a boxing match and the desire to evade the law on a single occasion. Underlying the official defiance was a common desire to use El Paso's sister city to circumvent American law on a regular basis, and the most distinguished of citizens and businessmen participated prominently in this regionalized behavior. The business elite, for instance, generally looked at gambling as a lucrative and necessary business for the border region that could be safely promoted on the other side of the border, beyond the watchful eyes of state authorities seeking to enforce prohibition laws and other such "progressive" statutes. State authority, in other words, represented an intrusion in local affairs, and local elites found ways to evade the law almost at will.

Average local residents also resisted the governor's mobilization of the Rangers, suggesting that the defiance of state authority went beyond the local elites. One of the Rangers in El Paso explained that the crowd that gathered for the prizefight had openly threatened the Rangers while they patrolled El Paso. Several cases of violence, including gunfights between the Rangers and local residents, occurred within the city limits.[34] Popular discontent toward the Rangers was widespread throughout the city and among all ranks of society, including the city administration and police.

West Texas Lawlessness—"Pirate Island"

In the closing years of the nineteenth century, Texas Rangers in West Texas not only struggled in building alliances with local authorities and residents but also were unable to successfully negotiate the precarious nature of border geography and jurisdiction. Some believed that lawlessness and criminal activity in West Texas had outmatched local law enforcement officials and ranchers. The center for El Paso's criminal activity was an area known as Pirate Island. The "island" was comprised of 15,000 acres of land that lay between the original riverbed and the channel of the Rio Grande. According to the International Boundary Commission, the original dry riverbed was the boundary line, making the "island" part of the United States. However, half a mile across the line was Mexico, which made for an easy escape for smugglers or suspected cattle thieves.[35] It was covered with brush and became a rendezvous point for a large criminal element in the area. Texas authorities had difficulty patrolling the area since the Mexican line was so close and could place the Rangers out of their jurisdiction and at the mercy of Mexican officials. A small Ranger detachment, Company D, consisting of four men and led by Captain Frank Jones, along with the help of El Paso deputy sheriff R. E. Bryant, enforced the law on the island.[36]

The Holguin "bandit gang," as Rangers called them, controlled smuggling and other clandestine activity on Pirate Island. They were led by three brothers, Severo, Sebastián, and Priscellano, and their father, Jesus María. The gang rose to notoriety following the shooting death of a relative at the hands of Rangers during the San Elizario Salt War.[37] According to Ranger John R. Hughes, who was a sergeant under Captain Frank Jones in 1893, "the gang grew stronger and stronger . . . they [laughed] the 'gringos' to scorn."[38] On June 30, 1893, Captain Jones was ambushed and killed by what was believed to be members of the Holguin gang. The Texas Rangers and the Mexican police, in a joint effort, succeeded in capturing the murderers and imprisoning them in a Juárez jail. However, Mexican authorities later released the individuals and revenge came quickly for Jones's Ranger comrades.[39] Almost immediately upon their release, one of Jones's murderers died. A second was found dead from "apoplexy" near the fallen captain's murder site. Finally, the third assailant was found hanging from a tree from an apparent suicide. Some believe that all of Jones's murderers met an untimely death at the hands of the Texas Rangers.[40] A reckless cycle of violence, hatred, and retribution permeated the region as the memory of injustices burned in the collective conscience of the Mexican and Anglo community. The Ranger force continued to struggle as it sought to establish its authority in the region.

The death of Captain Jones ushered in new leadership and more problems for the Rangers. Under the captainship of John R. Hughes (1893–1915), the Texas Rangers sought more collaborative relationships with both local and Mexican officials to aid in the apprehension of suspected criminals. This was due primarily to Hughes's ability to nurture cooperative relationships with authorities in the region as well as in Ciudad Juárez. For example, Hughes, along with other Ranger officers, developed a relationship with some of the most powerful revolutionary figures in northern Mexico during the revolution.[41] Hughes was also instrumental in grounding the authority of the Rangers on positive relationships with some of the local Mexicans. Hughes understood that the Mexican population in West Texas greatly outnumbered Anglos and that challenges to local Anglo-American authority would be frequent.[42]

Despite the friendly relations that Hughes and others were able to develop with some Mexican revolutionaries, increasing violence undermined hopes for lasting racial peace. Efforts to bridge the gaps between the two communities never fully succeeded. By 1907, depressed economic conditions in northern Mexico and the advent of the Mexican Revolution created fertile ground for revolutionary activity and banditry.[43] Livestock thefts and border raids plagued ranchers living in remote areas of West Texas.[44] Many of the bands exploited the lucrative business of smuggling arms and livestock to advance their own financial agendas or to seek retribution for injustices that the Anglos had visited on the Mexican population. The conditions instigated by the revolution, especially depredations on West Texas ranches by raiders that the US authorities considered bandits, prompted the Rangers to utilize brutal tactics and crude justice aimed at Mexicans who were suspected of participating or collaborating in the raids. Border depredations in the early 1900s became more frequent, and criminality became increasingly synonymous with "Mexican." Throughout the period of the Mexican Revolution, all Mexicans would emerge as a target of the Texas Rangers, and, as a result, Ranger treatment of Mexicans became harsher and more indiscriminate.

At the turn of the twentieth century, smuggling, ranch raids, and political instability in Mexico contributed to tension and the official and public perception of lawlessness. In one report, Captain Hughes of Company D stationed outside of El Paso in Ysleta claimed that there were "more calls for Rangers than I have been able to fill since I have been stationed in El Paso District. I could find places for twice as many men as I have in my company."[45] In his reports dating back from 1907 to 1917, Hughes and his men were kept busy by making several arrests for a variety of crimes.[46]

Tensions between the Mexican community and the Rangers became highly localized and retained an element of racial animosity. In 1908, yet another example of local and racialized defiance occurred in West Texas. Vigilantes confronted Captain Hughes in the area near the Shafter Mines and San Antonio Canyon. Ranger Alex Ross, Ranger Sergeant J. D. Dunaway, Sam McKenzie, and a justice of the peace from the Shafter Mines had gone to San Antonio Canyon to arrest S. A. Wright, an Anglo, for killing a Mexican.

When they returned, approximately thirty-five armed Mexicans demanded that Wright be handed over to them. The Rangers refused and the situation grew tense. According to Hughes's report, "the Rangers refused to give [Wright] up and it looked for awhile like there was going to be war between the Rangers and the Mexicans."[47] The situation was finally resolved when the vigilantes backed down and the authorities took the prisoner to Marfa.

Hughes's reports show little variation in the manner in which laws were violated and enforced. However, as companies of Rangers were dispatched to affected areas, many agitated the volatile situation and were, at times, asked to leave the area. Although they did not note the source of their concern, there was one instance in which the citizens of Clint, a town located southeast of El Paso, petitioned the adjutant general for aid in keeping the peace and, with this petition, Justice of the Peace Homer Wells specifically requested the assistance of the Rangers. Adjutant General James A. Harley responded by sending a group of Rangers led by Jeff Vaughn.[48] The outsiders failed to quell the "troubles" and instead escalated them, according to Wells:

> Some months since Clint and [the] surrounding country petitioned the state for some Rangers and in answer to that petition you sent four men, but the one whom was put in charge of the bunch (They call him Jeff Vaughn.) has acted in such a way as to cause more trouble in the past few months than has been here for months before . . . I hope some action will be taken at once as the longer he remains here the more liable is there be trouble.[49]

According to the petition, Vaughn assaulted an innocent Mexican man for no reason. Wells also noted in his letter that if the Rangers stayed in the area, there was "liable to be serious trouble." Many area residents expressed to the judge that if Harley did not act, they would take matters into their own hands.[50] The Vaughn case clearly demonstrated the disorderly and inflammatory nature of some Rangers and the Mexican community's willingness to defy the group's authority and presence in the area.

Ranch Raids and *Bandidos*

An increasing number of raids on Texas ranches and other forms of violent behavior also contributed to a deteriorating situation in many parts of the state, especially in areas close to the border. Unstable economic conditions in northern Mexico during the revolution forced the working class to reject their oppressed and impoverished condition and act against the landed elites. Anglo-American society viewed these raiders, or "bandits," as outlaws, fugitives, and criminals; however, for some outside observers, they were victims of the Anglo invasion of northern Mexico, later known as the American Southwest.[51] These Mexican bandits viewed the Rangers, Mexican revolutionary soldiers, and US military units as outsiders and were simply protecting their homeland.[52] Eventually, such responses to injustice expanded across the border, and an increased number of Mexicans decided to even scores in Texas. The sparsely patrolled border created an opportunity for many of Mexico's poor border residents to prey on the provisions and herds of ranchers. For some bandits, the decision to raid American ranches was shaped by need, hunger, and most of all, mistreatment at the hands of many gringos.[53] The US soldier, H. F. Bonner, stationed along the border, observed that "although I am gunning for Mexicans constantly, I feel that I too would be a bandit if I were treated as some of these people have been treated."[54] By the mid-1910s, relationships among Mexicans, local authorities, and ranchers were divisive, highly complex, and did not always reflect the simple dichotomous character of good citizen versus bandit.

Further blurring the lines between good and evil, some ranchers in West Texas had business and personal dealings with the same bandits they complained about to the Rangers and local authorities. Ranchers often forged contracts with bandits to recover their cattle or steal livestock from rivals. However, such dealings were volatile and fluid. Ranchers oftentimes later manipulated their relationships with Rangers to opt out of contracts with bandits and therefore fostered distrust and animosity between the two sides.[55]

The relationships between the bandits, ranchers, and Rangers grew increasingly ambiguous as the political tides changed in Mexico during the revolution. In order to obtain some protection for property, the landed elite forged alliances with revolutionary factions near the area. These alliances did not always coincide with the revolutionary-minded bandits in the region. For many area residents and Rangers, it was difficult to tell if a Mexican was a bandit or if he was a friend:

> We knew what we were up against when we seen a bunch of Comanches; there were two things to do, fight or run. You meet a bunch of Mexicans and you don't know what you're up against, whether they are civilized or not.[56]

Although observers like Ranger Sam Neill wondered about the loyalty of locals, he was not unlike many Anglos who ultimately opted for classifying virtually all Mexicans as criminal and threatening. A daughter of a Ranger made the following observation to underscore the fact that whites were infuriated with the Mexican raids on Anglo ranches:

> The [Rangers] were popped off easily and the outlaws stole more Texas cattle than ever [and] they also carried more contraband back and forth across the Rio Grande . . . These conditions made the Texans furious.[57]

The loss of property and lives led to public demand for state and federal officials to provide more protection. The response was a massive military campaign directed at the violence associated with the San Diego revolt in deep South Texas in 1915. The rebellion primarily involved the Texas Rangers and the US Army.[58] Its focus may have been South Texas, but its message of the capacity for Mexican banditry and a disloyal Mexican community spread throughout the border region.

The Bitter Feud: Texas Ranger Joe Sitters and Bandido Chico Cano

Confrontations between the Rangers and bandits often resulted in a great deal of violence and retribution. One factor that augmented violent outcomes was a clear understanding among Rangers that no time should be lost in avenging a comrade's death.[59] These singular vengeful acts often resulted in a broad netting of culpable targets. At times, innocent members of the Mexican community were victim to the harsh treatment and punishment of the Rangers pursuing a suspected bandit. In one such case in West Texas, the violent relationship between Texas Ranger Joe Sitters and so-called bandit Chico Cano reflected the overall conflict evident throughout the Texas-Mexico border and the complicated rendering of social justice.

Chico Cano's name was well known along the border in the Texas Big Bend region. His enemies regarded him as a "bandit," but his supporters regarded him as a hero.[60] Joe Sitters owned a ranch near Valentine, Texas. He worked as a border guard and Texas Ranger, and it quickly became evident that Sitters despised Cano and his defiance of Anglo authority. Sitters adamantly believed that Cano orchestrated and participated in every ranch raid that occurred in the area. In one incident, some of Sitters's neighbors had lost thirteen horses to four armed Mexicans who claimed to be from Pecos. Sitters refused to accept that the Mexicans were from Pecos and insisted that the notorious Chico Cano, who resided some 120 miles south in the Big Bend region, and his friends had taken the horses.[61] Cano violently engaged law enforcement officials and ranchmen as a result of the ill repute Joe Sitters fostered him.[62]

On January 23, 1913, Sitters; Jack Howard, a US customs inspector; and J. A. Harvis, an inspector for the Texas Cattle Raisers Association, set out to capture Cano. Their first move was to raid a Mexican wake on the Texas side of the Rio Grande in Presidio County believing that Chico Cano was present. Sitters called for Cano to come out while his father tried to stall the authorities. The house was surrounded by mounted officers, thus limiting any possibility Cano would have of an escape, and, in an attempt to force Cano out, the Rangers threatened to burn the house down if he did not surrender. After a series of inquiries regarding the safe release of the women and children present at the wake and Cano's safety while in custody, the bandit gave himself up to Sitters.[63]

Everyone at the wake knew that Cano would not make it to Marfa alive. The Rangers had a reputation of killing Mexicans who they alleged had attempted to escape. Before the posse could get too far from Pilares, Cano's younger brother organized several family members and friends to rescue Chico. A gun battle ensued and all three of the law enforcement officers were wounded. Howard later died from his wounds. The incident spawned a series of blood oaths and vows of vengeance. The group that rescued Cano became known as the "Cano Gang." A succession of ranch raids occurred a few weeks after the episode and was reported to be the work of Cano's gang.[64] Although the accuracy of the accusation was questionable, the fact that the Mexicans were armed and willing to engage US authorities created great anxiety among Anglos in the area. The problems between Sitters and Cano reached a boiling point in May 1915.

On May 21, Ranger Captain Jim M. Fox of Marfa, Texas, organized a party of Rangers and local ranchers to investigate fresh claims of stolen horses. A group of Pancho Villa's soldiers, allies of Joe Sitters, informed him that Cano had a large herd of smuggled horses and mules. Sitters saw the opportunity to help Villa and finally kill Cano.[65] The feud reached its climax on May 24, 1915, when Cano ambushed and killed Sitters.[66] Although personal vendettas were the catalyst for this incident, the actions of the Rangers and bandits would later transcend their personal feud and escalate into full-blown racialized conflict.

Tough-Acting Men with a Scared Look:
The Brite Ranch Raid and the Porvenir Massacre

In the late 1910s, Ranger and Mexican violence in West Texas reached a violent apex that firmly placed Mexicans as "enemy others."[67] American civilians wounded or killed along the entire border reached nearly 150 residents by 1920.[68] Texas Rangers in the Big Bend region moved beyond the narrow retributive pursuit of Chico Cano and instead used the series of so-called bandit violence committed in the area to persecute all Mexicans regardless of their innocence or guilt. The massacres at the Brite Ranch and Porvenir demonstrate how a single violent act transcended into the wholesale vilification of ethnic Mexicans in West Texas.

On December 25, 1917, the L. C. Brite Ranch headquarters, located some fifteen miles north of the Rio Grande and near Valentine, Texas, in Big Bend, was raided by a group of Mexican bandits. Ranch foreman Van Neill and his family, all of whom were at the ranch and engaged in a ferocious gun battle with the bandits, succeeded in killing one bandit and fatally wounding several more. The bandits viciously killed a mail carrier and his two Mexican assistants, who recognized the outlaws, and who, to their misfortune, happened to be at the wrong place at the wrong time.[69] The prized items of the ranch's general store were their target, and the raiders quickly filled their bags with various goods.

Word finally got out to Marfa, Valentine, and Van Horn that the Brite Ranch was under attack. In Marfa, ranch owner Lucas Brite immediately organized a posse of law enforcement officials, soldiers, and civilians, a common practice that blurred the lines of official authority and vigilantism, to render aid and pursue the bandits. Soldiers from throughout the area were some of the first to arrive at the ranch and saw the bandits riding off toward the border. However, the soldiers arrived in a car and were unable to pursue the bandits immediately because of the rough terrain of the Candelaria Rim. More people came to the ranch and gave chase after the bandits wounded and killed several of them.[70]

The bold attack on the ranch marked a turning point in the violence that area ranchers had endured. Until Christmas Day 1917, Brite Ranch was immune to much of the violence associated with the revolution. The ranch headquarters, which housed a well-stocked general store, was nearly inaccessible with a natural barrier of mountainous terrain on its southern and western border. Two trails led to the ranch and were traversable only with great difficulty by horse or wagon.[71] The raid on Brite Ranch not only shocked the residents who were attacked but also demonstrated that inland

Figure 1.
Brite Ranch after raid.
Photo courtesy of the Archives of the Big Bend, Bryan Wildenthal Memorial Library, Sul Ross State University, Alpine, Texas.

Figure 2.
Sam Neill at the Brite Ranch after raid.
Photo courtesy of the Archives of the Big Bend, Bryan Wildenthal Memorial Library, Sul Ross State University, Alpine, Texas.

ranchers and residents, those who were several miles from the border and previously were isolated from much of the atrocities of the revolution, were no longer an exception to the threat and reality of violence and raids.

Responsibility for the attack became another source of intense controversy and scrutiny. Rumors and conflicting reports circulated regarding who organized and led the attack. The *El Paso Morning Times* identified one of the bandits killed as Antonio Avila.[72] Eyewitnesses of the raid identified Avila as the leader because he was in front of the pack and he was the first man Sam Neill shot.[73] Others believed that Pancho Villa played a role in the attack. Several eyewitnesses placed the notorious revolutionary leader near Pilares, Mexico, not far from the Brite Ranch.[74] According to Dorothy Messey, many residents believed the raids were politically motivated by Villa, who tried to recapture control of Mexico's northern region from Carranza forces.[75] His imminent presence in the area stirred fear and distrust among Anglo residents in the region:

> In fact, we lived in fear. This is the main thing I remember, is the great fear and dread that we had of the things that went on. They never came to Van Horn, but we'd go to bed at night without lights because we were afraid that lights might attract them or that they could find the place . . . of course [Pancho Villa] was responsible for all the dread and terror that we experienced . . . just his name meant terror, you know. He was a raider, a desperado.[76]

Villa's presence in the region prompted many authorities and civilians to believe he had joined forces with some of the known bandits in the area, and US authorities seriously considered theories of possible alliances between Pancho Villa and Chico Cano. However, at the time of the Brite Ranch raid, the two men were at odds with each other.

Cano left the Villa outfit and sought a higher military commission with the Carranza army and government.[77] In addition, matters were complicated by the fact that bandit gangs often acted independently from Villa and other revolutionary groups. Cano family members reinforced this important point by stating that many of Cano's men, including Jesus "Pegleg" Renteria, did not always ride with him because their services were usually "for sale."[78] The duplicity of Chico Cano and other bandit gangs suggests that fidelity was dependent on survival and not necessarily related to a political cause or philosophy. Strategic positioning and anticipation of political or military change allowed local actors to survive in a hostile environment. Nevertheless, these fluid alliances did not fully protect the likes of Chico Cano from domestic foes like the Texas Rangers and local ranchmen.

Van Neill, foreman of the Brite Ranch, and his Ranger associates immediately pointed the finger at Chico Cano. They identified Cano associates "Pegleg" Renteria and Placido Villanueva among those in the raiding party. The day after the raid, a detachment of Texas Rangers and army soldiers followed a set of tracks to a small village called Pilares, which was a well-known hideout for Chico and his men. The Rangers set Pilares ablaze in order to instigate a confrontation with Cano. At this point, according to reports and Cano family accounts, the soldiers and rangers were determined to "bring Chico to his knees" whether he was involved with the Brite Ranch raid or not.[79]

Lucas Brite, on the other hand, was not fully convinced that Cano was a part of the raid. A secret meeting was held soon thereafter between Brite and Cano to clear the air on who was responsible. Cano adamantly declared his innocence and Brite took him at his word. Both men shared a mutual respect for each other for the work each did for the Mexican community on both sides of the river.[80] The Rangers' willingness to blame Cano despite Brite's hesitation to lend his full support in Cano's capturing demonstrates the narrow focus of the Rangers on Chico Cano and those "affiliated" with the bandit. The razing of Pilares failed to yield the capture of Cano, and the

Texas Rangers set their sights on another of his "hideouts," a small Texas village along the border called Porvenir. Vilification for the Brite Ranch atrocity took a violent turn as culpability befell an entire community simply for being Mexican.

The responsibility of maintaining the peace in the area east of El Paso fell upon Captain Jim M. Fox and Texas Ranger Company B.[81] In many cases, Fox recruited local cattlemen who had grown increasingly impatient with Mexicans suspected of being bandits.[82] As Fox investigated the Brite Ranch raid, he focused his attention on a small village known as Porvenir.[83] The small community lay on the banks of the Rio Grande and was located approximately 170 miles southeast of El Paso, across from Pilares. The village consisted mostly of farmers and small-scale ranchers. Some of the inhabitants lived there for up to six or seven years and were United States citizens.[84] Local area ranchers harbored ill feelings toward the Porvenir villagers and expressed their bad reputation to Fox. Based largely on suspicion and the community's ill repute provided by the ranchers, Captain Fox agreed that the village harbored bandits and needed to be cleaned out.[85] The posse also believed that the residents and its sister city across the river acted as spies and accomplices for Chico Cano.[86]

On the evening of January 23, 1918, the Rangers and several local ranchers surrounded Porvenir, rounded up the Mexicans, and held them at gunpoint while they searched the houses for stolen "loot" from the nearby recently raided Brite Ranch. The Rangers claimed to find some items like soap and other small articles from the ranch and proceeded to disarm the village. They turned over beds and forcibly looked into trunks and boxes in search of arms. Only two firearms were located in the search: one was a pistol belonging to John J. Bailey, the only white man living in the village, and the other was a Winchester rifle that belonged to Porvenir resident Rosendo Mesa. Both were family men and innocent of any wrongdoing according to local schoolteacher Harry Warren.[87] Despite these insignificant discoveries, the Rangers arrested three Mexican residents, Manuel Fierro, Eutimio Gonzales, and Román Nieves, and questioned them before releasing them the following day. The lack of evidence linking Porvenir residents to the Brite Ranch raid did little to protect the community from the wrath of the Ranger force. In the eyes of the Rangers the residents were at least guilty by association.

The Porvenir Massacre, 1918

A few days later on January 28, the Texas Rangers approached Camp Evetts (Diez y Ocho Camp), an Eighth Cavalry border outpost located near Porvenir, where they presented Captain Henry H. Anderson with a letter from his commanding officer, Colonel George T. Langhorne, requesting army assistance.[88] The Rangers believed that Cano and his gang would be there around midnight, and they expected trouble. The US Army's Eighth Cavalry had previously investigated the Brite Ranch and found that the Porvenir residents were innocent of wrongdoing. In addition, Captain Anderson found that all of the men in Porvenir were accounted for on the day of the Brite Ranch raid, and none had previous knowledge of what occurred.[89] Some of the soldiers suspected an ulterior motive by the Rangers. Intelligence reports gathered by army scouts had placed Cano on the Mexican side of the river wearing a Carranza uniform and patrolling the river as a military officer. The military outfit was familiar to the residents, who knew them to be innocent civilians who "wouldn't harbor outlaws."[90] Many among the Eighth Cavalry were reportedly suspicious of the Rangers' intent because none of them had ever been to the army camp. One soldier went further and recounted that the Rangers had never visited the area and were "in reality the only group of officers in the county, who knew nothing about river conditions, their head-quarters [were in] Marfa, sixty miles from where all of the Big Bend trouble originated."[91] After confirming the validity of the letter and order, Captain Anderson mobilized his men, the Rangers, and several local ranchers, in-cluding Buck Pool, John Pool, Tom Snyder, and Raymond Fitzgerald, to Por-venir.[92] Despite Captain Anderson's suspicions, the soldiers and Rangers acted with impunity and ambushed the village in the late hours of the night.[93]

Accompanied by masked soldiers, the Rangers forced themselves into the homes, removed men from their beds, and beat them on the way to an isolated area a few minutes away from their homes.[94] The Rangers ransacked Porvenir while the cavalrymen stood watch over the inhabitants, who were disoriented and huddling around a makeshift campfire.[95] As the Rangers finished searching the homes, they rounded up fifteen men and boys and corralled them down a river road along with the soldiers. According to local schoolteacher and witness Harry Warren, the soldiers veered off the main road toward their camp, leaving the Rangers alone with the fifteen men and boys. After a few moments, a fusillade of shots was heard and one of the soldiers rode back to witness what the Rangers had done.[96]

The Rangers shot the Mexicans in cold blood. Ranger Captain J. M. Fox later reported to the adjutant general that they were fired upon in the dark and were forced to defend themselves, thereby killing all the men.[97] The women of Porvenir later reported to the army that the men were lined up against the rock bluff and were never interrogated.[98] The Rangers rode away in a drunken stupor, shouting "Comanche yells."[99]

The army collected the bodies on the morning of January 28, 1918, and interrogated some of the survivors. Harry Warren policed the area and in-formed the women of the circumstances of the mass killing.[100] Many of the families collected their loved ones and took them to Mexico for burial. The village and the surrounding area of the upper Big Bend were abandoned for fear that the Rangers would return to "finish the job."[101] Residents left their harvest and livestock and fled to Mexico. Sheer animosity for the Mexican residents of Porvenir was evident on some of the bodies that were mutilated by stab wounds to the face or "chopped up with a knife" by the Rangers.[102] According to reports filed by the United States Army, the survivors had few options regarding justice or legal retribution. Only one of the twelve widows interviewed, for instance, mentioned that she had any contact with Mexican officials.[103]

The Texas Rangers present that evening and their captain, J. M. Fox, came under fire from Adjutant General James A. Harley in Austin. The men were discharged from the force but never brought to trial for the murders. Harley drafted a letter to Fox and later had it reprinted in the El Paso Times chastising the ranger captain and exposing the notorious behavior of the force:

> You know, as all peace officers should know, that every man, whether he be white or black, yellow or brown, has the constitutional right to a trial by jury, and that no organized band operating under the laws of this state has the right to constitute itself judge and jury and executioner, and shooting men upon no provocation when they are helpless and disarmed . . . you were not forced to resign by the governor for political reasons but your forced resignation came in the interest of humanity, decency, law, and order.[104]

Public castigation of the Ranger Force offered little recourse for ethnic Mexicans in West Texas. The mass murder of innocent Mexican residents of Porvenir by the state ranger force suggests that all ethnic Mexicans were culpable for the deaths of white Americans along the border. The accumulation of retributive acts between law enforcement and suspected bandits had now escalated to a full-blown race war that included innocent civilians on both sides of the racial and international divide.

Mexicans from both Mexico and the United States expressed outrage and threatened to retaliate against the Rangers and Anglos.[105] The threat of violence from Mexicans was serious as far as Captain Anderson was concerned. He insisted that the governor remove the Rangers from the vicinity immediately because, "instead of proving themselves [observers] of the peace & dignity of the state, they are proving themselves its worse enemies."[106] The wholesale murder at Porvenir exposed the extent of the Ranger violence against Mexicans as well as the sense of impunity with which they acted. The massacre also exposed the deep divisions that emerged during the 1910s between Anglos and Mexicans in West Texas. All of the brutal tactics used by the Texas Rangers and ranchers vastly deteriorated racialized relations in the area. However, the US Army, especially those troops stationed along the border in the Texas Big Bend region, requires further evaluation as to their role in targeting and killing residents of Mexican descent in the area.[107]

The State Ranger Force Investigation

Crimes committed by the Ranger Force did not go unnoticed. Texas state representative José T. Canales of Brownsville filed nineteen charges against the Ranger force largely for their violence against Mexicans in South Texas.[108] Following an investigation of the force by the Texas legislature and state representative William H. Bledsoe of Lubbock, who chaired the committee that conducted the inquiry, the investigation discovered major violations and human rights infractions in South Texas as well as in other places throughout the state. Rangers in El Paso County, for example, were accused of treating "prominent citizens roughly" and murdering a military policeman at a local saloon.[109]

The charges by the investigative committee ranged from murder, wanton killing, flogging and torturing prisoners, drunkenness, to assault.[110] Most of the charges originated in the Rio Grande Valley region of South Texas; however, major incidences of mass murder, like Porvenir, were among the list of charges Canales presented. After a lengthy and colorful hearing that included threats on Canales's life, the committee concluded that the dead men of Porvenir were innocent of any wrongdoing. However, full vindication of Porvenir's Mexican residents fell short when the committee further determined that the villagers were shot because they had conspired with some of the ranch raiders. The Porvenir case underscores the tenuous relationship between Mexican residents along the border and state authority figures like the Rangers.

Despite the wide range of charges brought forth by state representative Jóse Canales, an awkward political compromise was arranged after nearly two months of investigation.[111] The understanding was that the Rangers' excesses were unacceptable, but that their function as a state police force was necessary to protect cattlemen from thieves and other "bad characters."[112] The committee recognized the abuses of the Rangers but also highlighted their exemplary services. Initially, Canales introduced a bill to reorganize and upgrade the Rangers by raising their pay and qualifications.[113] However, he faced considerable opposition from Ranger Captain Frank Hamer and committee chairman William H. Bledsoe for his harsh criticism of the force. Bledsoe in turn proposed a substitute bill for Ranger reform that the legislature subsequently accepted. The Bledsoe bill provided for Special Rangers to be recommended by district judges and attorneys. This was intended to deny ranchers the opportunity to solicit the help of the adjutant general in deputizing their own private police forces and to use these private Rangers to kill Mexican ranchers and deprive their families of their properties.[114] The bill also called on the Rangers to surrender their prisoners to the local sheriff's department where the arrest could be made. The objective was to put a stop to the mysterious killing of Mexican prisoners in legal custody, a practice that had seriously impaired racial relations in Texas.[115] In addition, charges of abuse were to be heard by a local magistrate if the adjutant general decided it was necessary to initiate an investigation. Nominal salary increases were also proposed but were later reduced before the bill left the House. The Bledsoe-sponsored bill passed both the House and Senate with little opposition. Despite the reduction in the authority of the Rangers, the force remained relatively intact. The governor and adjutant general were left to utilize the Rangers as they saw fit.[116] This extensive investigation of the Rangers highlighted the violence the Rangers directed against Mexicans and their contribution to the racialization of relations between Mexicans and Anglos in South and West Texas.

Conclusion

A reexamination of the Texas Rangers as the state's primary police force in South and West Texas throughout the late nineteenth century and early twentieth century offers a lens into the historical construction of ethnic Mexicans as "enemy others" and transcends the racial binary of white and nonwhite others. Their work in pacifying and displacing Native Americans and Mexicans to make way for Anglo settlers in the late nineteenth century worsened an already troubled relationship, especially between whites and Mexicans. In the Anglo community, the Rangers were welcomed as a necessary police force although they were later questioned when they began to disrupt common social practices. The violent response by Mexicans to the heavy-handed methods of the Rangers ushered in another conflictual period, during which the Rangers targeted the Mexican community in an effort to pacify the region and discipline the resident Mexican population. Anglos welcomed this shift in the exercise of Ranger authority. The West Texas region, however, posed special challenges for the Texas Rangers, including a general state of lawlessness, distance from centers of authority, and the geographic proximity of Mexico as a safe haven for illicit behavior and a staging area for violent forays into Texas.

The El Paso Salt War in the 1870s defined the social context among Anglos and Mexicans in West Texas. Privatization efforts and the use of the Texas Rangers to protect the common salt licks prompted local residents to arm themselves, and opposing factions divided along racial lines. The conflict underlined several important developments that persisted throughout the nineteenth and early twentieth century. Residents resorted to vigilantism and violently expressed latent racial feelings. Opposing groups eclipsed citizenship and class and identified themselves along racial lines. In addition, the conflict assumed a regional characteristic as Mexican residents organized to resist the efforts of outside entrepreneurs whose actions disrupted local practice. Tensions resulting from the Salt War remained predominant throughout the remainder of the century.

The Ranger approach to law enforcement in the 1890s, under the captainship of John R. Hughes, initially sought to nurture close relationships with some of the area's most influential and notorious individuals, including the revolutionary Pancho Villa.[117] Rangers understood that local support in the form of informants and alliances with local ranchers and revolutionary figures could help them do their job. Still, despite the collaborative efforts, racial tension continued to escalate during the early years of the twentieth century under the leadership of Captain Hughes.

Ranch raids caused great distress among property owners living along the international boundary line. The economic and political instability in Mexico during the early twentieth century marginalized much of Mexico's poor, and, driven by need and retribution, various individuals sought social justice through banditry. Many Mexican residents residing on both sides of the river accepted the bandits as heroes, champions, and fighters for justice. However, Anglo ranchers and authorities, specifically the Texas Rangers, viewed the bandits as nothing more than arrogant outlaws who threatened the lives and livelihood of residents in West Texas. The violent relationship between Sitters and Cano reflected the larger struggle between law enforcement and social bandits.

The skirmishes between the Rangers and bandits remained largely isolated but impactful events that were the by-product of complex alliances between ranchers, Mexican revolutionary factions, and American law enforcement. Throughout the early 1910s, however, their confrontations developed into an environment of extreme distrust and animosity. The Texas Rangers utilized humiliating and brutal tactics that, at times, Anglo residents accepted. Mexicans captured by Texas Rangers were often murdered before legally charged or tried in a court of law. Many Anglo residents in West Texas categorized Mexicans as bandits and potentially dangerous. By the mid-1910s, social relations in West Texas had become thoroughly racialized.

CHAPTER 2

¡Muerte a los gringos!
The Santa Ysabel Massacre and the El Paso Race Riot of 1916

Entonces estaba el Segundo Barrio lleno de pura mexicanada, se imagina.
(Then there were the residents of the Second Ward, full of *mexicanness*, can you
believe it?)
—Hortencia Villegas, eyewitness and survivor of the El Paso riots of
January 13, 1916

THEIR BODIES WERE STRIPPED NEARLY NAKED AND STREWN
about the train like fallen leaves. Pools of blood marked their final resting
place. This was the scene near the Cusihuiriáchic (Cusi) Mines in Santa Ysabel, Chihuahua. Nineteen engineers and staff of the Cusihuiriáchic Mining
Company traveling on the Mexican Northwestern Railroad to their reopened
mines under the protection of their passports and their *salvo conductos* furnished by de facto Chihuahua governor Ignacio Enriquez met this brutal de-
mise.[1] A band of soldiers led by *villista* officer Pablo López hijacked the train
and demanded that all Anglos disembark. Their subsequent fate hung at the
end of bayonets and rifle shots as they were mercilessly executed for simply
being "gringo."[2] This event, the Santa Ysabel massacre, served as a catalyst
for one of the largest race riots ever to occur in West Texas.[3]

The Mexican Revolution had a major impact on the social, cultural, and
political landscape of Mexico and the United States. The horror and ideals of
the revolution extended their reach into the United States, especially into the
Southwest, as revolutionaries migrated across the international border during the early 1900s. For the United States, increased political activity associated with the fighting in Mexico required vigilance and expanded authority
among its border patrolling organizations. People in places like Columbus,
New Mexico; and Marfa, Presidio, and El Paso, Texas, were drawn into the
conflict as Mexican insurgents claimed to embrace a broad transnational
cause or redress local wrongs. Others participated in General Pershing's
Punitive Expedition or signed on to Mexico's army of Dorados in Chihuahua
headed by General Francisco "Pancho" Villa.[4]

The "border troubles" associated with the revolution gave shape to a disciplined society that reinforced racial segregation within El Paso and, to a
certain extent, between El Paso and Ciudad Juárez. The troubles began in
1916, when members of Pancho Villa's army killed approximately fourteen
American engineers in cold blood in Santa Ysabel, Chihuahua.[5] A critical
review of the events of 1916 will explain how transnational circumstances
reinforced long-standing characterizations of Mexican Americans as being
"un-American" by examining the violence suffered by an innocent population. First, a reassessment of the 1916 events in West Texas will address latent
racial tension that persisted in the region, one that paralleled the friction that
38   prevailed in central and northeast Texas between whites and blacks.[6] A brief

analysis of the region's history of racially motivated violence and resistance will provide an understanding of the events leading up to 1916. Second, an evaluation of these events will demonstrate that international militarization during the Mexican Revolution, specifically in 1916, contributed to the definition of Mexicans as an "enemy other." As a result, for most of the twentieth century in the southwest United States, "American" generally meant white, while "Mexican" referred to race and not citizenship.[7] Last, an appraisal of the riot demonstrates in stark fashion that Mexicans, despite their citizenship or long residence in El Paso, could be easily identified as proxies for the Mexican revolutionaries responsible for taking American lives.

The episode gave rise to ill feelings that had been brewing in El Paso since the dawn of the revolution. Many Anglos were increasingly fearful of an armed insurrection by the revolutionary-minded local Mexican community. The riot also raised security concerns among city and military officials and further polarized the city along racial lines. Various law enforcement officials, military personnel, and vigilante groups played a major role in defining a racial line of separation while Mexicans in El Paso and Ciudad Juárez simultaneously contributed to the separation with their own self-defining activities. Most observers became convinced that the revolution had reached home. In order to better appreciate the significance of the riot in Chihuahuita, it is necessary to first review the history of the border area of El Paso and Ciudad Juarez. In the process, we will outline the development by which Mexicans became the "enemy other."

Economic, Social, and Demographic Transformation in El Paso/Ciudad Juárez, 1880–1910

The riot and its consequences can be better understood by examining the history of the development of the El Paso/Ciudad Juárez district. The industrialization of the area began around the time that the Southern Pacific Railroad reached El Paso on May 19, 1881. Prior to its arrival, El Paso was known as a quiet, practically irrelevant village of just eight hundred residents. Change, however, came quickly. One of the most notorious lawmen in El Paso's history described the transformation, or "social activity," that affected his world:

> Bankers, merchants, capitalists, real estate dealers, cattlemen, miners, railroad men, gamblers, saloon-keepers, and sporting people of both sexes flocked to town. . . . A saloon was opened on almost every corner of the town with many in between, but if one wished a seat at the gaming tables he had to come early or he could not get within thirty feet of them.[8]

Local Anglo leaders sought to effectively manage the rapid and often chaotic development of a social economy made all the more complicated by a volatile international setting. Prerevolutionary activity made its way across the river in the arrival of increasing numbers of destitute immigrants, including political exiles with radical ideas. It is no accident, then, that the intensification of law enforcement and border surveillance began in tandem as the region witnessed "booming" growth at the close of the nineteenth century. The events of the time period revealed the unavoidable ties shared by border communities and their residents. In the process, law enforcement and border patrolling officials conflicted with the local residents, especially Mexicans from both Mexico and the United States.

El Paso began to look like a modern industrialized US city by the late 1880s, with banks, newspapers, churches, a fully functioning city government, and a hotel. A school board was elected in December of 1882, and the first public school opened in March 1883. The first "Black School" was built and Olivas V. Aoy organized a school for Mexican-origin children.[9] Moreover, the Mexican Central Railroad Company connected Mexico's northern outpost to its interior in 1884. Mexico's industrialized northern region attracted foreign capital and stimulated the importation of northern Mexican agricultural and mining products into the United States. By the 1890s, Mexican railroads reached the urban centers of the north from central Mexico, and places like Ciudad Juárez began to prosper and exhibit the accouterments of a modern city. Mexico's labor population grew substantially during the late nineteenth century, especially along the international boundary line. Such expansion contributed not only to the population growth of a sparsely inhabited area but also to the overall economy and spending power of the region.[10]

To be sure, Ciudad Juárez, known as El Paso del Norte until 1888, lagged behind El Paso economically and consequently requested special concessions from the Mexican government. Residents of northern Chihuahua had signed a petition requesting that the government extend the Free Trade Zone to their region because of lack of employment opportunities and the high cost of living. In January 1885, the Mexican government responded by extending the trade zone along the entire northern border for a distance of twenty kilometers from the boundary line. El Paso del Norte subsequently entered the more modern era of economic development. The standard of living rose along with wages. Exotic and profitable foreign goods made their way into the Mexican city.[11]

The Free Trade Zone was not without controversy. El Paso merchants, for instance, opposed it because they feared that smugglers would import duty-free goods and undermine their businesses. Many of them pleaded to the US government to intervene. Officials in the United States acted with a series of articles and decrees that placed hefty tariffs on goods produced and imported from the Free Trade Zone.[12] As tariffs began to place unbearable restraints upon the Juárez area, by 1905 the economic potential of the region began to wither slowly. Businesses in Juárez closed their doors while some relocated across the border to El Paso.[13] Laborers in need of a livelihood searched out work in El Paso, further depopulating Ciudad Juárez. El Paso, on the other hand, faced overpopulated neighborhoods, health issues associated with a growing poor population, and rising unemployment.[14]

The "great migration" beginning in the early 1900s, with its roots in the economic destabilization of northern Mexico and broadened by the Mexican Revolution (1910–20), caused both social and racial tensions to simmer among the Anglo-American population of El Paso.[15] Many among the city's business elite supported an order by the president of the United States in 1916 to racially identify and classify Mexicans separate from whites in order to have a "better grasp of the population on social and economic problems."[16] Reports of the period in the national press described the refugees, exiles, and immigrants as "homeless, poverty stricken, chronically hungry, [and] alien in speech, manners, habits, and ideas."[17] They seemed no more than social stressors bound to complicate racial matters in the United States. At the turn of the twentieth century, larger issues of an international nature, including immigration and revolutionary turmoil in Mexico, often acted to bring local policy in line with state approaches then redefining relations between Mexico and the United States.[18]

International Tensions:
The United States and Revolutionary Mexico

Apart from straining diplomatic relations between the United States and Mexico and begetting ill feelings between citizens of the two countries, the Mexican Revolution expectedly caused distress in the United States over the welfare of American citizens in Mexico. The clashes of rival revolutionary factions forced many American workers and residents to abandon their homes in Mexico and head north to the United States. Conversely, anti-American feelings ran high in Mexico and along the border.[19] Anglo residents in El Paso feared that assaults and casualties inflicted on Americans in Mexico would translate to attacks upon whites in the city. In their apprehension, citizens and local officials requested protection by Texas Rangers and the US Army.

The economic backlash of the revolution equally concerned Americans as chaos plagued the Mexican landscape. American investments throughout Mexico faced serious risks as Americans abandoned private property and industries in places where battles raged. Businessmen in El Paso, home for one of the largest smelting companies in the United States, worried as revolutionary forces closed or occupied mines in Chihuahua.[20] The economic ties between the United States and Mexico, magnified in El Paso, brought the revolution to the United States' doorstep.

American residents in Mexico as well as those along the international boundary line did not escape the violence of the revolution. Ranch raids caused great distress among Anglo property owners living along the border on the US side. Some of these attacks were the work of individuals who, driven by need and the opportunity to retaliate for past wrongs, sought justice through banditry. Many local Mexican residents accepted some of them as heroes, champions, and defenders, but Anglo ranchers and authorities, specifically the Texas Rangers, viewed the marauders as nothing more than arrogant outlaws who threatened the lives and livelihood of residents in West Texas.[21]

In El Paso, furthermore, Anglos grew increasingly suspicious of all things Mexican, especially of Mexican refugees and their intentions. White El Pasoans simultaneously entertained dreaded fears of attacks on their city, either by revolutionary troops or soldiers from Mexico's army. In response, US military officials moved to fortify El Paso and other strategic locations along the border.[22] Racialized tensions spread unchecked throughout the region.

Racial Antagonism on the Border

A review of the conflictual context of West Texas and Chihuahua is critical to understanding border race relations during the early decades of the twentieth century. The events and setting that have been briefly analyzed might act as a lens through which the complex struggle between authority and the populace, as well as the underlining racial tones of conflict, may be understood. Further, these events afford a comparison to violent actions that took place in other parts of the state in more or less the same time period. What occurred in El Paso also discloses patterns of racial antagonism. The El Paso region, including Ciudad Juárez, emerged as the epicenter of the Mexican Revolution, and both concurrent and subsequent events that pitted the United States against factions of the Mexican Revolution translated into an ethnic struggle between Anglos and Mexicans in El Paso in particular.[23] The events of 1916 demonstrate how diplomatic and military struggles between the United States and Mexican revolutionary agents resulted in the arbitrary categorization of the Mexican population in El Paso as more than the "non-white other" and as the "enemy other." This classification was solidified as local, state, and federal authorities mobilized, identified, and contained the Mexican population as oppositional to "Americans" in the aftermath of the Santa Ysabel massacre and race riot of 1916, as we will later see.

Rapid population growth caused by the dramatic shift in racial demographics and economic hardships affected race relations between Anglos and Mexicans in El Paso. By 1916 the ethnic Mexican population of El Paso city proper outnumbered that of whites emerging as the majority population in the city.[24] Again, similar to the "Africanization" in northeast Texas towns in the late nineteenth century, El Paso's "Mexicanization" in the early decades of the twentieth century contributed to racial tensions between the city's Anglo population and newly arrived Mexicans.[25] The influx of refugees and displaced laborers from Mexico resulted in heated discussion among Anglo laborers and residents regarding Mexican immigrants.[26] However, labor disputes were not the only source of tension. Diplomatic and political tensions escalated with the dramatic shift in power within Mexico.

On October 19, 1915, Francisco "Pancho" Villa's political rival, Venustiano Carranza, emerged as the political leader of Mexico when the Wilson administration extended him de facto recognition and special military concessions. Villa saw these actions by the United States as both a betrayal and a clear violation of neutrality laws. His subsequent anti-American rhetoric forced state and federal governments to reexamine security concerns along the border. Villa's antipathy is well documented in various academic and popular works; however, few historians have measured the significance of these international incidents on local social relations in places like El Paso.[27]

On October 26, 1915, Villa assembled the inhabitants of Colonia Morelos, Sonora, and delivered one of his most notable public speeches. His speech was heavily anti-American, as evidenced by his proclamation that he would, "rescue the settlers from the tyranny of the North American Mormons, who exploit, vilify, and assassinate the Mexicans in the region."[28] His willingness to generalize the "tyranny" of Americans to a specific population, such as the Mormons, is a strong indication that his growing hatred toward Americans was not limited to the Wilson administration.

Relations between Villa and Carranza continued to deteriorate as Villa began to criticize the United States. General John Pershing, who had taken command of Fort Bliss, attempted a diplomatic intervention by inviting Carranza's chief general, Álvaro Obregón, and Villa for conversations in El Paso. The attempt to reconcile the opposing revolutionary camps may have sought to pacify matters on the border. The results, however, were peculiar. Villa became the man of the hour among the Mexicans in the city. One El Paso resident recalls Villa in exciting terms:

> Pasó por la Calle de El Paso cuando vino con el General Pershing. ¿Comó no lo voy a recorder, joven? Pero ni el golpe [the young girl sustained a minor injury falling down some stairs] sentí por llegar hasta ver a Pancho Villa. (He came through El Paso Street with General Pershing. How could I forget, young man? Not even my injury was going to keep me from seeing Pancho Villa.)[29]

The Mexican community clearly welcomed him into the city, a sort of home-coming that alarmed members of the Anglo community.[30]

The Santa Ysabel Massacre

Events in Chihuahua acted as a major source of uneasiness among Mexicans and Anglos in the city of El Paso. On December 30, 1915, El Paso honored *carrancista* officer General Álvaro Obregón with a banquet and an audience with notable individuals.[31] Various political and military dignitaries, including El Paso mayor Tom Lea, Consul Andrés G. García, Mexican American businessman and local politician Félix Martínez, and General John J. Pershing, attended.[32] The spectacle attempted to promote the beginning of a peaceful era in Mexico by emphasizing the removal of Pancho Villa (following his defeat at the Battle of Celaya in April 1915) as a threat to American mining interests in Chihuahua. Martínez furthered the rhetoric at the occasion by stating that Obregón had assured him that US capital and American personnel would be safe and protected in Mexico. Days later the statement proved false when *villista* troops led by Colonel Pablo López hijacked a train carrying seventeen American citizens on their way to Cusihuiráchic, west of Ciudad Chihuahua.[33]

General Alvaro Obregón and the de facto government overlooked two critical facts with their proclamation. First, the supposed deposition of Pancho Villa as leader amounted to an overstatement as his downfall did not minimize his influence over his loyal soldiers and officers. Second, the de facto government had grossly underestimated Villa's furor toward Woodrow Wilson when the US president recognized Venustiano Carranza as the de facto president of Mexico and extended to him special military concessions. Villa saw these actions by the United States as betrayal, disrespect, and a clear violation of American neutrality. Public anti-American rhetoric from Villa forced both the Texas and federal governments to examine security concerns along the border. Again, Villa's antipathy is well documented in various academic and popular works; however, it is relevant to note for this discussion that Villa's reaction to the recognition of the Carranza government served as a catalyst for intense racialized conflict and for attacks on Anglos and Mexicans alike.[34]

In December 1915, just a few weeks prior to the massacre, Villa delivered a statement before the Cusihuiriáchic mining district in front of manager C. R. Watson and his men warning them that they would no longer be protected and they should leave the country:

> Since your government has seen fit to recognize Venustiano Carranza, I no longer consider myself responsible of the safety of you or your countrymen in the territory dominated by my men. Your government has advised you to leave Mexico. Now leave. If you ever come back I'll kill you and kill you quick.[35]

Following Villa's speech, Watson quickly gathered his men and boarded a train and safely arrived in El Paso. But several weeks later *carrancista* troops reoccupied Ciudad Chihuahua and secured the region. At the behest of Obregón and in defiance of the ominous threat by Villa on that fateful night in December, Watson and his men contacted customs collector Zachary Lamar Cobb and Mexican consul general Andrés G. García for passports and *salvo conductos* for their trip back to the Cusi mines in Chihuahua.[36]

Watson and several men made their way back through Chihuahua to the properties of the Cusihuiriáchic (Cusi) Mining Company.[37] At approximately two o'clock in the afternoon on January 12, a band of one hundred soldiers under the command of Colonel Pablo López attacked a "stalled" passenger train that contained the Cusi mining men. One eyewitness claimed that the band shouted, "Viva Villa!" and "Death to the gringos."[38]

According to another person at the scene, Juan Vásquez, the rebels lifted a rail to side track the locomotive, which consisted of two passenger coaches, one carrying Americans and the other about twenty Mexican male passengers. Pablo López and his men quickly surrounded the train, entered the coach occupied by the Mexican men, searched all passengers, and stole their "bread and lunches."[39] Five Americans jumped from the train upon hearing shouts from the *villista* band, but the rebels easily captured them and summarily executed the hapless miners.

The soldiers marched to the "American coach" and commanded, "all Gringos step out" of the car.[40] They ordered the Americans to line up and strip themselves of their clothing. López then ordered two troopers with Mauser guns to prepare and kill the Americans; the soldiers walked down the line and shot them one by one. Americans attempting to flee fell prey to other rebels who mortally shot them in their tracks.[41] According to reports, bodies lay strewn about in grotesque positions. The top of one American's head had been shot off and his brains had spilled onto the ground.[42] According to the affidavit of J. O. H. Newby, one of several Americans who viewed the bodies soon after the incident, the bodies had been robbed of everything, including their clothing, and showed evidence of brutal treatment:

> Practically all bodies . . . showed evidence of brutal treatment. For instance, the body of Maurice Anderson, which was lying on the top of the pile of bodies, had his arm up before him as if endeavoring to protect his face. Other bodies had either been kicked or struck with some blunt instrument, as the heads of some were twisted around from the original position in which they fell. The body of R. H. Simmons . . . had the entire upper portion of the skull shot off.[43]

Various American newspapers reiterated descriptions of the murders, which quickly fueled tensions between Anglos and Mexicans.

The targeting of Americans aboard the train took an interesting turn when Colonel López identified a brown-skinned man, ostensibly Manuel Bonifacio Romero, a Mexican American native of Las Vegas, New Mexico. López inquired suspiciously of his association with the "gringos." Romero replied, "I too am an American." "*Pues se quede allí entonces* / well then stay put," López shrugged, and Romero died with the rest of the Americans.[44] In an ironic twist of fate, a Mexico–United States Claims Commission later refuted Mr. Romero's citizenship because the absence of a birth certificate could not authenticate his New Mexico residence thus American citizenship. Romero's wife presented other forms of evidence, including their marriage certificate, to support his American citizenship claim but to no avail. The Mexican representatives doubted his American status and therefore denied his widow compensation in the lawsuit.[45] Manuel Romero died proclaiming his "American" identity and in death was categorized as Mexican. In the eyes of the law, he didn't belong.

Killing of Americans during the revolution did not commonly occur; however, the Santa Ysabel incident underscored the failure of the Chihuahua government to guarantee Americans safe passage. The activities of *villista* forces further angered Americans who feared for the security of their fellow citizens. Villa's anti-American harangues and his public denunciation of President Wilson made Villa a persona non grata, especially among the Anglo residents of El Paso.[46]

While Anglos viewed Villa as a callous murderer, many Mexicans in El Paso held an opposing opinion of him. In the early years of the revolution, Villa had often visited El Paso for diplomatic and personal reasons and, as evidenced by his loyal followers, enjoyed considerable and favorable support from many of the Mexican residents in El Paso's Mexican district, called "Chihuahuita."[47] Even after Wilson's official recognition of Carranza, Villa still wielded extraordinary power and influence, a fact that made Mexicans grateful and respectful toward him and Anglos fearful and resentful of the revolutionary leader.[48]

El Paso Race Riot of 1916

The death train carrying the bodies of the seventeen Americans murdered at Santa Ysabel, Chihuahua, arrived in Juárez on the morning of January 13.

Figure 3. Maurice Anderson and other American victims in Santa Ysabel massacre.
Photo courtesy of the National Archives at College Park, Maryland.

Figure 4. American killed in Santa Ysabel massacre.
Photo courtesy of the National Archives at College Park, Maryland.

Figure 5. American shot near water source in Santa Ysabel massacre.
Photo courtesy of the National Archives at College Park, Maryland.

Figure 6. American shot dead in the back in Santa Ysabel massacre.
Photo courtesy of the National Archives at College Park, Maryland.

From there, it crossed the river to the Santa Fe railway freight depot in El Paso where citizens unloaded the corpses and an armed escort accompanied the bodies and took them to various undertaking establishments.[49] The local police and military guard took precautions against any disturbances.[50] However, many Americans refused to stand idly by as they witnessed their comrades arriving in caskets.

In the early afternoon hours of January 13, shortly after the bodies of the dead Americans reached El Paso, a mob of Americans jeered and verbally attacked United States consul T. D. Edwards. Many screamed, "Villa's consul, not ours," and "go back to Juárez with the Mexicans where you belong." The protestors felt that consul Edwards had not done enough to protect the men traversing Chihuahua despite the fact that he had personally received assurances by top Carranza officials of safety measures to be taken and the assignment of a military guard to protect them. Nevertheless, a petition circulated throughout hotel lobbies and the city asking President Wilson to remove Edwards because he allegedly gave Villa advice whenever the general visited Juárez.[51] The verbal and political ambush of Edwards soon gave way to a much more aggressive, retaliatory initiative by a mob.

Several groups of Americans took to El Paso streets and organized a variety of retributory responses to the atrocities committed in Santa Ysabel. Thirty or so men of various backgrounds, including prominent local businessmen, conducted a meeting in El Paso proposing to organize a volunteer "foreign legion" of one thousand men for service in Mexico under the protection of the Carranza government. The men felt confident that their unit could be financed and outfitted by a majority of those present at the meeting but more fully by mining interests in Mexico.[52] There exists, however, no record of anyone heeding the call to ride into Mexico. Mine workers and cattlemen elsewhere in El Paso organized a secret meeting to gather a second expedition into Mexico to capture those responsible for killing the American engineers.[53] Apparently, such a plan did not materialize either. But as fate would have it, people of all sorts responded to their instincts and amassed for action on the streets of El Paso.

Tensions escalated throughout the afternoon close to downtown El Paso that fateful day in January. American soldiers stationed at Fort Bliss attacked two Mexican men near the Chihuahuita district. Scuffles between other US soldiers and Mexicans occurred later that evening, and many police wagons returned to their respective stations with Mexicans who had been attacked and with "civilians" who had participated in the sporadic disturbances.[54] Before long, soldiers and Anglo civilians in saloons began to take their drunken escapades to the streets and assault Mexicans they apprehended. Women, children, and the elderly did not escape the terror of the vigilante group. According to Hortencia Villegas, who recalled the rioting years later: "me acuerdo que a toda la gente dándoles golpes, a viejitos y a jóvenes y a todos (I remember everyone receiving blows, the elderly and young people, everyone).[55] Hundreds of Americans amassed in the principal downtown streets that outlined Chihuahuita, clearly intending to exact revenge on local Mexicans.[56] The confrontation then morphed into a full-fledged riot, turning into a shadow of a war that involved two primary sides: Anglos and US soldiers on one side, Mexicans on the other. The crowd bent on retaliation swelled to nearly 1,500 men, and it would take another two to three hours after the first reports of the fighting began before the police successfully dispersed the deluge. Military reports claim that the disturbances surprised police officials, who concluded earlier that "there will be no trouble that evening."[57]

The Anglo rioters, however, met resistance. Once the word of the turmoil spread throughout the *colonia*, groups from "El Segundo Barrio" began to show up with sticks, bats, pipes and anything else they could muster to defend themselves.[58] According to Villegas, residents of Ciudad Juárez, including soldiers, joined their Mexican brethren from El Paso:

> No le digo que se vino toda la mexicanada, y luego los de Juárez. Creo que eran todos los soldados de allá de Juárez, porque los tranvías empezaron a pasar con gente que se fue pa' Juárez y avisaron allá como andaba aquí el mitote. (I tell you that all the Mexicans came and then from Juárez. I believe they were the soldiers that were stationed there in Juárez because the trolleys began to take people to Juárez to tell everyone there of the ruckus that was going on.)[59]

Toward the climax of the rioting, General John J. Pershing, who commanded forces at Fort Bliss, ordered the Sixteenth Infantry to take charge of the downtown area since police officers seemed unable to control the melee. Lines of troops four abreast bulldozed through the streets and established sentries on street corners and in the middle of the plaza. American soldiers conducted a search for weapons and for additional Villa sympathizers in Chihuahuita well after midnight. The troopers prohibited residents from walking the streets without a permit signed by the provost marshal.[60] Despite the military occupation, soldiers and Mexicans continued to brawl in the streets. A war zone was established as American soldiers and civilians moved from protective duties to acts of aggression. All ethnic Mexicans despite innocence or guilt were the enemy and were collectively responsible for the tragedy at Santa Ysabel.

After the riot, General Pershing and the El Paso Police Department sent their respective units on a "clean-up" mission of the Mexican quarter in order to avert further violence. About fifty soldiers and as many police officers went "looking for Mexicans" and rounding up "suspected" Villa associates during their "clean up" of the Chihuahuita streets.[61] As the "clean-up" campaign diminished and soldiers and police officers spread out over the bustling downtown area, General Pershing declared martial law. Despite this drastic military measure, Anglo rioters defiantly frequented saloons and other public establishments searching for more trouble. A few intrepid Mexicans also congregated in open places, but police officers ordered them to leave because of "concern for their safety."[62]

An article in the otherwise progressive *Labor Advocate* revealed the outrage smoldering among Anglos who increasingly saw the conflict in nationalistic terms. The writer called on "Americans" to defend their country, suggesting

49

that doing so would avenge the murder of American engineers and other foreigners in Mexico.[63] Such exaggerated nationalism that gave meaning to the attack on Chihuahuita only deepened a racial line of division as real as the international border that separated Mexico from the United States.

General Pershing reinforced racial divisions by instituting martial law—based on a policy of containment—on Mexican neighborhoods. One of his more creative enforcement practices included the enactment of "dead lines": physical demarcations that set aside the Mexican neighborhoods from the rest of the population. As Pershing concluded, Mexicans needed to be separated from Anglos in order to halt any further rioting. As he phrased it: "the excitement on Friday was still intense, and but for the presence of the troops on the streets separating the Mexican from the American part of the city, there would certainly have been serious rioting."[64] The Pershing directive prohibited Mexicans from leaving the Chihuahuita district and Americans from entering it.[65] General Pershing next closed the international bridge, thereby extending the "dead line" to a separation of the United States from Mexico. This order denied American residents access to Ciudad Juárez and prohibited Mexicans from crossing into El Paso.[66]

While the "dead line" intended to quell the disturbance, it reinforced the racial division that incidentally indicted the larger Mexican community for the atrocities associated with the Santa Ysabel massacre. Moreover, the order and its execution recalled the imaginary point beyond which prisoners during the United States Civil War could not cross lest they be shot. In the case of Chihuahuita, Mexicans who violated the "dead line" faced legal and physical repercussions. Many residents, including Hortencia Villegas, feared to cross the line: "Yo pa' la Plaza no me voy, no me vayan a golpear" (I don't go to the Plaza; they are not going to assault me).[67] In one case, a dark-skinned Mexican left a bar after the curfew established by the "dead line" and received a severe beating by soldiers. It would not be until he claimed to be a "nigger" that the soldiers released him.[68]

Pershing's containment measure also made it possible for the Army to continue searching Mexican homes for "armed Villa sympathizers." Subsequent declarations by officials that they had "cleaned up El Paso Street" further implicated Mexicans in the rioting and stigmatized them as a threat to the social order in El Paso.[69] The military strategy of separating the races, ostensibly for the protection of the Mexicans (who suffered an injustice during the upheaval) represented a repressive measure that strengthened Anglo anti-Mexican feelings and reaffirmed the position of Anglos as the final arbiters in cases involving racial conflict.

Conclusion

The 1916 El Paso riot stands as one of the most blatant expressions of ethnic animosity ever to be directed toward Mexicans during this time period. The Santa Ysabel massacre evoked past conflicts between Anglos and Mexicans in West Texas, and it unleashed entrenched anti-Mexican feelings. According to one newspaper report, fifty thousand cards that read "Remember the Alamo . . . Remember the Cusi" were ordered for distribution the day after the riot.[70] Subsequent to the mass rioting, plans for "revenge" were still being hatched throughout El Paso, showing how historical memory could spark mob violence, pitting Anglos against Mexicans.[71]

Local newspapers, among them the *Labor Advocate*, played on the exaggerated nationalism of white El Pasoans, encouraging them to seek retribution against the "non-white and non-American" Mexicans in the city. The emphasis on race galvanized various segments of the white population, from private citizens to professional associations, into assuming their civic duty to intervene and make themselves available lest the large Mexican population rise up and retaliate. The remarkable appeal to active citizenship and nationalistic expression evidences the argument that whiteness often became a call to arms when people of color endangered white society.[72]

The exponential population growth among Mexicans in El Paso had further heightened suspicions of Mexicans in the city and inflamed passions in the moment of crisis. Whites sensed their numerical disadvantage and moved to defend themselves at every cost, including violence. US officials assisted them by pursuing strict punitive measures. Fort Bliss soldiers ransacked many Mexican homes in search of guns and other weapons, heeding rumors that Mexicans had heavily armed themselves and prepared to attack Anglos in the city.[73] Similar to events that developed in northeast Texas, whites used violence in cases where racial groups needed to be put in their place.

Aside from illustrating that what occurred in El Paso conforms to patterns of racial violence toward other minority groups elsewhere in the state, the El Paso riot of 1916 offers other lessons. First, it indicated that when under stress, local authorities and Anglo citizens would use the opportunity to reinforce their position as the final mediators when racialized social conflict erupted. In fact, the episode legitimized the role of authorities (such as General Pershing and the US Army) to segregate El Paso through militarized separation of the races. They had the consent of the dominant Anglo population to dictate a line of separation that could be militarily enforced and beyond which Mexicans could not travel. The separation of Mexicans from the rest of El Paso, the prohibition of passage across the border, and the establishment of martial law with the accompanying "dead lines" reinforced the verdict that Mexicans stood as a defeated minority. Mexican isolation and vilification, culminating from the massacre and the riot, succeeded in identifying them as an "enemy other."

Second, the riot exhibited a transnational character, as the Mexican Revolution figured prominently into relations between Mexico and United States and into local affairs. On the border, race relations had become increasingly problematic as Mexicans expressed mixed political allegiances and cultural attachments. Villa's assertion that Anglos were no longer safe in Mexico and the subsequent proof of this statement through the racially motivated Santa Ysabel massacre ignited rage among the Anglo community, whose members then indiscriminately lashed out at all Mexican residents residing in the city. Anglos became anxious over the threat posed by the revolution and acted out fears through violence in 1916.

Third, Anglo conduct during the riot validated the long-standing image whites held that Mexicans, regardless of citizenship status, were foreigners or, more specifically, the "enemy." The special census of January 1916, designed to identify and "segregate" Mexicans from Anglos, had practically confirmed the Mexicans' position as such.[74] Immigration scholar Mae Ngai states that "foreignness" became a racialized concept extended to all Mexicans and Mexican Americans in the 1920s and carried the opprobrium of illegitimacy and inferiority.[75] American citizenship provided few benefits to Mexicans born in the United States or naturalized therein, states Ngai.[76] Public statements by Hispanos from New Mexico expressing their support for an American punitive operation against Villa went unheeded and received secondary coverage in local newspapers, suggesting that Mexican American loyalty was suspect and unwelcomed.[77]

Last, the El Paso race riot of 1916 demonstrates that resistance against violent aggression—as occurred during the disturbance—is very much a mark of Mexican American history. Many have been the times when Latino communities defended themselves against white aggression or aided and abetted one of their own who resisted Anglo injustice. Obvious cases where Mexican Americans retaliated against wrongdoings occurred in 1859 when a segment of the Tejano population around Brownsville joined forces behind Juan Cortina, or in 1888 when Tejanos in Rio Grande City threatened whites for an attempt on the life of Catarino Garza. Three years subsequent to that incident, Mexican Americans in South Texas shielded the same Catarino Garza from Texas Rangers who were hunting Garza down for violating the neutrality laws, and a decade later, Tejanos gave succor to the fugitive Gregorio Cortez who was wrongly accused of horse stealing. In 1938 Tejanos extended moral support to Emma Tenayuca and the pecan shellers of San Antonio, who were then striking against the Anglo-dominated pecan shelling industry; in 1949 Mexican Americans coalesced behind Dr. Héctor P. García and the GI Forum, who protested the refusal of the Three Rivers mortician to hold services in his funeral home for the slain World War II soldier Félix Longoria; and more recently, communities have stood behind Mexican American activists challenging the malicious bashing of undocumented Mexicans. Such has been the stridency of a people unwilling to accept their condemnation as outsiders in the land of their birth or naturalization.[78]

The 1916 riot deepened racial divides between Mexicans and Anglos in El Paso, and for many years following altered relations between Americans and Mexicans in the border region. The riot exposed underlying anti-Mexican feelings and reinforced derogatory views of Mexicans. It provided local authorities and Anglos the opportunity to reinforce their positions to judge in cases involving racialized social conflict. Further, the episode sanctioned the role of authority to segregate El Paso through the militarized separation of the races with "dead lines."

"How Mexicans Die"
The El Paso City Jailhouse Holocaust

IN THE DAYS FOLLOWING THE RACE RIOT IN EL PASO, SOME American officials believed that the excitement subsided and relative peace permeated the city streets. American military reports stated that *carrancista* general Gabriel Gavira in Ciudad Juárez took strong measures to prevent any move on the part of Mexicans to the US side of the river. In addition, relations between American and *carrancista* officials were "very cordial."[1] However, the facade of tranquility was unnerved by the undercurrent of bitter resentment among Anglos and Mexicans on both sides of the border and the conflicting reports that emerged from various local officials. Citizens called for their respective governments to intervene in the chaos that ensued.[2] Americans, including New Mexico senator Albert B. Fall, demanded that retributive action take place immediately. The United States consul in Juárez, Thomas D. Edwards, reported that the cry for American intervention "enraged the Mexicans and they [were] preparing to meet such a condition."[3] A possible invasion originating from the Mexican side was augmented when former chief of staff for General Villa, General Manuel F. Medina Vieta, claimed that Villa called all of his chieftains and planned to attack Juárez and then open fire on El Paso.[4] Calls for American intervention and Mexican retribution reached every corner of the United States and fanned the flames for military recourse.[5]

In the early months of 1916, the vindictive cycle came full circle and deepened the divide between Americans and Mexicans on both sides of the river and their respective nations. An array of factors was put into play and formed a perfect storm of distrust and hatred between American and Mexican communities. Firstly, interventionist rhetoric between civilian and political circles in the United States galvanized Mexicans to resist such an effort by any means necessary. Secondly, economic depression and acts of banditry in and around Ciudad Juárez undermined any semblance of cordial relations between American and *carrancista* officials, which consequentially destabilized the fragile hold Carranza forces had on the city. Finally, the lack of authority and control by the military on both sides of the river invigorated a civilian response to justice and retribution for the violent acts committed in the region. The events between January and March 1916 demonstrate that the militarization of the US-Mexico border by American and Mexican troops triggered the mobilization of the populace and reinforced the categorization of Mexicans as a dissident "enemy other" by American officials and residents. Suspected banditry and sporadic acts of violence that targeted both Americans and ethnic Mexicans proved that the undercurrent of tension expressed by United States customs agent Zach Cobb materialized and created a battle zone drawn along national and ethnic lines. In addition, chemical baths conducted on Mexican immigrants and residents in El Paso along with the explosion and resulting deaths of over twenty Mexican prisoners at the El Paso city jail in early March serve as stark examples of the expanded powers of justice local American authorities and citizens assumed. There is little doubt that in the wake of a publicized peace by the Carranza government in the closing months of 1915 and the diplomatic trust and support by the Wilson administration the following year proved that relations between the two nations and their respective ethnic communities were far from stable.

The Aftermath of Santa Ysabel and the El Paso Race Riot

Carrancista authorities struggled to keep order in Ciudad Juárez since villista forces surrendered it in December 1915.[6] Sporadic acts of violence committed by individuals along with threatened hostilities and inadequate pay for soldiers caused dissent along the carrancista ranks. For instance, an American trainman, while standing on a freight car in El Paso only a few yards from the river, was shot and killed by an "irresponsible Mexican soldier firing from the Mexican side."[7] United States customs and intelligence agent Zach Cobb reported that Juárez officials made efforts to squash any friction that could potentially erupt between El Paso and Ciudad Juárez. The wanton acts of violence were not the only problem General Gavira's army confronted. Soldiers from various revolutionary factions filled his ranks, and order was difficult to maintain as many refused to carry out orders.[8] Gavira's men grew increasingly dissatisfied when army officials paid them with worthless paper currency instead of that from the silver circulation.[9] Ciudad Juárez businesses refused to honor the paper currency and shut their doors, preparing for an uprising among civilians and soldiers alike.[10] The closing months of 1915 and the dawn of the New Year revealed civil and economic instability in Ciudad Juárez that for some demanded military and civilian recourse from El Paso and the United States. A blood feud would ensue that would fall along ethnic and national lines.

Tensions between Americans and Mexicans continued to spiral out of control following the Santa Ysabel massacre and the race riot in El Paso. Zach Cobb astutely observed that "feelings had been running very high" in El Paso and Ciudad Juárez.[11] On January 21, 1916, two Americans were attacked and one of them, Bert L. Akers, was murdered just opposite Ysleta, Texas, in Mexico. Several Americans in El Paso began to stir up calls for intervention and retribution. Carrancista officials quickly arrested, tried, and executed two suspects.[12] Federico and Bernardo Durán stood shoulder to shoulder against a whitewashed adobe wall of a cemetery death house in Ciudad Juárez. They faced the military firing squad with undaunted bravery and said, "Watch and see how Mexicans die you American [sic]."[13] The only evidence of a plea prior to the volley of bullets was the plea Bernardo Durán made. In his native Spanish, he turned to an American reporter covering the execution and said:

> We are dying for you Americans. Tell the world that. I shot the American because he was trying to force entrance to my home. I was defending my rights, as any man would have done. My brother here is entirely innocent. He did

not fire a shot. But they are going to kill him, too. Tell me, is that justice? He is being sacrificed to your American public opinion. We are not afraid to die . . . someday we will be avenged. They are killing two for one.[14]

The brothers refused to be blindfolded and fell together at the first volley from the executioners' rifles. Bernardo's arm lay across his brother's chest as though trying to protect him from death. Captain Alfredo Ortiz issued the mercy shot through their heads. Church bells rang from Our Lady of Guadalupe Cathedral in Juárez's main plaza, calling for early mass and inadvertently marking the passing of the two brothers.[15] Although a seemingly minor episode in a string of deaths and executions during the revolution, the Durán deaths reflect a precarious diplomatic relationship between American and Mexican officials and residents on both sides of the river.

The execution of the Durán brothers did not smother the brewing animosity between Americans and Mexicans in Juárez and El Paso. El Paso newspapers brought Gavira's swift act of justice into question. Secretary of State Robert Lansing expressed "grave concern" that "inflammatory articles" reproduced with "little modification" by the press throughout the country would instigate violence among Americans seeking revenge.[16] According to Cobb's report, Akers's companion, Douglas Downs, expressed doubt as to the identity of one of the attackers. Local newspapers ran with the story, inflaming public passions. Cobb quickly moved to suppress what he called "heightened race feelings."[17] On January 23, with the permission of General Gavira, Cobb accompanied Downs and other American officials to identify the exhumed remains of the executed men and confirmed their identities.[18] Despite this vote of confidence, American military personnel and Cobb confirmed that hostilities between Mexicans and Anglo Americans were at their peak:

> The race feeling was apparent, and the feeling which we experienced was creepy. The conditions are becoming more difficult here. I am growing afraid that things may break loose and get beyond control any time. . . . I have delayed writing this, so as to endeavor not to be influenced by the recent abnormal conditions.[19]

The "abnormal" conditions Cobb described were in direct reference to the hatred that permeated among the "rank and file of Mexicans" and "among some of our Americans, [where] the feeling is intense against the Mexicans."[20] Fodder for the contempt that Americans and Mexicans held for one another did not disappear with Douglas Downs.

General Gavira requested that an investigation be made regarding a shooting that occurred between Mexican and American soldiers on January 22, 1916.[21] Two Mexican soldiers crossed the line while recovering their mounts, which strayed across into the El Paso city limits. One of the soldiers was on the American side near the Stanton Street Bridge when a border guard warned him not to bring the animals over. The soldier drew his carbine as if to fire, but the American quickly drew his pistol and fired at the young Mexican, forcing him to retreat to the other side. It wasn't clear if the young man was wounded in the firing. The commanding general at Fort Bliss who submitted the report of the firing stated in unequivocal terms, "there exists an undercurrent of bitter resentment that might easily lead to personal acts of violence against individual Mexicans on either side of the line."[22]

Many within the Mexican military and civilian ranks grew increasingly hostile toward American authority figures along the border. The same report also indicated that the "lawless bandit class of Mexicans along the border without a doubt dislike Americans intensely."[23] A reference to Mexicans as the "bandit class" was a blanket term used by Consul Edwards to identify the *carrancista* soldiers who broke rank and were at an uproar over salary and other problems. Interestingly, both American and Mexican military officials in addition to Cobb expressed caution not to instigate another "Brownsville situation in Ysleta."[24] Cobb did not specify which "Brownsville incident"; however, the Plan de San Diego did instigate hints of Mexican uprising in various parts of the state and as far west as San Angelo.[25] The furor attached to the Plan de San Diego had little if any effect on El Paso. However, tension along the border did not cease, and the commanding officer at Fort Bliss indicated that the racial tension in the El Paso region was similar to that in the lower Rio Grande.[26]

Some scholars argue that tensions between Anglos and Mexicans following the race riot were subdued with only the sounds of "coyote yelps of the peanut sellers and sulfurous thump of moving-picture men lighting their fuses."[27] However, this could not be further from the truth. The process of categorizing Mexicans and Anglo Americans as proxies to the atrocities committed along the Texas-Mexico border persisted throughout the early months of 1916. The American National Livestock Association, which met in El Paso in late January, adopted a resolution promoting American intervention into Mexico. Although the charged act of the organization is not unique, Cobb's response reinforced the "failed state" of relations between Americans and Mexicans:

> [The American National Livestock Association] will adopt resolutions prepared for it by elements promoting intervention. Those adopting the resolutions are as a rule ignorant of the problems involved. . . . Between agitated race feeling and promoted expressions, based upon selfish interest, it is very hard to keep posted on actual facts. . . . Yet, trying to study the question dispassionately, and certainly not intending to be influenced by those with axes to grind . . . I have become reconciled to the hopelessness of the situation as it now exists.[28]

Cobb's despondency over the situation was deepened when one of his *carrancista* sources relayed the desperate state of the de facto government's economy. Ciudad Juárez was without industry, employment opportunities for its residents were limited, and closed railway lines isolated the northern border city from central Mexico. Cobb and several of his Mexican confidants believed that Carranza's government and forces in Juárez would "go on the rocks within less than ninety days."[29] Compounding the tenuous situation were the delousing baths performed on all Mexicans entering the United States.

Delousing Baths and Indignation

In 1916, health officials observed an increase in the typhus fever in Mexico combined with the growing immigration of Mexicans into the United States. Dr. Carlos Husk, a physician for the American Smelting and Refining Company, issued a report on typhus conditions south of the border to the El Paso Medical Society in January 1916. In the report, Husk documented five thousand cases of typhus in the town of Aguas Calientes and more than one hundred thousand cases throughout the country. He closed his presentation by stating, "I think typhus is going to come here."[30] A typhus scare out of Mexico reached the borderlands; El Paso city health officials, with the cooperation with Carranza officials in Ciudad Juárez, subjected all Mexicans crossing into El Paso to a chemical bath. Public health officials prompted concerns that Mexicans could at any time "slip through the border and get into the country without passing through the usual government quarantine stations," thus making all Mexicans along the border suspect.[31]

Because of the typhus scare, Mexicans were consequently labeled as a threat to public health and safety. In order to protect American residents from a typhus epidemic, health and city officials considered aggressive action and purification necessary. Mexican immigrants crossing the border at the El Paso port of entry were subject to a delousing bath and health inspection. Typhus and other communicable diseases were a public health issue in the region, especially in El Paso's Chihuahuita. El Paso city surgeon Dr. George B. Calnan explained that the "most effective way of stopping the spread of [typhus] has been found to be the extermination of body and head lice. . . . Kerosene kills the lice and vinegar kills the eggs."[32] Mexican officials in Ciudad Juárez cooperated with authorities on the American side. General Gavira declared that all trains coming from the south would be stopped two miles below the city of Juárez for an examination of all passengers and a boiling of their clothing. In addition, he promised to step up efforts to reduce the number of immigrants crossing the border outside of recognized ports of entry.[33]

El Paso lacked the facilities to address the flood of hundreds of the "dirtiest Mexicans ever [seen]," according to United States Public Health Service doctor John W. Tappan, who was assigned to El Paso in 1916. Tappan and his colleague C. C. Pierce rejected using Juárez's steam-shower-disinfecting facility and instead undertook the arduous task of securing funds and constructing one in El Paso. In the meantime, the doctors resorted to older and more dangerous methods of delousing: bathing in a mixture of kerosene, gasoline, and vinegar.[34] Many Mexicans on both sides of the river found themselves targets of this archaic method of "cleansing." Doctors Pierce and Tappan persuaded the El Paso Health Department to require gasoline baths for those Mexicans admitted to the city hospital and jail.[35] A concerted effort was made to target other sectors of the Mexican community in El Paso.

On March 2, the El Paso school board moved to prohibit Mexican students from attending El Paso schools due to fears of contagious diseases coming over from Ciudad Juárez.[36] City health inspectors ran through the Chihuahuita neighborhood ordering all bedding and rags infested with lice to be burned at once.[37]

Health officials in El Paso took extraordinary precautions. Dr. Pierce suggested that all trains coming in from Mexico should cease immediately and requested that the United States immigration service establish a complete disinfecting plant.[38] Militarization efforts were also set in motion. Soldiers were sent to patrol the border north and south of the American city to stem the flow toward the bridges where they can be inspected. In another effort to suppress a typhus outbreak, county physician Dr. G. N. Thomas stated that all prisoners of the county jail were subjected to coal oil and vinegar baths as a "precautionary measure."[39]

Private residents were also asked to get involved in the "clean-up" campaign. Individuals who employed domestic servants from Mexico were asked to bathe their employees with coal oil and vinegar and prohibit them from entering the southern part of the city after dark or on Sundays.[40] As stated earlier, schoolchildren were not excluded from this sweep, and the El Paso school board identified sixteen students known to be living in Ciudad Juárez banned from their respective schools.[41]

However, evidence shows that much of the hysteria in the border region was unfounded and largely racialized. Health officials in El Paso conducted a thorough sweep of Chihuahuita and found "unusually healthful conditions" in all districts visited. Not a single case of typhus was found.[42] Inspectors canvassed the homes and workplaces along or near the river, which incidentally were neighborhoods with high concentrations of Mexicans.[43]

An extensive review of newspaper accounts of the typhus scare in January and March 1916 failed to reveal any citywide campaign targeting white Americans to perform any precautionary or preventative health exercises in order to minimize the spread of the disease. General Gavira eventually found the treatment of Mexicans crossing into the United States disconcerting and threatened to disrupt the inspection process and prohibit American crossing into his side of the river:

> I would have it understood, however, that the manner in which our citizens have been treated when entering America has not been courteous and I also wish to state very positively that our policy is to be one of reciprocity. If you refuse to give passage to our people we shall also deny passageway to yours. There has been considerable lack of courtesy with the authorities in El Paso. I hope there will be no repetition of it, as the two cities have interests that are identical and friction between the two can never result in good.[44]

All American public health efforts targeted Mexicans and categorically stigmatized them as a threat and a degenerative lot. Moreover, the typhus scare allowed inspectors and law enforcement officials access into people's homes regardless of their level of exposure to the disease. In one "clean-up" case, two federal health inspectors along with immigration officials inspected the Mexican quarter of El Paso and instead of finding cases of contagious diseases they rounded up a "large number of Mexicans who had smuggled themselves across the river without passing through the immigration station and [undergoing] inspection."[45] Tensions simmered on both sides of the river.

After a thorough review of the border, Dr. Tappan concluded that not a single case of typhoid was reported from Ciudad Juárez. However, extra health personnel were placed at the American end of the international bridges.[46] Dr. Raul Argudin, chief of the medical staff of the Juárez medical corps, confirmed Tappan's report and declared, "there was not a single case of typhus or a single suspect in the border city."[47] Mexican residents on both sides of the river were not the only targets for delousing campaigns. Prisoners housed in the El Paso city and county jails were also subject to baths and inspection.

Their treatment was often the target of ridicule. A local newspaper column documented the delousing event and identified the prisoners as "vags," "floaters," and "rock pounders."[48] On Saturday, March 4, 1916, male and female prisoners underwent a bath at the expense of the city. The anonymous columnist sarcastically described the process and clarified that the baths were not a "warm bath with Florida water in it and perfumed soap on the side," but rather consisted of 50 percent kerosene—"called coal oil in the pine belt—and old fashioned vinegar." The dipping of prisoners was a part of the city health department's crusade against the "lowly louse," said to be the common carrier of typhus germs.[49]

Prisoners stripped nude and dipped themselves into the oily mixture. The process assured that any evidence of lice on their person would be killed. Their clothing was also subject to fumigation. As a consolation for their trouble prisoners were rewarded with an "extra portion of meat at dinner."[50] There were substantial fears among the prisoners that the heavy dosage of kerosene posed not only a health hazard but also a safety concern if a spark should be ignited. Their fears would come to fruition only two days later.

Jailhouse Holocaust

On March 6, A. B. Perry and several of his fellow prisoners housed in El Paso's city jail repeated the bathing ritual and were led into a delousing bath in the old cell room part of the jail. The ritual became all too familiar for the inmates and their jailers who conducted this process for at least a few months. What awaited the prisoners was a solution of coal oil and vinegar for bathing and unbeknownst to some a solution of gasoline as a "disinfectant" for saturating their clothes.[51] The men came out from their cells into an area known as the "roundabout" and were ushered into the old cell room in the lower tier. Before them were two tubs approximately twelve to fourteen feet apart.[52] One at a time, prisoners dipped their naked bodies into the flammable solution and returned to their cells to wait for their clothes to dry. Several medical and jail officials were present in the delousing room, including police surgeon Dr. G. B. Calnan, city jailer Frank Scotten, Dewey Johnson, chief trustee of the city jail Roy H. Bagby, and fellow trustee Harry Morris. All men later served as witnesses in the grand jury investigation and all emphatically insisted that prisoners were warned of the dangers of lighting matches. Scotten went as far as to proclaim that all of the men were searched and that they "begged them to give up their matches."[53] Well, not all of them.

Edward McGowan and H. M. Cross were arrested and admitted into the city jail for allegedly shoplifting a small black baseball glove from the Kraukauer, Zork, & Moyer hardware store in downtown El Paso. Moments after their arrest the two men were subject to the delousing baths conducted on all prisoners. McGowan stood in line as he awaited his kerosene baptism when he proceeded to light a match. Chief trustee R. H. Bagby darted toward him to put out the flame. It was extinguished but at roughly the same time Cross, McGowan's shoplifting partner, struck the deadly match and instantly lit the entire room on fire.[54] Prisoner A. B. Perry was stepping out of the coal oil and vinegar tub dripping from head to toe with the flammable solution when he saw a flash and the entire room burst into flames.[55] Cross was at the end of the jail farthest from the "vats of gasoline in which the prisoners were being bathed."[56] At least ten prisoners were near the big washtubs of kerosene and gasoline when the match was lit and two dozen more were standing without their clothes in the "bullpen."[57]

Dr. Calnan and Frank Scotten both vehemently testified that prisoners were constantly warned of the dangers of the matches near the bathing solution. Several of the witnesses corroborated the doctor's claim of constant warnings and reprimands. However, A. B. Perry testified to a different story. During the grand jury testimony, Perry claimed that he was never warned not to smoke. In fact, he claimed that he smoked a cigarette about forty-five minutes prior to the bath and was not reprimanded for the act. He further claimed that "they did not tell us what we were bathing in. I had no idea what it was."[58] The obvious contradiction in stories suggests that jail officials were trying to cover their missteps by reiterating a common story of warnings and reprimands. However, if Perry's account is accurate it also suggests that city jailers underestimated the potency of the concoction and essentially placed little value on the prisoners' lives. Nevertheless, a disconnect between jail officials and prisoners was evident.

In addition to warnings issued by the city doctor, other precautions were taken. The windows of the jail were left open to allow some ventilation in the facility. Most of the doors, including those of the lower cells and those leading out of the cage, were unlocked. Trustee Harry Morris was thought to have the keys to the few locked doors in the area. The tubs were located in front of the door that led prisoners to their cells. In other words, when the fire broke out, all the prisoners had to pass through the gasoline flames to get out.[59] Morris was stationed near the door of the lower tier, letting prisoners out to the bath and admitting those who had bathed. When the explosion occurred he flung the door open and rushed outside, leading few prisoners with him. It was estimated that it took anywhere between fifteen to twenty minutes for the jail to empty.[60]

Few prisoners made the brave attempt to escape the room. The fire enveloped the entire area, blistering the paint on all the cells. Some men buried their faces into their blankets but soon they caught fire. Temperatures in the jail rose exponentially and soon made the "floors of the cells, particularly those of the upper tiers, so hot that it was impossible to stand upon them even in shoes, and all the prisoners were barefooted."[61] Ernesto Molina, a seventeen-year-old prisoner, was within a few feet of the tub when the explosion occurred and ran to the iron steps leading to the courtroom on the second floor of the building. He ran across the courtroom leaving bloodstained footprints until he leaped out the window onto the roof of the patrol wagon shed. Another prisoner, Ocario Soto, was one of the first bodies firemen dragged out of the burning building and left out in the alley to die. He suffered intense agony and could not see out of his swollen and bloody eyes. Some eyewitnesses claimed that Soto's body emitted such great heat that the "black asphalt was drawn to the top of the pavement and the spot where [he] laid resembled a sun blistered street on a summer day."[62]

Chaos erupted in and around the jail as prisoners sought relief for their painful burns. An American who was badly burned about the arms escaped and ran down the streets of downtown El Paso. He found refuge in a drug store where he was given medical attention. However, a Mexican prisoner who escaped the fire by running through the wall of flames and into the city streets was apprehended by police officers after a lengthy pursuit.[63] Numerous men found themselves in agonizing pain before they met their death. Cross was immediately killed in the explosion and McGowan suffered for six days before expiring on March 13 and becoming the twenty-third victim of the blaze.[64]

One newspaper account stated, "many unusual incidents marked the fire in the city jail."[65] On the morning of March 7, 1916, Judge Dan M. Jackson of the Thirty-Fourth District Court called for a grand jury investigation. He instructed the members to be thorough and in the case that the explosion was a result of criminal negligence to return indictments regardless of who may be implicated.[66] Although many in the grand jury believed that they would have exclusive control of the investigation, it was revealed to them that Justice James M. Deaver and Assistant County Attorney Frank Feuille Jr., would investigate the affair by interrogating the witnesses prior to the grand jury's line of questioning.[67] The publication of the testimonies revealed several inconsistencies that would suggest a conspiracy and fuel the fears that had many Mexicans in the area believing the incident was not accidental.

The grand jury probe exposed several testimonial inconsistencies by key witnesses that suggested neglect and conspiracy. First, the question of ventilation and exit strategy was addressed and details were asked of city jailor Frank Scotten. During a line of questioning by Assistant County Attorney Frank Feuille, Scotten reiterated that "as far as ventilation was concerned, every precaution had been taken," and that all the windows and doors were open.[68] Scotten went further to say that since the doors of all the cages were unlocked they didn't need to be open for prisoners to escape. Dr. Calnan was in charge of the bathing program at the city jail. He corroborated Scotten's statement and reiterated that the doors of the lower cell were unlocked and the door leading out of the cage was unlocked as well. However, he failed to recognize that the area where the bathing occurred was in the south end of the jail and one of the two exits in that area was locked. In addition, the upper-tier cells were not open or unlocked and at least six men were trapped in their cells when the explosion occurred. Dr. Calnan later contradicted his earlier statement when he testified that at least two of the men trapped in the upper tier died from the flames.[69]

Fire chief John W. Wray recounted that he and his men first tried to gain entry from the north side of the jail rooms but found the door locked. They went around toward the back to the alley and found that door closed.[70] They hacked their way through and extinguished the flames with chemicals and water. Chief Wray stated that he and the firemen had to fight the fire before they were able to reach the prisoners and carry them out. Some were lying on the floor and some were in cells, he said. Chief Wray recalled that the firemen had to step over one dead prisoner who was lying near the doorway.[71]

The bathing area was an inferno and yielded few opportunities for escape. A door leading into the bathing area, approximately forty feet from where Cross lit the fateful match, was badly damaged, and the paint blistered in all the cells. Prisoners housed in the bathing area had to pass through the wall of flames in order to exit the room. The door leading from the cell room to the police station proper was kept locked since the completion of the new cell house and the establishment of a new office for the jailer in the rear of both cell houses. The locked door blocked the only way out for the prisoners.[72] Few men attempted or made the escape largely because the entire room was instantaneously engulfed in flames.

Carmela Alonzo, a nurse, was at the police station when the explosion occurred. She testified that she smelled fumes of gasoline, and at approximately three twenty-five in the afternoon she heard an explosion. Two men who were burned came running out, and she poured some olive oil over them. One of the grand jurors, A. H. Anderson, asked her if she noticed if any windows were open and she answered, "The windows where the patrol goes in must have been closed because they were all broken out. The rest of the windows were open." Nurse Alonzo recalled that the jail didn't seem to have any facilities to treat the burned prisoners.[73]

Another major concern that arose from the grand jury probe was the contradictory testimonies regarding the precautionary measures taken to ensure inmates did not possess or strike matches during the bathing ritual. Justice Deaver questioned R. H. Bagby and Harry Morris, who swore that the prisoners were repeatedly warned not to strike matches in the jail:

> (Bagby's testimony): I was in charge of the trust[ees] of the city jail and was in [the] cells on the east side supervising the dressing of the men and seeing that none of them struck matches. I had assisted a Negro, Dewey Johnson, in fixing up the baths under instructions from Dr. Calnan. We had two tubs, one for the bath and one for washing their clothes. In the bathtub we put a bucket of gasoline, one bucket of coal oil and a bucket of vinegar, and in the tub for the clothes we had a bucket of gasoline and a bucket of disinfecting solution.[74]

Dr. Calnan, who directed the bathing process at the time of the alleged accident, confirmed Bagby's assessment. When asked if any precautions were taken against matches, he emphatically stated that he and his staff repeatedly instructed the prisoners to not strike any matches. However, as stated earlier in this chapter, inmate A. B. Perry testified to the contrary.[75] At the time of the explosion, Perry was standing next to the door that led to the large bathing room and was quickly overwhelmed by the flames when the match was struck. He sought refuge in an adjacent room with two or three other prisoners and concluded that he would kill himself before the flames got to him. However, someone broke open a door and they all escaped.[76]

The grand jury probe dug deeper into the preparation process Calnan and his staff undertook in warning prisoners and securing the area of matches. In a follow-up question, Dr. Calnan was asked if a search was made of individual prisoners to see if any of them had matches. He replied that searches were not made, despite the fact that several prisoners made requests for matches. Frank Scotten partially refuted Calnan's statement by claiming that every man was searched thoroughly for matches the Saturday before when the prisoners were bathed.[77] However, when Frank Feuille, the assistant county attorney, later questioned Scotten, he said that a search of the prisoners was made prior to the March 6 bath and that "in most cases we put our hands in the men's pockets to find matches."[78] When asked if everyone was searched, Scotten admitted that some were not searched. However, R. H. Bagby, prisoner and head trustee, testified that he didn't think prisoners were searched, only warned not to have matches.[79] Harry Morris testified that he did not perform any searches on prisoners and was instructed by Dr. Calnan and Scotten to simply warn them "to be careful about matches."[80] In fact, he claimed that an "old Mexican" asked him for cigarette paper just thirty minutes prior to the explosion. The lack of a thorough search of prisoners was evident when H. Cross and E. McGowan were brought in by city detectives while the prisoners were being bathed and not searched for matches.[81]

Nineteen of the twenty-seven dead prisoners were of Mexican origin. Many of the Mexican survivors recalled harrowing stories of escape and excruciating agony. Prisoners Molina and Soto were just a few of the stories echoed in local newspapers of the horrific scene at the city jail. Daniel Yrias, a Mexican with a wooden leg, saved himself by standing on his wooden leg with one hand firmly grasping the iron supports of the cell. He sustained severe burns about the head and hand but would have sustained more serious injuries if he had not drawn himself out of the wall of flame and held himself up on his wooden stump.[82]

Accounts of heroic escapes took a dramatic and interesting turn when Diego Acebes fled the burning jail. City detectives arrested Acebes, who crossed into El Paso from Juárez, for selling empty bottles on the streets. It wasn't clear where Acebes was exactly when the explosion occurred, but he was close enough to get burned and was seen running nude through the downtown streets and frantically crossing the Rio Grande into Ciudad Juárez. Acebes's escape albeit dramatic wasn't unique; however, it was what he proclaimed to the people south of the river that caught the attention of many. As Acebes ran nude and in intense agony from his burns he claimed that Mexican prisoners were being burned to death by Americans.[83] The *San Antonio Express* newspaper reported that two Mexicans reported from their hospital beds that El Paso authorities rounded up Mexican men for no good reason, poured gasoline on them, locked them up, and then threw in a lit cigarette to finish them off.[84] Many in Juárez, including *carrancista* troops, agitated to a frenzy and threatened to cross into El Paso and defend their Mexican brethren. However, Gavira and his officers were able to keep the men from crossing and maintained a semblance of order.[85] Nevertheless, within hours of Acebes reaching Ciudad Juárez, a uniformed Mexican soldier took matters into his own hands. Again, a state of war emerged as military personnel sought to avenge the unjustified deaths of their comrades. The tragedy at the city jail transcended localized conflict and inspired international intervention drawn along racial lines. Citizens and military officials alike sought retribution.

C. A. Phelps, a motorman on a racetrack trolley car, made a turn onto Constitution Street in Juárez where a man stood in the center of the track and motioned for the car to stop. Phelps brought the car to a stop and opened the front door; a uniformed Mexican soldier stepped in and drew an automatic pistol, firing four times at the driver. Phelps was shot through the right shoulder and jaw and collapsed to the floor. There was a stampede of passengers on board who paid little regard to Phelps and trampled upon the man who was still alive. After a few moments, Phelps exited the car and somehow made his way to the Mexican customs house. His condition was reported to the American consulate and Ciudad Juárez mayor Manuel M. Prieto. Mayor Prieto took Phelps across the Santa Fe Bridge to the emergency hospital and later to Rolston Hospital. All streetcars operating in Juárez were immediately stopped for the night. Mayor Prieto expressed regret and assured American officials that the identity of the shooter was known and that he was a well-known bandit wanted by local police.[86] The Ciudad Juárez mayor, however, did repeat that rumors were running rampant in the city and that many Juarenses believed El Paso police were herding Mexicans, covering them with gasoline, and applying the torch. Prieto stressed to El Paso police chief Don Johnson that the rumors caused considerable excitement and asked that all Americans be turned back at the bridges and not permitted to enter Ciudad Juárez from El Paso, "for fear they might be molested."[87] General Gavira quickly mobilized his troops to suppress any disturbance or uprising.[88]

In an attempt to suppress the rumors of intentional murder and inciting a race war, the American press moved quickly to extinguish any blame targeted toward the police. On the front page of the *El Paso Herald* on March 7, a day after the fire, El Paso city alderman and chairman of the sanitary committee, J. P. O'Connor, made a statement claiming that it was "wrong to censure the police department in any manner for the horrible accident yesterday afternoon, as they had nothing whatever to do with the sanitary work being done in the police station."[89] Mayor Tom Lea returned from Albuquerque two days after the fire and adamantly condoned the efforts of Dr. Calnan and renounced the statements made by some Mexicans that this was not an accident but an intentional act:

> I deeply deplore the occurrence of Monday afternoon and consider it an accident. I feel that Dr. Calnan took every precaution. Sometimes with every care and precaution taken, the unexpected happens. I deeply deplore the statements made by irresponsible people which would almost make the public believe that the health department ordered these men burned . . . no sensible person would pay any attention to any such report or talk.[90]

Lea's quick judgment and dismissal of any wrongdoing agitated many Mexicans in Juárez and El Paso, as well as those in Villa's ranks. Lea further commented that "this kind of accidents happen pretty often to Mexicans in Texas and it was just as unavoidable as the lighting of the cigarette."[91] Ethnic Mexicans thought otherwise and distrusted the police and Anglo authority.

Herbert H. Thompson, a Stanford journalist stationed in El Paso, related to a colleague that Mexicans' distrust of the police is not completely unfounded. Thompson argued that "what the police have done here (El Paso), the Texas Rangers have done all down the line. . . . Mexicans commit their crimes on our side of the line, but too often merely in retaliation."[92] The Acebes proclamation that Americans were burning Mexicans alive resonated throughout Ciudad Juárez and the rest of Mexico. Susanna Houghton, a British subject leaving Chihuahua en route to Arizona a few weeks after the fire, stated that the "lower classes of Mexicans" believed that the El Paso city jail fire was deliberate and meant to kill Mexicans.[93] Francisco Villa subscribed to this school of thought.

Residents and civilian law enforcement officials in West Texas and along the US-Mexico border mobilized their efforts to combat Mexicans in two ways. First, the mishandling of the kerosene baths at the city jail suggests that local police in El Paso supported retaliatory operations on Mexican residents in the city. Furthermore, the front page of the El Paso Herald on the day of the fire ominously printed the headline, "It Is Just Eight Weeks since Santa Ysabel—and Nothing Done Yet." The El Paso jailhouse holocaust suggests that El Paso police and jailhouse officials enacted their own level of justice when a fire broke out and killed nineteen Mexicans, a few white transients, and a "negro."[94] Mexicans on both sides of the river perceived the act as "pure hatred."[95] A grand jury was assembled and failed to return any indictments, thus finding all medical and city officials innocent of any wrongdoing for the burning deaths of twenty-six prisoners.[96] In a bold move, American public health officials concluded that more, not fewer, rigorous methods of prevention were needed.[97] Mexicans on both sides of the river continued to express discontent and anger to what they believed was systematic murder.

News of the atrocity reached Villa prior to his raid on Columbus, New Mexico, just a few days after the fire on March 9. According to some rumors circulating around El Paso and Juárez, Villa said, "Now I'll show them how to set people aflame."[98] Prior to his attack on Columbus, Villa gathered his men and gave a passionate speech denouncing the Americans for their role in his defeat in Agua Prieta, accusing the United States of selling him defunct ammunition, and of the El Paso jailhouse holocaust. Villa and his men were suspicious of the incident and believed it was a deliberate act largely because of the dozens of Mexicans lynched in the lower Rio Grande Valley and throughout Texas.[99]

Conclusion

The early months of 1916 set the stage for war between Americans and Mexicans and to a certain degree the United States and Mexico. Following the Santa Ysabel massacre tensions ran high, and many Americans anxiously awaited retribution. The typhus scare out of Mexico led many US health and immigration officials to aggressively protect American communities from a perceived threat. As a consequence, ethnic Mexicans were forced to delouse and bathe in a kerosene solution that was thought to kill the disease. However, the bath did more than subject Mexicans to inspection; it further marginalized and stigmatized the community as a threat to American security.

By March 1916 elevated tensions between Americans and Mexicans were at a boiling point. The process of delousing Mexican immigrants, residents of Chihuahuita, and Mexican prisoners housed in city and county jails categorically criminalized ethnic Mexicans and further reinforced their status as an "enemy other." Anglo residents in El Paso who employed Mexican servants, for example, were not subject to chemical baths, therefore squarely identifying Mexicans as dirty and a threat to the public welfare of the city. The appropriated stigma of being Mexican by the authority structure consequentially required vigilance and purification by Americans. Regardless of whether the jailhouse holocaust was an accident, the failure of assigning accountability and mayor Tom Lea's dismissive attitude toward ethnic Mexicans suggests that Mexican lives were of little value. Immediately following the jailhouse holocaust, Pancho Villa made sure revenge would be had and that his stamp on American and Mexican relations would be immortalized.

¡Viva Villa!
The Columbus Raid and the Rise of the Mexican Enemy

I've done my fill of the border, / Of greasers and border men, / I've done my bit and I stand to quit / And never take on again, / But I seem to know, when the bugles blow / And I hear the reveille, / That my blood will heat and my pulses beat / No matter where I may be. / And I'll yearn to go—with a burning yearn / That only the soldier feels.
—Unknown author

ON MARCH 3, 1916, ZACH COBB REPORTED TO SECRETARY OF State Robert Lansing, "[Francisco] Villa left Pacheco Point, near Madera, Wednesday, with three hundred men headed toward Columbus, New Mexico. . . . There is reason to believe he intends to cross to United States and hopes to proceed to Washington."[1] Cobb sent a follow-up letter on March 6 that stated that Commanding General Gavira in Ciudad Juárez announced to reporters that Villa was indeed on his way to Columbus and that American military authorities should be on the "look out for him."[2] In the early hours of March 9, 1916, Francisco Villa invaded American territory at Columbus, New Mexico. At least sixteen Americans lay dead and several hundred fatally wounded *villistas* were scattered across the desert landscape. The Columbus Raid was the culmination of a vengeful war that not only pitted two ethnic communities against each other, but also solidified the Mexicans' position as the enemy and a threat to the United States and its Anglo community.

Events such as the Santa Ysabel massacre and the El Paso race riot racially delineated between the guilty and innocent. The mediatory role of the United States military came full circle by March 1916. The largest military base in West Texas, Fort Bliss, had served the borderlands as a protective institution against an "enemy other" since its establishment in the mid-nineteenth century. Increased militarization at the turn of the twentieth century agitated race relations and encouraged violent retaliatory response from civilians. By 1916 a military approach to the border and the apparent shortfall in manpower prompted civilians to arm themselves and organize in vigilante groups known as Home Guards.[3] Collectively they identified Mexicans as an enemy with little regard to military protocol or distinguishing the guilty from the innocent. Military presence in Mexican neighborhoods resulted in the social categorization of its ethnic residents as a threat to society and a marginalized community. Reinforcing the point that a militaristic approach to border violence spread to the civilian sector as Home Guards felt compelled and justified to organize and fight the Mexican enemy.

Home Guards, as civilians and political officials alike called them, were volunteer paramilitary units intended to protect communities from raids and to secure justice through extralegal methods. The various units were endorsed and, at times, supported by the state. Governors Oscar Colquitt and later James Ferguson rallied towns across Texas, especially along the border, to organize able-bodied men and consequentially receive ammunition and other resources from the government.[4] However, the state's militarization efforts proved to be problematic as Mexicans became more reactionary. Some Anglo Texas farmers objected to Ranger treatment of Mexicans because it made relations more tenuous and tense.[5] In El Paso, the mayor published tirades against Washington, fueling the agitated state of many in the city.[6] In addition, Mexicans' and Mexican Americans' resistance to the impunity of Anglo authority and civilian efforts made them look like the "enemy" in the eyes of many in El Paso. The efforts of a loosely organized Mexican community contributed to the perception that Mexicans were "enemy" combatants who diverted from their submissive or passive stereotype. The actions and presence of the increased military personnel translated to a highly sensitive and militarized citizenry.[7]

Villa's attack on Columbus and the mobilization of the National Guard provides a lens through which to view a seemingly interdependent and highly complex relationship between the military and civilian sectors. The deputization of civilians and the creation of Home Guards blurred the lines between innocent and combatant. A militarized citizenry increased steadily throughout the early period of the Mexican Revolution.[8] However, as Francisco Villa's disdain for President Wilson's policy toward his revolution and his anti-American rhetoric materialized in Santa Ysabel and northern Mexico, many US residents increasingly militarized themselves and targeted all Mexicans as enemies of the state. Scholars suggest that white Texas residents in the early twentieth century straddled the line of maintaining order through legal means and violently securing justice through extralegal methods, such as lynching.[9] Not to suggest that the lynching of African Americans in Texas were not retaliatory actions, but Mexicans as white suggests that violence toward Mexicans was a matter of defending the country from an internal and external enemy. In other words, the citizenry mobilized and outfitted itself militarily as a means to identify the Mexican as an enemy and subject to justice. The Punitive Expedition into Mexico in March 1916 and the mobilization of the National Guard along the US-Mexico border, along with the organization of Home Guard units, promoted a call to duty to the idea of a Mexican "enemy."

After Pancho Villa's attack on Columbus, the borderlands of West Texas, southern New Mexico, and northern Mexico emerged as ground zero. Civilians, servicemen, and politicians had fully engaged the problems on the border, waged punitive measures against Mexico, and managed the intense racial tensions that erupted. Agencies that included the National Guard, the Home Guards, local police, and newspapers attempted to establish order at the same time that they reinforced the idea of the Mexican as the "enemy." Also, the massive military buildup on the border, led by the National Guard, contributed to the separation of the neighboring regions that had long been interdependent. Lastly, the infamous "dead line" imposed on El Paso continued to divide people a year after the race riot.[10]

The mass mobilization of the national guardsmen to the border in 1916, especially to El Paso, established yet another layer to the authority structure already in place and complicated social relations even more.[11] The National Guard, or state militias, had long engaged the western frontier. This was evident soon after the US-Mexico War of 1846–48, when the border became a point of diplomatic and economic interest.[12] The interest continued during the late nineteenth century when railroads connected the southwestern states to the Pacific Ocean, Gulf of Mexico, and Mexico City. Conflict on the border also encouraged official interest. Mexicans residing in the annexed territories, for instance, resisted the takeover and often came into conflict with Anglo settlers. Anglos, on the other hand, often reacted with violence to defend themselves; they also initiated land-grabbing schemes toward Mexican landowners. Federal and state authorities who sought to resolve the conflict often reinforced it with their own violent methods as well as with their partisan ways.[13]

The "border trouble days," meaning the border conflict stemming from the Mexican Revolution, required border institutions to move beyond local vigilance and punitive measures and request that state and federal institutions assume greater responsibility in securing the border.[14] The federal response to the growing security concerns assumed international importance and reinforced a popular view of the Mexicans as the "enemy." Border institutions evolved from their localized and state settings into more federalized and complex power sources that extended beyond assuring border security to maintaining social order. As the US-Mexico border witnessed pacification, two distinct and racially divided communities emerged. The US military assumed a major responsibility in this process, as its relationship with local Mexicans worsened along the international boundary line. Moreover, the National Guard's intense militarization of the border complicated intergovernmental relations as Mexico came to see the buildup as a direct threat to its national security. Additionally, as border conditions assumed a greater federal and international context, the local mobilization of the citizenry remained a pivotal aspect of border security despite the mobilization of over 111,000 guardsmen to border duty immediately following the Columbus Raid.[15] As a result of an active militarized citizenry and the dominant presence of the National Guard along the US-Mexico border, the Mexican community on both sides of the river secured its place on the military stage as the "enemy."

President Woodrow Wilson's recognition of Venustiano Carranza's Constitutionalist government in October 1915 encouraged Villa to commence a series of violent acts that targeted American citizens and property. His subsequent attack on Columbus turned an intergovernmental initiative that sought greater security along the border into another source of conflict. Predictably, Secretary of War Newton Baker responded to Villa by federalizing the state militias into the National Guard under the National Defense Act of 1916 to enforce the United States' neutrality policy and border security. While the US Army marched into Mexico in pursuit of Villa, the newly organized National Guard under the direct command of the president and US Army assumed the responsibility of patrolling the border, protecting American property owners from raids, and disbanding Mexican revolutionary *juntas* that were organizing on US soil.

Martial law in El Paso may have stilled the political waters somewhat, but the revolution still ran deep, and its current continued to carry the fortunes of many in its wake. This was especially evident in Villa, still smarting from Wilson's recognition of Carranza and the US's arms embargo that was undermining his revolutionary cause. His eventual attack on nearby Columbus, New Mexico, demonstrated that the revolution continued to spill over into the United States and influence both intergovernmental relations and race relations in places like West Texas and southern New Mexico.

The Invasion of Columbus, New Mexico, and Racialized Justice

A review of Francisco "Pancho" Villa's invasion of Columbus, New Mexico, follows the trajectory that civilian involvement in policing and protecting the border was an active part of the official authoritative structure. Blurring the divide between innocent and guilty was also present as Villa's troops kidnapped and killed several innocent civilians who crossed their path on the way to Columbus. Maude Wright's firsthand account describes Villa's movements and objectives prior to attacking the small New Mexico border town. After the invasion, Americans in Columbus mobilized a "home guard" that pursued not only retreating *villistas*, but also ran out several Mexicans who peacefully resided in town. Juan Favela, a Columbus resident, recounts his unheeded warnings of the invasion and his exile from Columbus following the invasion. The attack on Columbus highlights yet another racialized conflict but sheds light on a massive American federal response that further complicated social relations between Americans and Mexicans.

Maude Wright lived on a small cattle ranch with her husband, Ed, some thirty miles from Pearson, Chihuahua, Mexico. In August 1912, the Wrights had their first contact with Mexican revolutionaries. Members of Pascual Orozco's revolutionary faction called Los Colorados, or Red Flaggers, would leave their tired horses and take whatever fresh horses were available on the ranch. In 1913, conditions worsened and the Wrights, along with her parents and several other Americans, moved to southern New Mexico. Ed took on several odd jobs for about a year and by February 1916 they made their way back to their ranch in Pearson. A garrison of Carranza soldiers at Pearson provided added safety for the Wrights. However, this false sense of security was shattered on March 1, 1916.[16]

Roughly fifty to sixty mounted Mexican men approached the Wright ranch. Maude Wright advised them that she didn't have much but offered to feed them. Ed arrived shortly thereafter and one of the Mexican men asked where he could get some feed for his horses. Ed never returned to the house. According to Maude, the men began to ransack the house and take whatever supplies they could find. The young mother was then taken captive. Ranch raids along the border and in the northern region of Mexico were not unusual. However, the Wrights did not fully understand that their presence in Mexico agitated Villa's growing hatred for Americans following the

Wilson administration's recognition of Carranza as the de facto leader of Mexico in late 1915. Nevertheless, on the morning of March 2, after marching all night, Wright arrived at Boca Grande Ranch on the Casas Grandes River some twenty-five miles southwest of Columbus. There, Wright first saw Villa and roughly 2,500 to 3,000 of his men. Her husband and a young ranch hand named Frank Hayden rode past her with their hands tied. *Villistas* led the men to a nearby hill and killed them. When Ed and Frank's killers returned to join the main Villa army, Maude overheard the group discuss a raid on Columbus.[17]

Officials in the United States monitored Villa's whereabouts in 1916. A number of military and civilian officials as well as run-of-the-mill Anglo residents from El Paso aided in the intelligence gathering of Villa near the international boundary line. Zachary Lamar Cobb, the city's collector of customs and intelligence during the Mexican Revolution, expressed a popular local concern over the instability in Mexico to Secretary of State Robert Lansing:

> As seen from here, the Carranza authorities have lost their opportunity to have established the trend toward improvement. The trend has set in against their success. As seen from here, I am reconciled to the expectation that conditions in the state of Chihuahua and along the border will grow worse.[18]

Cobb also warned of possible German influence in Carranza's administration, a point that must have piqued the interest of the security-conscious Wilson. In addition, he sounded the first alarm of a possible invasion by Villa or his sympathizers on American soil.[19] Villa's continued influence in Ciudad Juárez explained the United States' interest in El Paso and the intelligence reports that came from the border city. Villa had maintained military control over Juárez at least until late December 1915. Cobb maintained that his influence was still evident. He reported, for example, that Villa's family continued to live in El Paso.

As early as January 1916, Cobb relayed a message from Carranza authorities indicating that Villa would be crossing "to U.S. somewhere in Columbus, New Mexico district."[20] By early March, Cobb was eventually able to confirm Villa's movement toward Columbus, New Mexico:

> Villa left Pacheco Point, near Madera Wednesday [March 1] with three hundred men headed towards Columbus, New Mexico. He is reported west of Casasgrandes [sic] today. There is reason to believe he intends to cross to United States and hopes to proceed to Washington. Please consider this possibility and the necessity of instructions to us on the border.[21]

On March 6 and 8, Cobb was able to locate Villa's forces in the Palomas region, just south of Columbus on the Mexican side.[22]

Villa made his presence known to all in northern Chihuahua by slaughtering cattle and raiding small ranches. Innocent residents of the region were not spared from his rampage. For instance, Villa's soldiers abducted Buck "Babb" Spencer, a black man who was working on an American-owned ranch. As they made their way north toward Palomas they raided one bunch of cattle from the Palomas Land & Cattle Company, which was led by company foreman Juan Favela. Villa took the cattle and several captives, including local judge Hilario Fraere and a cook named O'Neill, who was later shot and killed in cold blood by the *villistas*. Arthur McKinney, an American cowboy on the ranch, was hanged with a strand of barbed wire instead of a rope.[23] The reckless abandon in which Villa killed these Americans served as an example for all of his men as they approached the border. After the execution, he made his way toward Columbus, and in the ranches El Chale, Rancho Verde, and others just outside of town, Villa recruited an unknown number of local Mexicans.[24]

On the morning of March 8, Villa was within sight of the border and set up camp. Spies returning from a reconnaissance mission in Columbus met with the general and divulged detailed information about the situation in Columbus. According to Maude Wright, the spies informed Villa that the American soldiers were scattered all over the region and that only a skeleton crew remained, and the town was theirs for the taking.[25] Villa and his officers held a conference and inspected the men and equipment. Due to a shortage of ammunition, they selected six hundred men for the siege and outfitted them with at least three belts of cartridges.[26]

Meanwhile, Juan Favela of the Palomas Land & Cattle Company, who escaped Villa's raid on his cattle, hurriedly made his way to the border for safety. Juan approached Lee Riggs, a US customs inspector, and relayed to him that Villa was coming to the border and was intent on killing every American in gunshot range. Riggs then took Favela to Colonel Herbert Slocum, commanding officer of the Thirteenth Cavalry stationed at Columbus. Slocum was with a few other officers when Favela started to spill the details of the impending raid. Slocum shushed Favela and dismissed the other officers in the room. He then locked the door and sat down with Juan alone. After completing his story and warning Colonel Slocum of the raid, Favela was dismissed and told to go about his business and not utter a word to anyone. "Look here, Juan, you take care of your business and I will take care of the running the Army."[27] Slocum declared that such a declaration by Favela would only cause unnecessary worry and concern among Columbus's residents. The colonel proceeded to run the business of the army by dispersing a "couple of companies to the Gibson Line Ranch some fifteen miles west of Columbus and another couple of companies some fifteen miles east of Columbus."[28] After dispersing the various companies to the outreaches of southern New Mexico, Slocum ordered that all arms in the camp be locked up. The remaining officers and their wives, along with Slocum, then took off to a party on a ranch some fifteen miles east of Columbus. Lieutenants Castleman and Edwin Lucas were the ranking officers remaining in the camp the morning of March 9, 1916.[29]

"I Am Going to Make a Torch of Every Man, Woman, and Child": The Columbus Raid

Wright continuously heard Villa tell his men not to forget the burning of the El Paso city jail just a few days prior to his arrival at the Columbus and Palomas area.[30] Villa accused the Americans of deliberately starting the fire with the intention of killing Mexicans. He garnered intense hatred toward Americans and kept his soldiers "keyed up and desiring revenge."[31] On the morning of March 9, 1916, Columbus claimed approximately four hundred residents and a skeleton crew of the Thirteenth Cavalry.[32] At around four thirty that morning shots and battle cries rang out, "Viva Villa!" and "Muerte a los gringos!" (death to gringos).[33] Private Fred Griffin, the sentinel on post number three at Regimental Headquarters, challenged the rebels and was mortally wounded.[34] Villistas made a strong push forward, setting ablaze Ravel's Commercial Hotel.[35] Officers were absent and the soldiers had to rip down the locks to the guardhouse to get to their weapons. Chaos spread like wildfire. Civilians and some soldiers made a run for the desert to escape the attack. Lieutenant Edwin Lucas, fresh from the Philippines and a machine-gun company commander, broke open the lock on the arms closet and had four Benet-Mercier machine guns in operation, getting off some four thousand rounds.[36] The spewing of machine gun fire forced the villistas to make their retreat; however, they quickly realized that one of the machine gun units cut off their access. This proved to be the deciding factor in ending the raid.[37] The raiders were finally outnumbered and outgunned when the few officers and units began to organize and the arms storage was unlocked. The attacking party was repulsed an hour and a half later at approximately six o'clock.[38]

Hundreds of villistas raced back to camp near Palomas, among them General Pancho Villa himself. Maude Wright recalled that Villa entered Columbus on a paint stallion taken from the Palomas ranch. However, the stallion was shot from under him and as soon as the melee of machine gun fire forced the villistas to retreat, Villa returned with a gray horse.[39] Many of Villa's men did not make the retreat and found their final resting places scattered throughout various parts of the town alongside seventeen American casualties, mostly civilians.[40] Villa allowed Wright to be released and directed her to Columbus where she made her way to the ranch of J. K. Moore, a dry goods merchant killed in the attack. Deputy sheriff Jack Breen and a group of American soldiers soon picked her up; they immediately took custody of her and prohibited any of the civilian law enforcement officers to question her. She was transported to headquarters to meet with Colonel Slocum, who arrived in Columbus later that morning a few hours after the final Mexican retreat.[41]

Former Columbus resident Mary Lee Gaskill was a young girl at the time of the raid and she recalled in an interview that there "were hard feelings towards Mexicans then."[42] Colonel Slocum immediately went on the defensive and ordered military police to pick up Juan Favela. He gave Favela a pass that allowed the Mexican national to travel anyplace in the United States, along with some cash. Slocum then instructed Favela to "take this pass and get out of town. Go wherever you want, but I don't want you hanging around here. Don't come back for a couple of weeks. Now get!" Favela simply went up to nearby Deming and drifted back to Columbus after a few days.[43] Fortunately for Favela, tensions were riding high immediately after the raid and Mexicans became the prime target. Several white residents issued a warning to any "stranger" caught around town that they had five minutes to get five miles out of town.[44] People who had fled to Deming, New Mexico, and El Paso made their way back to Columbus. Among them was a Mexican from El Paso, who was hoping to open a barbershop in Columbus. Late that night, on March 9, when their train arrived, a group of Americans assaulted the Mexicans and killed them. According to an interview with an observer:

> (Armendáriz): Y hubo otros Mexicanos, eran tres, tres Mexicanos, que llegaron en la noche, también por ahi de Deming. Y los agarraron, y luego . . . Les soltaron los balazos y dos cayeron . . . los mataron. (And there were Mexicans, three, three of them that came that night from Deming. And [the Americans] got them and then shot them and two of them fell . . . they killed them.)

> (Sánchez): ¿Los Americanos? (The Americans?)

> (Armendáriz): Los Americanos los afusilaron. (The Americans executed them.)

> (Sánchez): Y esos muchachos nomás venían, no tenían nada que ver con el ataque ni nada. (And those men just arrived; they didn't have anything to do with the attack or anything.)

> (Armendáriz): No, nada nada. Si nomás venían de por ahi de otros pueblos. (No nothing. They just came from other towns.)[45]

More Mexicans, some arriving from Asunción and Janos, Chihuahua, encountered the same fate that night. After the Columbus attack, a vigilante group made up of Anglos took justice into their own hands, just like in El Paso, and began to assault any Mexican they saw.

Daniel J. "Buck" Chadborn, his family, and J. F. "Jack" Thomas were at home about a mile east of town when Villa attacked the town. When the firing died down, Chadborn hid his family in an old cellar behind the house; then he and Thomas started for town and caught a glimpse of Villa's troops retreating, and US military forces were "rounding up whatever stragglers they could find with the help of a citizen here and there."[46] Major Tompkins took command of two troops in pursuit of the *villistas*, and Chadborn seized the opportunity to organize a posse of citizens who were armed and mounted in support of Tompkins. Chadborn's vigilante group quickly confronted many of the retreating *villistas*, who were either badly wounded, unable to keep up with the escape, or were under orders to stay behind and provide cover for their retreating comrades. According to Jack Thomas, the posse pursued the *villistas* for about a mile into Mexico and was ordered back to the US side. On their return they completed their "mop up duties" and didn't bring any prisoners with them.[47] Approximately twenty-five men comprised the civilian posse and were led by customs inspector Jolly Garner (half-brother of the 32nd vice president of the United States, John Nance Garner), customs inspector Ben Aguirre (whose father was US Consul in Ciudad Juárez), and Buck Chadborn.[48] It did not matter if the Mexicans were

Figure 7. Columbus, New Mexico, Home Guard.
Photo courtesy of Archives of the Big Bend, Bryan Wildenthal Memorial Library, Sul Ross State University, Alpine, Texas.

associated with Villa or not. Little is known about the violence after the attack, but it is clear that it was used to justify the racially inspired reprisals and the continued vilification of ethnic Mexicans in Columbus and other towns and cities on racial grounds.

The attack on Columbus resonated among residents and government officials in El Paso, all the while acknowledging the complex circumstances that could potentially arise with an intervention into Mexico. On one hand, Zach Cobb petitioned Secretary Lansing that the Wilson administration act swiftly and with force. He feared that Villa's attack would "hasten the disintegration of the Carranza government" and "make [Villa] a national hero," since many among Carranza's military ranks were in a desperate state.[49] Cobb's concern over the strength and capability of Carranza's forces to pursue Villa were echoed by Consul Edwards, who reported that the garrison was poorly equipped and housed a mere three hundred men.[50] However, Edwards understood that the crossing of US soldiers into Mexico, although initially tolerated by General Gavira, could change the longer Americans remained on Mexican soil.[51] Villa successfully promoted his brand of propaganda by sending couriers to all Mexican states to incite the populace against Americans whom he termed as the "common enemy of Mexicans."[52]

Americans in the United States mobilized their retaliatory efforts in the broadest of terms, hoping intervention would come to fruition. For instance, four hundred El Paso residents represented by the city's Chamber of Commerce discussed plans for immediate organization and requested arms from the state or federal government.[53] The militarization of American civilians was in full swing in the aftermath of the Columbus Raid. Modest military encampments and civilian Home Guards, once organized in the

Figure 8. Citizens' Home Guard, Columbus, New Mexico.
Courtesy of the Columbus, New Mexico, Historical Society.

wake of American occupation of Tampico, Mexico, in 1914, quickly sprung into action.

Many "unruly" elements on both sides of the border eagerly awaited word for action.[54] The climate along the border was thick with anticipation and tension. In an editorial printed a few days after the Columbus Raid, the editor wrote that all residents were expected to offer their services in the case of "any local emergency" and cooperate with "civil and military authorities to protect life and property."[55] The excitement felt by many in El Paso, Ciudad Juárez, and southern New Mexico could not be underestimated nor was it by city, state, and federal authorities in the region. On the day after the editorial, March 14, law enforcement authorities admonished the call to duty by issuing the following statement:

> El Paso is protected for any emergency, but the authorities are not looking for any trouble. The authorities have but one request to make of the people of the city and that is that in the event of trouble—which is most remote—the men of the city remain in their homes, with their families, and not come downtown.[56]

Apprehensive and cautious American officials took note of the precarious support lent by Carranza forces in Ciudad Juárez and throughout the state of Chihuahua. Local papers, at times, censored their reports in order to not "inflame the public."[57] However, the rumor mill filled the void left by the newspapers and caused considerable unrest among the population.

Nearly two weeks after the Columbus Raid, two major developments were reported by the United States consul agent in Torreon, Chihuahua, George C. Carothers. He telegrammed Secretary Lansing on March 22, informing him that two thousand Carranza troops supposedly deserted and declared allegiance to Villa. Refugees fleeing Torreon reported that the city would fall to Villa within a few days.[58] Although Carothers expressed doubt of the actual desertion he pressed forward and claimed that Mexicans of El Paso "have arms and ammunition hidden in their homes which will create dangerous condition," especially as American troops pressed deeper into Mexican territory.[59]

The Columbus Raid on March 9, 1916, sparked a retaliatory response by civilian and military alike. Many along the border felt threatened by Villa's anti-American violent tirade and sought immediate action by organizing armed civilian posses and targeting any Mexican who crossed their path. The United States and its military responded to Villa's invasion with the Punitive Expedition.[60] However, the might of the American military and the diplomatic exchanges between Wilson and Carranza did not remove or diminish the civilian role in the militarization process after March 1916. A week following the Columbus incident, a committee on military affairs for the El Paso Chamber of Commerce met with the military brass of the Eighth Cavalry at Fort Bliss and discussed the possible formation of a citizen military training camp equipped by the federal government.[61] Not surprisingly, militarization of border residents following Villa's raid in Columbus continued a long history of securing the area and building institutions that included civilian, state, and local law enforcement entities.[62]

At the turn of the twentieth century, the US government reorganized the state militias to provide uniformity among all units and ensure that the federal government would have at its disposal the necessary state forces. This reorganization federalized the state militias and converted them into the National Guard. By 1910, the Mexican Revolution was a major security concern for the United States, especially in West Texas. Ultimately, the National Guard became responsible for responding to raids by Mexicans from Mexico and localities in West Texas, the activities of revolutionary *juntas* on the US side of the border, and American citizens killed at the hands of revolutionary forces in Mexico.[63]

The National Guard and Home Guards along the Border

Armed conflict attributed to the Mexican Revolution led Texas to mobilize its state militias and supplement the Regular Army soldiers already stationed on the border. At the beginning of armed conflict attributed to the Mexican Revolution in 1911, a single National Guard unit was headquartered in El Paso.[64] The company consisted of some fourteen officers and twenty-four privates. This was a small contingent considering that it was responsible for much of West Texas and parts of southern New Mexico. However, El Paso and Ciudad Juárez assumed an important role in the Mexican Revolution. El Paso's strategic locale for importing munitions and recruitment saw increased actions by both the state and federal governments; by 1912 three thousand US troops, including National Guardsmen, were stationed in West Texas.[65]

The call for military protection that often involved National Guard troops in places like West Texas usually came in response to fears that the revolution, or international incidents associated with it, could inspire Mexicans residing in the United States to take up arms.[66] All along the Texas-Mexico border, American residents expressed that "if serious trouble ensue between [the United States] and Mexico, no one can tell just what stand the Mexican residents [in Juno, Texas] might take against the whites."[67] A medical doctor in Presidio emphasized that the Mexican population grossly outnumbered the Anglo population "three hundred to one," and Rangers were desperately needed to curb the disturbances caused by "drunken Mexicans."[68] White fears of mobilized Mexicans went beyond the local scope. The landing of US Marines in Veracruz in 1914, for example, demonstrated that such faraway incidents could trigger local fears. As US-Mexico relations began to deteriorate after the American occupation of Veracruz, army troops at Fort Bliss and the National Guard were ordered to patrol the streets of Chihuahuita and place under surveillance a number of suspicious residents. Local and military officials feared aggressive or violent anti-American demonstrations. As a precaution, additional troops were placed on high alert and citizens were deputized to enlarge the police force.[69]

Letters from willing and able citizens from all walks of life flooded the governor's mansion, pledging their services for military action against Mexico in 1914 and 1916. Some eighty men of the Southwest Texas State Normal School (later Texas State University at San Marcos) informed Governor Colquitt that they were ready to enter military service of any kind if needed.[70] Another letter from Teague, Texas, not only asked for permission from the governor to organize a company of volunteers but also demanded that "every Texian should show his loyalty to this great Nation and *especially* to Texas." The term *Texian*, used by the letter writer, echoes the racial divide present during the Texas rebellion of 1836 to separate Texian Anglos from ethnic Mexican Tejanos.[71] A real estate agent from Houston wrote to Governor Colquitt remarking that "patriotism calls upon him to defend a people who fear a lot of 'Greasers.'"[72] The pleas to organize civilian regimens did not go unheeded. Governor Colquitt not only granted permission for Home Guards to be sworn in throughout the state but also he informed the Texas Rangers of their availability and allowed for "requisitions for guns come through Ranger captains."[73] The hysteria soon passed. Fear, however, continued throughout the state and along the international boundary line. This was especially the case among El Paso's Anglo community. The thought of revolutionary sympathizers operating in the city, the possibility that they would instigate violence in El Paso, and the limited presence of the federal military and National Guard deepened their concerns.[74]

The apparently ominous threat Mexicans posed led Governor Oscar Colquitt to further militarize the border. He rushed sixteen companies of the National Guard to supplement the Texas Rangers already on duty along the Texas-Mexico border.[75] El Paso residents offered to aid the National Guard and Rangers by submitting requests to organize volunteer guards for war with Mexico and border protection.[76] The Veracruz incident and the militarization of the border that it caused were accompanied by other political developments that increased security concerns along the border. For example, continued fighting between Mexican revolutionary forces in 1914 led the United States to contribute additional army troops and National Guard soldiers to border security. Area newspapers added conflicting reports to security concerns by reporting that thousands of Villa and Carranza officers and soldiers resided in El Paso and planned on invading the city.[77] Meanwhile, city officials repeatedly downplayed Mexican mobilization by emphasizing their confidence that the city was not anticipating any excitement due to the Tampico affair in 1914 or any other revolutionary stimuli. Nevertheless, city and military officials moved to militarize downtown El Paso and Chihuahuita.

Mayor C. E. Kelly conferred with Colonel C. A. P. Hatfield at Fort Bliss and announced that it may "be necessary to place the city under martial the law [and] the city hall would be turned over to Col. Hatfield" despite little evidence of unrest in the city and especially in Chihuahuita.[78] Sheriff Peyton Edwards had five hundred civilians along with a militia company and cavalry from Fort Bliss ready to respond to a fire whistle if an emergency arose.[79] Although Mexicans residing in El Paso were "on the friendliest terms with the Americans," extreme militaristic measures were taken in anticipation of an uprising by Mexicans on the US side. Following President Wilson's address to Congress requesting authorization for military action in Mexico, Governor Colquitt telegrammed the president suggesting that it would be "imperative that there be an immediate invasion of Mexico so as to take possessions of Matamoros, Nuevo Laredo, C. P. Dias and Juarez" to suppress the threat of 20,000 to 30,000 Mexican refugees on the Mexican border.[80] Wilson responded to the governor by stating that an invasion of Mexico was unlikely; however, it did not stop military and civilians alike to fortify El Paso.

A few days following President Wilson's address to Congress in 1914, El Paso residents offered to serve as policemen, and fifty men were added to the force. The patrolmen and mounted men on South El Paso Street and in the lower section of the city (Chihuahuita) were doubled.[81] El Paso emerged as an "armed camp largely for the reassuring effect of the troops on the more nervous citizens." Cannon were posted on the highlands of the city at the water reservoir. An additional two battalions of infantry with a machine gun platoon, and two squadrons of cavalry kept watch and ward over the city.[82] Colonel Hatfield took his headquarters in city hall at night with a variety of resources, including direct telephone connections with gas and electric plants, as well as Fort Bliss, that kept the colonel in touch with all points on the border. The people and soldiers of the El Paso area and southern New Mexico were reassured when three regiments of infantry—the sixth, twelfth, and sixteenth—were coming from San Francisco along with Brigadier General John J. "Blackjack" Pershing.[83] Small towns outside of El Paso took advantage of the governor's call to organize Home Guards due to citizens feeling uneasy over Mexican events.[84] Although Huerta fled Mexico not long after the Tampico event, tensions did not subside along the border nor did the militarization of the region.

By 1915 the climate along the El Paso and Ciudad Juárez border intensified when the Wilson administration turned to Venustiano Carranza as the de facto president of Mexico. In response to the increased violence and fears of invasion, the US military placed one of its largest troop concentrations in the El Paso area.[85] In August 1915, troops were again mobilized in response to a possible uprising among revolutionary-minded immigrants residing in "Chihuahuita."[86] Stationing of troops actions worsened a tense situation. They sowed distrust between Anglos and Mexicans.

Racial animosity and the fear of uprisings did not only exist in West Texas. Social uprisings laced with racial overtones emerged in South Texas around the same time. The discovery of the Plan de San Diego in 1915 was especially important. It originated in South Texas, and the Plan's call to arms was initially a race war against Anglos and the establishment of separate republics for Mexicans, Native Americans, and blacks in the territory lost by Mexico during the 1846–48 war. Subsequent documents issued by the revolutionaries, who waged a guerilla war mostly in South Texas, announced that they were acting against anyone who opposed their irredentist movement, particularly the Texas Rangers.[87]

The raids stemming from the Plan de San Diego forced both state and federal authorities to reevaluate their vigilance over the border region. The small network that included the federal military, the National Guard, Texas Rangers, and local law enforcement groups engaged the raiders with a level of frequency that alarmed federal officials.[88] The raids associated with the Plan de San Diego brought to light the broader context of border security throughout the Texas border region. Headlines of racialized tension in South Texas reached El Paso, and, as a result, its residents requested that more federal troops be stationed in the area.[89]

The fear that resulted from events like the Plan de San Diego, Tampico, and Columbus permeated the border region and prompted many Anglos to resort to vigilantism and indiscriminate assaults on Mexicans.[90] Anglo ranchers in Hudspeth and El Paso counties armed themselves after popular revolutionary leader Pascual Orozco was killed near Sierra Blanca, Texas, believing that the local Mexican community would retaliate his killing.[91] Increased vigilance was clearly required to handle a situation that was seemingly spiraling out of control.

Border Duty, 1916–17

Villa's attack on Columbus, New Mexico, jolted the nation back into an international crisis with Mexico. The Columbus Raid created the opportunity for the United States government to organize and deploy its army and National Guard to the US-Mexico border. The incessant call for more troops and federal redress by border residents and politicians since the outbreak of hostilities, stemming from the Mexican Revolution, had finally reached policy makers in Washington by May 1916. Soon thereafter, heightened security concerns stemming from Villa's attack on Columbus led Secretary of War Newton Baker to call on the governors along the border to mobilize their guardsmen and make them available to the president for border duty. In one communiqué to Governor Ferguson, Secretary of War Newton Baker underscored the importance of the mobilization:

> I am directed by the President confidentially to advise you that he may be obliged to call out the militia of your state for the defense of the Mexican border and to ask you to take such steps through your Adjutant General as can be taken without publicity to [expedite] immediate action upon such a call if it does become necessary for the President to issue it.[92]

Eight days later, the US government issued the order to activate all state militias into a National Guard and assign them to border duty. The US Congress and President Woodrow Wilson had approved the National Defense Act, which further expanded the National Guard's role through a unified federal effort and guaranteed that the National Guard would function as the Army's primary reserve force to serve along the border.

The legislation coined the term "National Guard" and granted the president the authority to mobilize it in case of war or national emergency.[93] By August 1916, about 111,954 National Guardsmen from across the country and nearly 11,000 Texas guardsmen were placed along the Texas-Mexico border. The commanding officers regarded West Texas as an area desperately in need of reinforcements.[94] The Fourth Texas Infantry and the First Texas Cavalry arrived at Marfa and immediately set up camp outside of town. Company K of the Fourth Texas Infantry was composed mostly of El Paso men and was one of the first ushered into service following the Columbus attack.[95] The responsibilities of the state militias mustered into national service were expanded to guard against a possible Mexican invasion, disrupt illegal revolutionary juntas that violated neutrality laws, and protect American property from raiding Mexican bandits.

National guardsmen were mustered from all over the United States and found the Texas-Mexico borderlands as foreign as its people. For outsiders coming to the borderlands for the first time, El Paso and Ciudad Juárez did not replicate the romantic vistas portrayed in movies. By June 1916, when much of the American military force was summoned to the border, El Paso was under martial law. Few police were on hand and directed traffic. However, the provost guards, or military police, detailed from the army patrolled the city streets. They were an intimidating lot carrying billy clubs and rifles. Soldiers were ordered to keep a strict eye on the Mexican population in El Paso as they were seen as the source for danger should an uprising occur. El Paso absorbed a significant number of Mexico's displaced and refugee population. As a result, the Mexican population outnumbered the Anglo population, which caused grave concern among civilians and military alike. A private in the machine gun company of the Eighth Massachusetts Regiment stated:

> Contrary to the general belief, the danger along the border States is not wholly from foreign raids, but partly from the great Mexican population within our own States in the southwest. The population of El Paso, for instance, is sixty per cent Mexican. As these aliens are segregated in one quarter of the city, and are closely united in every way, chiefly through mutual hatred of the gringo, they would prove a serious menace if an attack or uprising took place. And even at towns like Las Cruces, New Mexico, over fifty

miles from the border, a company of infantry is required to keep the foreign population in check.[96]

Private Roger Batchelder went further to describe the Mexican population as an unsavory community and echoed the popular southwestern opinion that Mexicans were "unscrupulous and untrustworthy."[97]

The mobilization of the National Guard in 1916 was a response to several key events. First, the Wilson administration's recognition of Venustiano Carranza as the de facto government in Mexico in October 1915, spurred a series of violent initiatives by Villa against American citizens and property. Moreover, the Carranza government posed a diplomatic problem as the Mexican Revolution continued to spill over into Texas and other parts of the border region, and Carranza did not seem interested in cooperating with the United States until Wilson recognized his government.

The government also militarized the border in response to the fear and racial tension that had escalated since the Mexican Revolution, most notably after the discovery of the Plan de San Diego in 1915 and the increased Mexican population residing in counties along the Texas-Mexico border. For many border residents, the Mexican threat was real and capable of erupting into a full-scale race war pitting Mexicans and whites on opposites sides of the battle. This was made evident when US consular agent George Carothers pointed out that the militarization of the border was necessary due in large part to the suspicion and fear of worsening conditions at places like El Paso. Following the tumultuous events of early 1916, the debate over national defense along the border became especially marked. Carothers reported an armed Mexican community to Secretary of State Robert Lansing:

> A large portion [of the] Mexican population of El Paso have arms and ammunition in their houses which will create [a] dangerous situation here . . . the possibility exists of them starting something serious.[98]

National guardsmen and army troops were often assigned to Chihuahuita as a preemptive measure, but it became evident to many Anglos in El Paso that the local population represented a potential threat to everyone.

The mass deployment of guardsmen to the border hit a peak in February 1917 and eventually redirected its efforts and presence elsewhere. Pershing and his men were recalled from Mexico after failing to capture Villa, and the United States was preparing for its entry into World War I. Removal of the Guard troops from the borderlands began in mid-February, and units were dispersed to various places away from the border. The Texas units were sent to Fort Sam Houston in San Antonio and Camp Bowie near Waco.[99] Units from Arizona, New Mexico, and California were stationed at Camp Kearney, California. Many of the units were some of the first to be deployed to France when the United States declared war on Germany April 1917.[100]

World War I left the border to fend for itself. State and local officials assumed a greater responsibility of protecting its citizens along the border. In 1933, the Guard was reorganized as a permanent component of the federal army, which the president could order into active federal service whenever

Congress declared a national emergency.[101] The formidable presence of the National Guard along the US-Mexico border during the period of the Mexican Revolution proved to be more of a facade of law and order. Many of the units faced considerable difficulty in establishing effective authority in the region or stabilizing tensions between the two ethnic communities.

"Conflict, Not Peace": The Trials and Tribulations of the National Guard in West Texas

Impending war with Mexico and the high concentration of Mexican residents along the border forced the US government to use guardsmen from across the country to reinforce what was thought to be an inadequate defense along the border. Villa's attack on Columbus was believed to have exposed the weaknesses of the American military. According to Senator George E. Chamberlain, chairman of the Military Committee, the United States had only 15,000 eligible men for border service, while it was projected that Mexico could organize 50,000.[102] Senators Reed Smoot and William E. Borah contributed to the argument by adding that Mexico had more field guns and was better equipped than the United States. The political critics were not only concerned with the lack of eligible men for border service, but they also did not underestimate the difficulty of manning an extensive boundary line.

In a published interview an anonymous "high ranking military official" recognized the immensity of the line and felt that the undertaking would be too great for the small military:

> Persons do not realize the length of the line we would be called upon to defend to prevent raiding-parties from attacking border-towns and treating them far more terribly than Columbus was treated. . . . The length of the Texas frontier is more than the distance from [New York] to Chicago. . . . We talk of invading Mexico. With every regular in the United States concentrated on the border we could not defend it properly from an attack, let alone inaugurate a pursuing punitive expedition.[103]

Congress and military officials then turned to the National Guard to supplement their low numbers. However, the National Guard soldiers reporting for border duty confronted a set of circumstances and obstacles that would affect their successful negotiation of the borderlands region, especially in West Texas.

The National Guard in West Texas faced a number of problems. First, the rough and vast terrain of West Texas kept the guardsmen from effectively executing their responsibilities of protection and surveillance. Small canyons and other nooks in the area provided ideal hiding places that made it nearly impossible to conduct effective searches.[104] Also, some Mexicans on the Texas side of the river sympathized with the raiders and revolutionaries. They furnished them information concerning the area ranches and patrol schedules of the National Guard and other authorities. These problems caused the guardsmen to assume the added responsibility of conducting surveillance over the Mexican community. They also recruited

Mexicans as guides and spies and urged local residents to provide for their own protection.

National Guard officers called on border residents to organize committees of defense and neighborhood guards under the supervision of a National Guard officer.[105] The local units, or Home Guards, patrolled the international boundary line and gathered intelligence on the movements and actions of Mexicans on the US side of the border. The commanding officers of the National Guard claimed that Mexicans in the United States were increasingly abetting revolutionary factions and activities, thus causing disorder and breaching federal neutrality laws.[106] Fear among the predominantly Anglo Home Guards, may explain why some of them began to apply their own brand of justice on innocent Mexicans.

Overzealous locals often took action into their own hands. El Paso chief of police Don Johnson and Captain Lee Hall held in custody alleged *villista* colonels Juan and Samuel Rodriguez as "suspicious characters and agitators, as a precaution against revolution or agitation of revolution," despite the fact there were no formal charges attributed to the men. They were simply arrested because of a rumor that they planned to "blow up [El Paso]."[107] In places such as Culberson, Hudspeth, and Presidio counties, citizens were quick to pursue suspected Mexican raiders who had attacked desolate ranches hugging the US-Mexico border. Again, a mere rumor was enough to trigger action. According to a former resident of Van Horn, Texas (some 120 miles east of El Paso), the town's people reacted immediately:

> A report came over the wires that Van Horn was to be raided. The men of the town gathered guns and ammunition to defend the town.[108]

The feared raid did not occur. Nevertheless, residents from all over West Texas were ready to seek out any Mexican they thought was breaking the law.

Guardsmen contributed to the campaigns against Mexicans in other ways. In some cases, they were reckless and aggressive with them. These problems became so serious that commanding officers found it necessary to issue general orders reminding soldiers of the Mexicans' rights and the need to observe them.[109] This explains the policy of "peace and friendship" that the National Guard and the Army implemented in 1917, primarily to avoid conflicts with Mexico and local Mexicans. The National Guard, for example, posted this policy in May:

> The policy to be observed toward Mexico and Mexicans is one of peace and friendship. The same treatment will be accorded to all Mexicans by our troops, whether on or off duty, as is required by law and custom to our own people. Following this policy in the past has resulted in much harmony between the two races.[110]

Tensions were riding high between the National Guard and local Mexican residents. Much of the reckless behavior the guardsmen exercised was related to aggressive tactics and indiscriminate pursuit of Mexicans.

Guard units were instructed to seek the "offensive" when confronted with suspected bandits and "hunt them down and exterminate."[111] This resulted in several occasions where patrols of the National Guard fired upon innocent Mexicans:

> There have been several instances where so-called Mexicans have been fired on in the dark by patrols of the National Guard, and where it has been altogether uncertain that the parties fired on were not attending to their legitimate business.[112]

Mexicans along the border grew increasingly distrustful of the National Guard and the US Army. As a result, the units amplified the feelings of animosity and distrust among Mexicans in the border region. In some cases, Mexican residents manipulated intelligence data to thwart National Guard operations.[113]

The mobilization of the National Guard consequently increased militarization of the border but did little to cement effective and adequate authority in the region. The vast and rugged terrain, especially in West Texas, forced the Guard to set up only short camps, as the regiments were "split up and scattered throughout [the Big Bend]."[114] Vigilance over the Mexican population was of the highest priority. General orders to monitor "suspicious" congregations of Mexicans were issued and carried out by the conjoined effort of both guardsmen and civilians.[115] Surveillance efforts were also evident within the city. The National Guard's presence in the El Paso area brought on progressive initiatives that resulted in economic hardship in many of the city's entertainment industries located in El Paso's Mexican sector, Chihuahuita.

The National Guard also conducted surveillance in El Paso. Its major challenge in El Paso, however, involved a reaction from reformers against the vice industry in Chihuahuita, which had grown in large part to service the increasing number of guardsmen and army personnel in town. Businessmen involved in gambling, prostitution, and drinking establishments eagerly promoted their services to the soldiers. As noted in a previous chapter, the call for restrictions on the vice industry caused many businesses simply to move their operations to Ciudad Juárez.

The commanding officers of the National Guard, on the other hand, responded to War Department warnings to "clean up" by restricting the movement of the soldiers.[116] According to one missive, "the war department is determined not to locate cantonments in communities maintaining a [red light] district."[117] Problems with soldiers were frequent. According to court-martial records from El Paso, many soldiers were arraigned for various infractions, including public drunkenness, leave without permission, and behavior unbecoming of an officer.[118] Problems became so serious along the border region that Congress addressed alcohol consumption and disorderly conduct in the Emergency Army Bill of May 1917. The directive read as follows:

> That the President of the United States, as Commander in Chief of the Army, is authorized to make such regulations governing the prohibition of alcoholic liquors in or near military camps and to the officers and enlisted men

of the Army . . . that no person, corporation, partnership, or association shall sell, supply, or have in his possession any intoxicating or spirituous liquors at any military station, cantonment, camp, fort, post, officers' or enlisted men's club, which is being used at the time for military purposes under this act.[119]

According to some commanding officers who reviewed units along the border, the accessibility of the vice industry at Ciudad Juárez and El Paso handicapped the Guard's ability to perform its duties and patrol the region effectively.[120]

City officials also acted on the soldiers' behavior. The city applied the "dead line" policy to them. The policy prohibited soldiers from frequenting El Paso's downtown entertainment district located in and near the Mexican portion of the city and adjacent to the international bridge. The enforced "dead line" placed many of El Paso's downtown merchants at an economic disadvantage as profits began to decline due to the absence of soldiers. Furthermore, customers were encouraged to go to other parts of the city deemed more desirable.[121]

Downtown merchants sought various options that would make the district more suitable for soldiers and citizens. One of them was to regulate the district with curfews and with medical examinations for the city's prostitutes.[122] Other merchants tried to cooperate with the National Guard and local police to rid the district of "undesirables" who were responsible for bootlegging and other forms of vice, presumably prostitution.[123] Despite their efforts to reopen Chihuahuita to soldiers and salvage their economic livelihood, the city and the Guard persisted with its enforcement of the "dead line."

Conclusion

The activation of the National Guard in 1916 signaled the elevation of local tensions and conflict to an international level. Villa's Columbus Raid served as the catalyst for the mass mobilization of the US Army and the newly minted National Guard. The amassing of troops served diverse purposes. In 1916 the US Army engaged an international agenda with the Punitive Expedition into Mexico, and the National Guard served as the source for national defense on the US side of the international boundary line. The National Guard provided an "added layer" to the security initiatives already in place by local, state, and some federal authorities.

The National Guard also faced problems. Its inability to effectively negotiate the terrain and overcome the existing racial tensions handicapped their effectiveness. Furthermore, reform-minded initiatives aimed at the military brought economic hardship to business owners in El Paso's "Red Light" and downtown districts.

The "dead lines" in El Paso's downtown "Red Light" district and the resulting segregation of Mexican neighborhoods reinforced a rigid line between Anglos and Mexicans. The complete elimination of vice was never fully realized, as many soldiers and patrons were simply encouraged to seek take their business to more "desirable" places outside the downtown or Mexican sector. Moreover, the issues of vice served as little more than a front to further isolate Mexicans from the rest of El Paso. The military's prohibition initiatives disrupted more than the economic structure of El Paso's downtown entertainment district. They crystallized the divisions between Anglos and Mexicans and encouraged the view of the Mexican community as the "enemy other."

"Agents under Fire"
Prohibition, Immigration, and Border Law Enforcement

IN MARCH 1916, MEXICANS LIVING IN SOUTH TEXAS, ALONG the Texas-Mexico border, complained to their local consul regarding the US Public Health Service's (USPHS) branding of their arms, in permanent ink, with the word "admitted," upon being bathed and physically examined at Laredo's international bridge. The Mexican consul sent a letter asserting his challenge to the United States' inhumane practice of "stamping Mexican citizens, who are looking for work." The USPHS medical inspector in charge of operations in Laredo, H. J. Hamilton, disagreed and believed the measures were not in violation of the individual's rights or dignity. In fact, Hamilton argued that the branding was necessary "to defend Texas from the lice, smallpox, and other germs usually carried by 'Mexican paupers,' and was a 'very good plan' that would help to deter 'future illegal entry.'"[1] In El Paso, Dr. Claude C. Pierce, the USPHS senior surgeon, began efforts to build a disinfecting plant in the city under the Santa Fe Bridge.[2] On January 23, 1917, Dr. Pierce announced that the moment had arrived for an "ironclad quarantine" against everybody entering the United States from Mexico and opened the disinfecting plant in El Paso, Texas.[3]

Militarization along the border grew to a crescendo as border security, labor needs, and immigration restriction took center stage in the US-Mexico borderlands during the closing years of the Mexican Revolution and into the 1920s and early 1930s. The United States Border Patrol, which was established in 1924, became an entity of federal authority in the region that was no longer local but national and transnational. Moreover, the permanent presence of a federal law enforcement agency suggests a shift in policing methods along the border. Over time the Border Patrol evolved into a militarized police outfit that followed a trajectory that went beyond policing and emerged as an aggressive force protecting the status quo in the United States. Enforcement practices, of course, reflected policy changes in immigration and prohibition laws as well as the accommodated needs of employers, mostly farmers. Also, an increase in the Mexican population created a "race problem" that encouraged restrictionists to call for stricter enforcement. Strong restrictionist sentiments gave greater significance to the enforcement of the Immigration Act of 1924, while "cultural nationalism of the late nineteenth century had transformed into a nationalism based on race."[4] Mexican immigration had increased exponentially since the outbreak of the Mexican Revolution and did not wane after armed conflict had subsided at the end of the second decade of the twentieth century. More importantly, Mexican exclusion from the quota rolls and Mexico's proximity to the United States presented a unique set of circumstances not necessarily seen among other immigrant groups; this augmented the notion that Mexicans were a severe threat to national security and American homogeneity.

By the early 1920s, nativist groups and immigration officials identified Mexican immigrants as a threat to the ethnic, economic, and cultural fabric of the United States.[5] Several policies, including the immigration laws of 1917 and 1918, which targeted Mexican labor, the landmark Immigration Act of 1924 that led to the establishment of the United States Border Patrol, and Prohibition are examined to demonstrate the importance of border security in the region and how it changed. Problems of banditry, smuggling, and mass immigration persisted; however, global and domestic factors, including World War I and stricter immigration policies, affected militarization efforts along the border, which consequently solidified the Mexican on both sides of the border as a subject "enemy other."

In August 1916, at the peak of border operations attributed to the Punitive Expedition, the massive American military arsenal of over 111,000 National Guard soldiers served along the border.[6] However, due to events escalating in Europe and Pershing's failure to capture Francisco "Pancho" Villa, General Frederick Funston recalled General Pershing's troops who were in Mexico to American soil on January 28, 1917.[7] By February 1917, the National Guard was ordered to muster out of the border, with the exception of some who would protect the "postal, commercial and military channels and instrumentalities of the United States" from possible German interference.[8] Pershing's regulars were redistributed along the border to relieve guardsmen sent to their home bases, resulting in a much smaller force to guard the border, a sharp contrast to the large support deemed essential to his long line of communications while in Mexico.[9] Ultimately, border residents were left to depend largely on local, state, and the unreliable Carranza government in Mexico to deal with the continuing problems of banditry, spillover violence attributed to the Mexican Revolution, smuggling, racial animosity, and mass migration.

Nativist concerns across the United States and restrictive immigration policies were played out on the US-Mexico border. Sanitation baths performed on Mexican immigrants prompted sharp criticism from Mexican officials and residents. As one scholar argues, "medicalization and militarization lead to a regime of eugenic gatekeeping on the U.S.-Mexico border."[10] Some Mexican women rebuked the practice and started a near riot on one of El Paso's international bridges. However, the perceived threat of a continued stream of Mexican refugees and laborers as well as the nativist alarms over immigrant flows from other parts of the globe, most notably southern and eastern Europe and Asia, led to a permanent federal law enforcement agency that would protect the white "American" family.

The diminished presence of the American military, growing nativists concerns over immigration, and progressive temperance initiatives led to the establishment of a more fixed and permanent federal law enforcement entity along the border. Since 1911, the United States federal government organized a handful of men called "mounted watchmen" to serve as the "first line of defense against the army of aliens who seek to enter the United States by illegal means."[11] In 1924, the United States Border Patrol headquartered in El Paso contributed significantly to social divisions and racialized conflict. This chapter addresses several policies, including the immigration laws of the 1917–18 period that targeted Mexican labor, and the landmark Quota Act of 1924 that led to the establishment of the Border Patrol. The National Prohibition Act of 1919 also figured prominently in the story of the Border Patrol. The agency was responsible for enforcing the law, which prohibited the manufacture, transportation, and sale of beverages that contained more than 0.5 percent alcohol. These policies contributed to the establishment of legal and political authority in West Texas and in worsening social relations between Mexicans and Anglos.

The precarious authority of the Carranza government along Mexico's northern border and conflicting temperance laws between those of the United States and Mexico destabilized political and social relations between Americans and Mexicans. For example, Mexican fiscal guards, or *fiscales*, engaged in extralegal practices by taking bribes to smuggle people and illegal alcohol across the river to the United States. American line riders and later the Border Patrol, lacked adequate resources to man the international boundary line and were overwhelmed by the sheer volume of cargo, participants, and violence attached to the lucrative business. The corruption of some within law enforcement agencies provided few collaborative opportunities between the two countries. The Border Patrol strengthened federal authority along the border; however, its presence and contradictory policies contributed to the image of the Mexican as the "enemy other." The agency did not just enforce immigration and prohibition laws but also mediated differences between nativists who called for stricter restrictions on Mexican immigration and farmers who wanted an uninterrupted flow of low wage labor.[12] In addition, Americans' insatiable demand for illegal alcohol created a nearly impossible task of disrupting the flow of liquor across the border as its financial benefits far exceeded any level of prosecution or risk.[13]

The Bath Riots

Immigration and health officials, including the United States Public Health Service identified typhus and other communicable diseases as some of the most serious public health threats on the US-Mexico border at the turn of the twentieth century. In the early 1900s, when the Immigration Service established its southwestern headquarters in El Paso, its concern was not with Mexicans, but with Chinese, Eastern European, and Mediterranean immigrants thought to be violating the Chinese Exclusion Act of 1882, the Disease Act of 1891, and the Immigration Act of 1903. El Paso was regarded as the back door through which, according to special immigration officer Marcus Braun, "diseased, criminal, and other classes of immigrants who have failed to get in through the regular ports" entered the United States.[14] Mexicans in the early era of the borderlands crossed the border with few restrictions. However, the Mexican Revolution compounded the public health threat as hundreds of thousands of refugees sought asylum from the violence and escaped to American border cities like El Paso. American residents and health officials grew increasingly fearful that typhus would follow the migrants into American neighborhoods.[15] Despite the fire in the El Paso city jail in March 1916 that killed over two-dozen inmates, border health officials continued with added vigor the controversial practice of disinfecting immigrants.

Historian Alexandra Minna Stern developed a simplified database of inspections and infections along the border in the fiscal year 1917. She noted that in June, Dr. Claude C. Pierce, one of the twelve senior surgeons at USPHS, reported that not a single new case of typhus was recorded along the Mexican border. Out of thirty-one cases of typhus recorded in the United States there were only three deaths, all in El Paso. However, taking into consideration the volume of human traffic flowing through the El Paso port of entry, the number of fatalities was miniscule. In the four-month period Stern studied, 871,639 bodies were inspected, 69,674 disinfected, 30,970 vaccinated for smallpox, 420 excluded on account of illness, seven denied entry for refusing disinfection, and eight retained for observation. According to Pierce, Texas border officials inspected 39,620 people per week.[16] The weekly baths took their toll on thousands of Mexican immigrants crossing into El Paso. In January 1917, many Mexican laborers, men and women, no longer submitted to the baths quietly.

A large gender-mixed group in Ciudad Juárez, incensed at the American quarantine regulations, led a riot on the morning of January 28, 1917. The rioting began when women were ordered to get off the streetcars and submit to being bathed and disinfected before passing to the American side. Reports circulated in both El Paso and Ciudad Juárez stating that the women were verbally assaulted in the bathhouse and photographed in the nude.[17] Mexican residents grew increasingly disenchanted with American health and immigration officials since at least March 1916 when General Gavira publicly renounced the discourteous treatment Mexican residents received when crossing into El Paso and by being subjected to kerosene baths.[18]

The women became indignant when they were ordered off the streetcar. For much of the day, thousands of Mexican women thronged the Ciudad Juárez side of the river and pushed themselves to the tollgate on the Santa Fe Bridge.[19] Many among the mob hurled stones at American civilians on the bridge and in the streets of the Mexican city. At least four streetcars were hijacked and their crew was forced to return to El Paso on foot after suffering minor physical injuries. The commotion on the bridge forced military personnel from both sides of the river to restore order. A Carranza cavalry appeared on the scene at approximately 7:30 that morning, while a dozen US soldiers pushed back the mob's advance toward the American side of the bridge.[20] Mexicans who pushed as far as the tollgate spilled over the railing and jeered at their compatriots who entered the bathhouses.[21]

Carmelita Torres, a seventeen-year-old "Auburn-haired amazon" and ringleader of the large gathering of male and female laborers, protested what she and the mob believed were unjust and inhumane health policies.[22] Reports circulated that American soldiers and immigration officials were photographing the women while nude and making the photographs public.[23] Some of the women not only resented the treatment they received by some American immigration and health officials but also the fact that the quarantine ordered "all persons of unclean appearance seeking to cross the bridge [to] take a shower bath" composed of a mixture of soap, kerosene, and water, which suggested that they were dirty and unacceptable.[24] Of course, several of the women who were stopped by American authorities and ordered to return to Ciudad Juárez could not help but recall the El Paso jailhouse atrocity of the previous year and circulated stories that all Mexicans were forced to take a bath in a gasoline mixture similar to that which killed over twenty-five prisoners.[25] The mob hurled mud, stones, and other objects at American civilians entering Ciudad Juárez. Finally, mounted *carrancista* soldiers led by General Francisco Murguía dispersed the crowd in Ciudad Juárez with a volley of gunshots into the air, and American soldiers physically forced the Mexicans back to the international line at the middle of the river.

Future rioting was avoided when federal health and civic officials from both sides of the border allowed Mexicans to cross into El Paso and bypass the sanitation plant if they obtained a certificate of disinfection in Ciudad Juárez.[26] Bathing certificates were valid for one week, and all crossings were subject to the discretion of the health official on duty.[27] Dr. John W. Tappan, an El Paso health officer, stated that the typhus cases found in Ciudad Juárez "are found among the refugees from the interior of the republic and they are *easily distinguishable* from the better classes of working people who [came] to El Paso."[28] Yet the good doctor offered no hint as to how Mexican refugees were "easily distinguishable" from those residing in Ciudad Juárez. In other words, it was a subjective process based on what the inspector and health official deemed acceptable and not acceptable.

The typhus quarantine did result in specific economic and social consequences suffered by American employers. Appeals were made to the El Paso Chamber of Commerce on account of "interference with business and household affairs resultant from the quarantine." For example, as many as two hundred laborers from El Paso's smelting company were absent, which proved a "serious handicap to that plant." Many El Paso families were without their servants as many preferred to stay in Ciudad Juárez rather than subject themselves to the weekly bathing process. Local and federal leaders from both sides of the river met and confirmed that a cooperative and reciprocal approach was necessary to deter any future rioting. Brigadier General George Bell Jr. of Fort Bliss announced that he would leave the situation to the care of local police and health officials and disperse the military only when requested. He further suggested to the local police that any future rioting should be handled by using "streams of water from fire hoses to disperse the mob."[29]

Rioting in Juárez halted, but tensions persisted. The United States' policy of disinfecting and sterilization continued into the late 1930s; it was then substituted with fumigation efforts, which lasted well into the late 1950s when Mexican workers participating in the Bracero Program were gassed upon entry. Raul Delgado, a bracero worker who came to the United States via Eagle Pass in 1958, described the fumigation process: "They put me and other braceros in a room and made us take off our clothes. An immigration agent with a fumigation pump would spray our whole body with insecticide (DDT), especially our rear and our *partes nobles* (genitals)."[30]

American sterilization and disinfecting efforts along the US-Mexico border demonstrate that immigration policy in the early decades of the twentieth century reached far beyond the enforcement of restrictionist policies. Eugenic philosophies and the proverbial ethnic cleansing became a marker of immigration enforcement during that time period. Immigration scholar Alexandra Minna Stern argues that the Mexican quarantine "hardened the boundary line between Mexico and the United States . . . and fostered scientific and popular prejudices about the biological inferiority of Mexicans."[31] As a result of the quarantine of Mexicans along the international boundary line in 1916 and 1917, Stern argues, ethnic Mexicans on both sides of the river were racialized as outsiders, which catalyzed anti-Mexican sentiment on a state and national level.[32] Beyond the El Paso and Ciudad Juárez borderlands region, newcomer farmers in other parts of Texas viewed Mexicans as racial inferiors who did not merit the rights and privileges of Americans; they belonged to that "class of foreigners who claim American citizenship but who are as ignorant of things American as a mule."[33] Militarization of the border played a critical role in establishing the Mexican as a threat to the United States and categorizing the Mexican as not only a racial other, but as an enemy of the state.

The authority structure present along the US-Mexico border was unable to enforce ambiguous immigration laws, and national security laws were found to be problematic. The Mexican governor of Coahuila made preparations in July 1916 to patrol the Mexican frontier in an attempt to prevent further raids into American territory by bandits or "irresponsible parties."[34] However, United States Vice Consul William P. Blocker, in Piedras Negras, Coahuila, Mexico, recognized that the military buildup on the Mexican side needed to be organized carefully and that the "most diligent and responsible of commanders be selected for this delicate work."[35] Vice Consul Blocker to some extent understood that various factors such as labor flow, commerce, and national security would be affected by militarization of the border. His assessment echoed the growing fear of a possible invasion by Mexican troops aided by Mexican residents living on the US side of the border: "If [Carranza troops, *villistas*, and old Red Flaggers (Orozquistas)] assemble an army of fifteen thousand . . . [they] could do immense damage in this valley [El Paso] before being stopped. Mexican population here so far are behaving admirably but could be expected to take active part if city were attacked."[36] Divisions within the revolutionary factions were blurred when Carranza soldiers evoked Villa's name to entice former *villistas* to join the cause against the Americans.

Nationalist rhetoric permeated the populace in Ciudad Juárez as soldiers and volunteers wore ribbon hatbands that read, "Volunteers to Defend Nation."[37] The elevated uneasiness of the political and social circumstances surrounding Pershing's presence in Mexico and rising nationalism among Mexicans in the borderlands culminated in a suspicion of all Mexicans by

American officials and civilians. Customs agent Zach Cobb reported on June 29 that a series of fires occurred in El Paso, but there was no evidence linking Mexicans to the crime. However, Cobb insisted that despite the lack of Mexican culpability, the unusual number of fires, coupled with the "strained conditions," caused general alarm among the American public that Mexicans were possibly involved.[38] Cobb went as far as to suggest that when guardsmen reached El Paso, they be authorized to "go through the Mexican district of El Paso with a fine tooth comb and take possession of all guns, ammunition, and explosives [to] eliminate the danger we continuously face of racial riots and consequent destruction of life and property in this city."[39] *Carrancista* soldiers responded in "retaliation or what the soldiers say is the general policy of disarming Mexicans in El Paso."[40] Heightened tensions and increased militarization resulted in the criminalization of ethnic Mexicans regardless of citizenship or guilt.

As hostilities between the two nations reached their climactic point in 1916, military buildup on both sides of the river, especially the presence of Pershing's troops in Mexico, concerned American officials. The instability of diplomatic relations between Mexico and the United States, combined with the extremely precarious military initiative of the Punitive Expedition, caused mounting tension and nationalistic fervor among many Mexicans residing on both sides of the boundary.[41] United States Vice Consul John Reid Silliman expressed in a letter to Secretary of State Lansing that *carrancista* officials in the northern state of Coahuila "plainly said that if American troops remained in Chihuahua after reception of American note, the situation would become immediately seriously grave" and determined that "all Mexicans [would] stand with him" and that in the case of a rupture "Mexico [would] receive assistance from many elements in the United States."[42] The ominous reports of a pending invasion by revolutionary troops in Mexico paired with the streaming flow of Mexican and American dispossessed refugees and Mexican laborers presented a highly complicated set of circumstances that synthesized labor concerns, immigration, national security, and, later, smuggling along the Texas-Mexico border.

Militarization of the international boundary in 1916 gave heed to a highly volatile social construct that continued to alienate and criminalize ethnic Mexicans. First, the Punitive Expedition unified to a degree the splintered revolutionary groups and narrowed their focus on the American invader. This heightened Mexican nationalism among Mexicans on both sides of the border posed a national security threat to the border residents on the United States side of the boundary. Second, the multipronged authority system on the border attempted to unilaterally deal with the complex crisis of migration, national security, and temperance without fully understanding the scope and long-term consequences of its actions. In other words, restrictionist immigration policies conceded to nativist and eugenic outcries while handicapping employers who were considerably dependent on Mexican labor by 1920. At the same time, temperance laws pushed vice into Mexico's border cities and gave rise to a lucrative smuggling business that engulfed almost every aspect of American society, the criminal and noncriminal alike.

Last, the militarization of border law enforcement forced various entities to assume militaristic characteristics and recognize the Mexican as the enemy. Mexican assimilation into the American social and political fabric was thus restricted.

Between 1916 and 1933, immigration policy and law enforcement evolved into an entity with multiple tentacles, including public health, national security, customs, labor control, and smuggling enforcement. However, restrictive immigration policies, labor controls, and Prohibition forced federal law enforcement into a dynamic authority structure that followed a militaristic blueprint. The realities of a volatile borderlands region with conflicting policies and practices positioned the Border Patrol into a complicated and contradictory position. As federal legislators passed America's most restrictive immigration policies of that time, employers' demand for foreign labor increased. Mexico's revolution and World War I presented a variety of national security issues that, after Pershing's recall in 1917, a fraction of military personnel, local and state law enforcement, and civilians were left to handle. The passing of the United States Constitution's Eighteenth Amendment prohibiting the consumption, manufacturing, and distribution of alcohol gave rise to a lucrative and violent smuggling enterprise that set law enforcement, smugglers, and civilians on a collision course that would not be settled until the repeal of the amendment in 1933.

Brief History of the United States Border Patrol

The culture and law enforcement methods of the modern Border Patrol can be traced to its predecessors. One of the earliest examples of the Border Patrol's tactics emerged with the passage of the Chinese Exclusion Act of 1882 and the establishment of the Chinese Division of the Immigration Service, which operated within the Department of Labor. The act reduced Chinese immigration and limited the immigrant labor supply for US industries like mining, railroads, and agriculture.[43] According to the Chinese Exclusion Act, Chinese immigration was to be limited until otherwise provided for by law.[44] Enforcement duties fell on the United States Customs Service, which had patrols known as the "line riders" or "mounted guard" serving principally on the Mexican border.[45] The mounted guard consisted of former and active Texas Rangers, sheriffs of border counties, and deputized cowboys.[46] The Customs Service had been entrusted to prevent all illegal smuggling, including that of Chinese immigrants. However, the task overwhelmed the Customs Service, and the apprehension of illegal immigrants fell on the shoulders of the Immigration Service in 1903.

By 1904, the El Paso area received its first mounted immigration officer to patrol the US-Mexico border looking for illegal Chinese immigrants. Jeff Miller, a former El Paso police chief, was the one-man border guard. He was selected "because he could ride and shoot."[47] At the time, those were the only qualifications required to serve. Miller patrolled a vast region that extended into New Mexico in the west and the Big Bend to the east. Although the US's southern border became a focal point at the turn of the century for apprehending illegal immigrants, Mexican immigration was largely inconspicuous. Prior to the breakout of the Mexican Revolution, crossing between Ciudad Juárez and El Paso was frequent and a part of everyday life for its respective residents. Native born El Pasoan Dr. E. W. Rheinheimer recalled that "there was not much attention paid to people crossing." Moreover, the doctor had a rather informal and cordial relationship with immigration officers in the early twentieth century: "We just went over [to Ciudad Juárez], took care of them, and came back. If a patient had to come over here [El Paso], to get [his] eyes examined or something, I just simply called the immigration people to tell them I had so-and-so over there."[48] The massive influx of European immigrants at Ellis Island and the geographic isolation of the American Southwest allowed Mexicans to remain under the radar screen.[49] Moreover, virulent anti-Chinese campaigns and the resultant declining numbers of Chinese laborers in agriculture and the railroads in the West and Southwest left a vacuum that Mexicans eagerly filled in increasing numbers.[50] Despite this, the primary focus of the Immigration Service remained on the restriction of Chinese immigration.

The Immigration Service created a section called the Chinese Division and labeled its officers Chinese Inspectors. Line riders aided the new division with arrests as they were familiar with scouting detail along the international boundary and border community residents.[51] According to Chinese inspector Clifford Alan Perkins, many of the illegal entrants continued to cross the Mexican border, but they began to abide by different patterns of movement:

> By the time I joined the Service [1910], few Chinese were coming in east of El Paso. Some continued to enter through gulf and west coast ports, but by far the greatest numbers were entering in the vicinity of towns on or near the Mexican border.[52]

Work along the line was difficult as few officers had been commissioned, the territory was extensive, and smuggling rings were very efficient. For instance, highly sophisticated civil or legal groups, such as the Chinese Consolidated Benevolent Association, better known to Americans as the Chinese Six Companies, operated highly successful human trafficking rings from Mexico and in the United States to smuggle illegal immigrants.[53] Also, many Chinese illegal immigrants kept a low profile and were considered law-abiding citizens despite their status, which deterred immigration officials from discovering or reporting them in El Paso neighborhoods.[54]

The Immigration Service officers inspected incoming traffic at major sea and airports, at rail terminals, and along vehicular access routes. Officers maintained surveillance of backcountry areas and forecast crossing periods by monitoring habits and trends. The officers increased their inspections over time, especially along railroad lines, as labor agents utilized boxcars to transport Chinese migrants.[55] A steady decline ensued as illegal immigration enforcement became stricter, Mexican immigrant flows increased, and laborers filtered into industries once dominated by Chinese workers, including railroads and agriculture.

In the 1910s the immigration office in El Paso was responsible for an expansive sector, with jurisdiction over the western portion of Texas including the area that stretched from Del Río to Yuma, Arizona. In 1913 the El Paso headquarters employed approximately thirty-five officers and over twenty-five staff members.[56] The Mexican Revolution changed this. Prior to the historic conflagration, Mexican immigrants had been entering in increasing numbers to work in the rapidly expanding agriculture, railroad, and mining industries. The economic dislocation and political instability associated with the revolution placed an added pressure on Mexicans to head north across the border in search of better and safer opportunities. Immigration authorities, consequently, assumed the added responsibility of housing and caring for destitute refugees fleeing the conflict. The US government constructed a temporary camp near the river that was guarded by US Army servicemen from Fort Bliss.[57] The crude and temporary detention facilities were used to aid and feed the refugees in addition to help curb the number of beggars roaming the streets of downtown El Paso. Once the fighting on the Mexican side of the border had subsided and a semblance of peace emerged in Ciudad Juárez, Border Patrol officers repatriated some of the immigrants.

The social and political instability caused by the Mexican Revolution complicated immigration matters. Ports of entry were flooded with destitute refugees as violence escalated in Mexico and especially along the Mexican side of the border. By 1914, Mexicans were a noticeable presence in the agricultural regions of Texas and California.[58] Texas A&M University professor William Edward Garnett identified the influx of Mexicans, or the "Mexican invasion," as "undoubtedly the most pressing race question that confronted Texas."[59] The significant Mexican population growth prompted restrictionists to reevaluate the social and racial value of Mexicans and to conclude that the integration of the Mexican population would disrupt the racial homogeneity of the Texas population. The immigrant flow continued relatively uninterrupted until the United States entered World War I, in 1917. Security concerns, eugenic movements, a growing restrictionist critique of immigration policy and enforcement, and the need for more efficient wartime methods for regulating the immigrant flow contributed to the new restrictive immigration policy that was passed that year. The new policy affected work on the border. In 1917 the former Chinese inspectors, who were now known as Immigrant Inspectors, assumed greater responsibilities.

The 1917 act, also known as the "Asiatic Barred Zone Act," included a new "head tax," literacy requirements, and time limits on labor contracts.[60] However, as the United States sought to limit the entry of persons believed to be public charges, immigration authorities along the border also relaxed the restrictions to encourage the entry of Mexican laborers and assist area agriculturalists to meet their harvest needs. After World War I, agriculture in the Southwest expanded even more. At least two consequences became evident. Since many of the immigrants increasingly chose to remain in the United States, Mexican communities throughout the Southwest and other parts of the United States grew significantly during the 1920s and early 1930s. Also, new immigration policies were enacted to regulate the existing flow in accordance with the needs of employers in the United States.

The Immigration Act of 1924, also known as the Johnson-Reed Act, established the Border Patrol.[61] It was a logical progression for border law enforcement since the enactment of prior laws brought about a "situation where the law enforcing agencies of the government were faced with the 'boot-legging' of aliens as one of their major problems."[62] The act of 1924 established the outfit as a uniformed law enforcement agency of the Immigration Bureau, which operated within the Department of Labor.[63] The Border Patrol's place within the Department of Labor spoke to the prominent role that immigration played in the story of labor supply and demand in the border region. Not surprisingly, a West Texas rancher with experience in the recruitment and use of Mexican labor became the strongest supporter of the bill that resulted in the Act of 1924. Congressman Claude Hudspeth owned a large sheep ranch near Del Rio, Texas, and served largely as a representative of the stockmen in the area. When Congress passed the Immigration Act of 1924, Congressman Hudspeth successfully pushed for a rider to the appropriations bill that provided for at least one million dollars for a land border patrol and the exclusion of Mexicans from the quota rolls. One hundred thousand dollars were to be made available immediately for the establishment of the agency.[64]

The first Border Patrol unit consisted of 450 "Patrol Inspectors" who were dispersed along the Canadian and Mexican borders as well as the Florida coastline. Veterans of World War I and those with other military experience made up a large proportion of the early agency, which marked the early militarization of the outfit.[65] The Border Patrol's first national headquarters were in El Paso, which also functioned as a regional sector. Its regional jurisdiction consisted of New Mexico and the three western counties of Texas. Approximately forty patrol officers manned El Paso; however, only a few were dispatched on scouting missions since it took months for the enrollees to train. The other sector headquarters included Marfa, Texas (1924); Gainesville, Florida (1925); Rouses Point, New York (1926); and Grand Forks, North Dakota (1939). Initially, inspectors wore their own clothing, received $1,300 a year, and furnished their own horses and feed.[66]

In West Texas, the Border Patrol was initially composed mostly of former "roughnecks" who had previously served as Texas Rangers or deputized cowboys. The Border Patrol unit at El Paso operated under the command of Lieutenant Colonel Hubert C. Horsley with twenty-five "cowboys" who only needed a passing knowledge of Spanish and the ability to ride a horse.[67] Border patrol service had lax requirements, unspecified duties, and the organization was unclear on the extent of its authority. According to one of the first recruits serving along the Texas-Mexico border in 1924, little was known of their actual duties, "no one knew what we were supposed to do or how we were supposed to do it."[68] Former Border Patrolman Wesley Stiles noted that his responsibilities were simple:

Catch Aliens. That's what we were supposed to do. The thing that established the Border Patrol was the influx of European aliens. Getting out of Europe from the depression there, coming through Mexico and into the United States. That was the main purpose of the Border Patrol that was organized and went into effect.[69]

They were simply equipped with the instruction to "look for aliens" and a short law book that gave them quick information on the recent and standing immigration laws in the United States.[70]

The overall responsibility of the Border Patrol was to manage the numerical limits specified in the Quota Act of 1921 and the Immigration Act of 1924.[71] In May 1921, Congress passed the Quota Act, which restricted immigration to 355,000 a year, and set a quota for each European country at 3 percent of the number of foreign-born persons of such nationality residing in the United States as determined by the census of 1910.[72] For many restrictionists, such as the Ku Klux Klan, greater restrictions were needed to "prevent America from becoming the melting pot or dumping ground of the world.[73] As a result of extensive political and social pressure from restrictionists, Congress passed a more comprehensive quota bill in 1924. The Immigration Act of 1924 made several key changes to the 1921 act. First, it revised the numerical value of the quotas from 3 percent to 2 percent. Second, it based the quotas on the 1890 census, which shifted the immigrant flow into the United States away from southern and eastern Europeans. The 1890 formula reduced the level of immigration to 155,000 per year and reduced the proportion of southern and eastern European immigration to 15 percent of the total.[74]

A standard procedure that involved a very basic legal process outlined the enforcement of the quota acts. Border patrolmen would request an arrest warrant from the Secretary of Labor if someone was thought to be in the country illegally. A court hearing would be held and legal counsel would be present if the accused requested it. If the immigrant was found guilty of entering the country illegally, paperwork regarding his deportation was sent to the Department of Labor. At this point the alien secured his legal documents and at the government's expense was sent to an appropriate port of embarkation depending on where he originated. In the case of Mexican deportation, many were given the option of "voluntary return" and were carted back to Mexico.[75]

Nationalism and race played a prominent role in both the Quota Act of 1921 and the Immigration Act of 1924. As a result of intense lobbying from the Ku Klux Klan, the American Federation of Labor, and restrictionist-minded politicians, a renewed emphasis was placed on patrolling the land borders and tightening up the enforcement of the law, especially along the southern border.[76] W. A. Whalen, the district immigration inspection director, underscored this point in bold bureaucratic terms: "[the US-Mexico boundary] must be guarded against the surreptitious entry of undesirable aliens."[77] In El Paso, the Klan's influence had reached nearly all aspects of city and county government, as well as law enforcement.[78] Mexican immigrants emerged as the focal point in immigration discussion primarily because of their exemption from the quota laws and the oversupply of labor pools in some urban areas.[79] The focus on Mexican immigration yielded yet another reorganization of the Border Patrol that recognized El Paso as a major point for the crossing of immigrants as well as alcoholic contraband.[80]

In order to restrict the flow of contraband and immigrants more effectively, the Border Patrol was placed under the authority of two directors in 1932. One was in charge of the Mexican border office at El Paso and the other the Canadian border office in Detroit, Michigan.[81] Liquor smuggling was a major concern because it was thought to accompany immigrant smuggling as well.[82] Smugglers used various methods to bring contraband across the international boundary. As a result, the Border Patrol was modernized and militarized throughout the late 1920s and 1930s. This involved standardized training. The first training school, Camp Chigas, was located in El Paso near the downtown area. Training included functional "border Spanish" and instruction in immigration laws; training lasted four hours per day.[83] Combat training was also part of the school's curriculum. Martial arts such as Jiu-Jitsu were introduced as a required course in 1936. Air patrols were another fixture within the agency at various times. In 1937, a US Coast Guard air patrol detachment was part of a campaign of the Southwest customs patrol against smugglers. The detachment consisted of two two-seat planes, and two four-seat planes, each equipped with a machine gun, short-wave radio receiver, and transmitter.[84] The training reflected the expanded function of the Border Patrol. It was not only regulating the labor flows, but it also increasingly assumed stricter law enforcement responsibilities that included the protection of America's moral agenda in prohibition, its ethnic purity, and national security. However, without a doubt at the close of the Roaring Twenties with the economic collapse the Great Depression brought the issues of labor and race to the forefront as prohibition laws were lifted in 1933.

The Border Patrol and Labor Flow

The stock market crash of 1929 and the resulting Great Depression decreased immigration flows for several reasons. First, employment opportunities became scarce. Second, the restrictionist critique gathered popular support. The Border Patrol thus became more aggressive in apprehending and deporting more Mexicans.[85] Consular offices in the United States also increasingly denied visas to Mexicans, and immigration authorities began to enforce more strictly provisions of the Immigration Act of 1917 that denied entry to individuals liable of becoming public charges. By 1930 all Mexican common laborers' visa requests were denied.[86] At the same time, arrests along the Mexican border significantly outnumbered those along the Canadian border.[87] The result was the deportation or voluntary movement back to Mexico of approximately 500,000 Mexican nationals and US-born Mexicans, the latter made up largely of sons and daughters of immigrants.[88]

On December 9, 1930, newly appointed Secretary of Labor William Doak announced that his solution to the high unemployment rate in the United

States was to deport immigrants holding jobs.[89] Although he did not identify specific immigrant groups, the initiative greatly affected the Mexican community. The effort, however, required manpower that far exceeded the capabilities of the Border Patrol. Agency officials responded to this by recruiting local and state law enforcement authorities to help in the deportations.[90]

The Border Patrol also coordinated publicity stunts to scare immigrants back to their native homeland. In some cases, press releases announced mass deportation drives and noted that local authorities would join in the effort in substantial numbers.[91] Mexicans and those of the Asiatic Barred Zone were specifically targeted.[92] The agency also coordinated sweeps. On February 13, 1931, for example, Border Patrol agents performed a raid in the El Monte area of Los Angeles, questioning three hundred people, of which thirteen were arrested. Twelve of the thirteen were Mexicans with no criminal record and were charged only with failure to prove legal entry.[93] Between 1929 and 1931, Mexican repatriation often involved raids in private homes and workplaces by the Border Patrol and other government officials.

Los Angeles city officials were especially concerned that Mexicans were taking an inordinate amount of the relief services made available to the large number of unemployed workers.[94] The raids yielded few results, and many of the Mexicans who returned to Mexico left voluntarily because of high unemployment and their destitute condition.[95] The Los Angeles roundups were repeated across the country.

Mexicans in the 1930s were at the center of the immigration debate. The heightened tension associated with the strict enforcement of immigration laws painted a negative image of Mexicans and contributed greatly to their assignment as scapegoats for the economic crisis.[96] Increased Mexican migration within and beyond the Southwest and high unemployment rates in the early years of the Great Depression also increased the restrictionist rhetoric. The Border Patrol found itself in the middle of the highly emotional debate between restrictionists and antirestrictionists, which became especially pronounced in the 1920s and 1930s. The Mexican was also caught in the anti-immigration rhetoric. Scapegoating and unsettling deportations caused much misery in the Mexican community. Their incorporation into American society was also disrupted.

The Border Patrol and the Mexican Community

The challenge of integrating the Mexican community into American society can be understood by examining the Mexicans' role as immigrant labor and their relationship with the Border Patrol. Mexican labor distinguished itself in the late 1910s and 1920s when it registered high immigrant figures and assumed a migratory character in agriculture. Immigration was primarily a response to the labor needs in southwestern industries, particularly in farming and ranching communities. Their movement across the border and throughout the Southwest, the far West, and the Midwest typically followed maturation patterns in agriculture and the recruitment activities of employers. This gave rise to a migratory work force that provided a number of challenges to the Border Patrol, as its patrolmen sought to enforce the law and avoid denying farmers the immigrant workers they needed. The mediating role that they played in West Texas can be appreciated by examining immigration policies and enforcement activities that preceded the Immigration Act of 1924.

Immigration policy was revised following the passage of the Immigration Act of 1917. The Department of Labor, for instance, established the Temporary Admissions Program, which permitted approximately 80,000 Mexicans to work as a "guest workers" in selected industries.[97] The growing demand for laborers, especially from Mexico, eventually led to the designation of the immigration inspectors as labor and immigration brokers who regulated and monitored the flow of labor from Mexico. They worked hand in hand with agricultural employers to meet labor demands in various industries.

In 1917 the Secretary of Labor, William B. Wilson, allowed for a labor importation program during wartime that introduced workers for the agricultural, mining, and railroad industries. Immigration officers and railroad companies from El Paso collaborated fully in the guest worker program. After a successful evaluation that included physical examinations and intensive interrogations, laborers were escorted by immigration inspectors to the rear of the immigration office building to hear labor agents "pitch" their company's services:

> The employer's representatives would make speeches about the delight-
> ful quarters, good pay and fine food they would have if they went to work
> for their company. When the promising was over, the [labor] agents would
> shout, "This way for the Santa Fe," "This way for the Southern Pacific."[98]

The obvious purpose of the change was to fill the void left by the previous strict immigration policies of the Chinese Exclusion Act, the US's entry into World War I, and the labor drop-offs resulting from the Immigration Act of 1917.

The first labor importation program guaranteed employers a legal process of labor contracting at the border. Agriculturalists, of course, could still depend on the larger number of workers who were crossing without the direct assistance of government officials. The labor importation program, in other words, institutionalized a process of close cooperation between government officials and farmers and provided prospective employers with a more rational and legal system to insure a ready labor supply. At a more general level, the Immigration Service continued to mediate the flow of labor to satisfy the requests of employers in the United States at the same time that it enforced immigration policy:

> Immigration officers will attend to the admission and distribution of [Mexi-
> can] laborers . . . respective employers of the agreements required under
> departmental orders . . . will cooperate with immigration officials in keeping
> track of laborers after they are admitted and in establishing and enforcing a
> follow-up system, to insure as far as possible, the eventual return to Mexico
> of those admitted.[99]

The amended policies of 1917 and 1918 introduced a seeming contradiction between the law and its enforcement. Although the policy itself was relaxed to allow for the admission of more immigrants and to coordinate their movement more effectively, officials on the border did not enforce the law strictly. As labor demands escalated due to "wartime" crisis, immigration enforcement was relaxed.[100]

The ebb and flow of Mexican immigration rested primarily on the actions of the Border Patrol. The agency enforced the official and private practice of placing immigrant laborers in needed industries and restricting the overflow of unwanted immigrants into nearby towns and cities. Border patrolmen E. A. "Dogie" Wright indicated this much when he told ranchers to "let me know when he's gonna leave so I can pick him back up."[101] The system of cooperation between the farmers and the Border Patrol systematically controlled Mexican movement.

The relationship between employers and the Border Patrol was significant in regulating the marginal social status of Mexicans. In the mid-1920s, farmers in Texas worked in tandem with the Border Patrol to fix Mexican farm wages by restricting the mobility of agricultural workers who sought higher wages. The average wage of Mexican laborers in Texas in 1926 and 1927 was the lowest in the south and southwestern region of the country.[102] Anglo farmers in Texas saw a clear distinction between Anglo wages and Mexican wages and sought the help of the Border Patrol to regulate those divisions. However, while the Border Patrol regulated labor flows and enforced immigration policy, prohibition laws inundated the agency as alcohol and drug smuggling grew increasingly more violent and prevalent.

Prohibition

The work of the Border Patrol became more complicated in the 1920s and early 1930s when its agents began to devote more of their attention to the smuggling of alcohol. Mexican border residents often engaged in a "cat and mouse" game with the border patrolmen, knowing that they were practically incapable of enforcing immigration laws as well as prohibition policies. Moreover, the high demand for alcohol in the United States created a lucrative and profitable market. A newspaper reporter covering the day-to-day activities of the El Paso police department recalled that "marijuana was common in those days (late 1910s and early 1920s) and narcotics addicts came to El Paso because it was easy to get drugs. The drugs were manufactured across the border. There were frequent fights and killings; every Saturday night we expected to have a shooting before the first edition."[103] El Paso's chief inspector, H. C. Horsley, a decorated military officer with the rank of lieutenant colonel, described the gun battles during Prohibition as, "guerilla warfare—firing from ambush."[104] Smugglers were willing to protect their valuable commodity by any means necessary and, as a result, violence often erupted between smugglers and the Border Patrol.

Once again, those in the Mexican community experienced things differently. Prohibitionists generally saw Mexican communities as bastions of alcoholic consumption that promoted "temptation, contamination, and damnation."[105] The general public also associated the contraband business with Mexicans, which was largely based on racialized feelings rather than facts.[106] Chester Chope, a newspaper reporter during Prohibition and living in El Paso, recalled that attempts were made in the American border city to "run bars openly," and "prostitution was an accepted thing in the early days."[107] Nevertheless, Ciudad Juárez's tolerance for alcohol and other vices reinforced the view of Mexicans as unsuitable members of American society despite Americans' thirst for vice and illegal liquor. In addition, violent clashes between the Border Patrol and Mexican smugglers also added to negative public perceptions.[108] In short, the Border Patrol's responsibilities of enforcing both immigration and prohibition laws deepened divisions between Mexicans and Anglos, especially within the working-class Mexican community in El Paso and Ciudad Juárez.[109]

Throughout the Prohibition Era (1919–33), El Paso and Ciudad Juárez became sites of tension and conflict. In one fourteen-month period during the late 1920s, nineteen Border Patrol officers were killed in the line of duty.[110] According to some newspaper reports, gun battles occurred almost daily near the international crossing.[111] This was a natural consequence of the fact that the West Texas region and the corresponding border area on the Mexican side had become a major staging and crossing point for smuggling alcohol, immigrants, and ammunition.

In a statement to the House of Representatives' Committee of Immigration and Naturalization, district director of immigration at El Paso Grover C. Wilmuth emphasized that much of the illegal contraband and human crossings occurred in the vicinity of the city:

> At El Paso—about 90 per cent of the crossing is done right in the vicinity of El Paso. . . . Yes, they cross all up and down the Rio Grande in the vicinity of El Paso. That is within, say, 5 miles . . . Most of the liquor and alien smugglers work close to town. The reason for that is that if they get farther out away from the settlements—on the banks of the Rio Grande all along near town there are Mexican settlements, and if they can get across safely they can run for harbor or shelter in one of these Mexican houses along there [on the American side], and unless you see them and trail them in you will never find them.[112]

The border was considered a wide-open enterprise for bootleggers. Every person had his or her favorite bootlegger, and by some rough estimates, a bottle of hooch ran about $2 more once it reached the American side of the river.[113] Tremendous profits were to be made by smugglers and bootleggers. One hundred cases of bourbon purchased in Ciudad Juárez at the wholesale price of $25, upon delivery in St. Louis, Kansas City, Denver, or Dallas could sell for $6,000 and up.[114] Price markup obviously reflected the difficulty of bringing illegal alcohol across the river, but it was also a result of the sometimes complex and costly method by which some booze made it to the United States. Some white El Pasoans with aviation experience and access to a plane used their expertise to fly liquor across the border.[115]

In 1927 alone, the Border Patrol seized over three thousand gallons of liquor and over 3,200 illegal immigrants in El Paso.[116] Despite their efforts, Border Patrol and Prohibition agents were in a losing battle. Whatever officials confiscated was only a fraction of what was making it across the river or what was made domestically in El Paso. Alcohol contraband was so prevalent in El Paso that one resident of the time recalled that "there was no trouble if you wanted liquor, there was no trouble getting it. People either made it themselves—bathtub gin or they made home brew—or they just had a rum-runner. They'd say, 'I want four bottles of something,' and they'd deliver it to his house."[117] Prohibition and immigration agents were aware of the illegal activity but found it difficult to apprehend anyone because much of their focus was on smuggling across the river.[118]

Mary Rak, a Border Patrol historian, noted that one of the more troubled locations existed in a peculiar strip of land near El Paso. It was "Cordova Island," a "small body of land, entirely surrounded by trouble."[119] During Prohibition, Cordova Island was a notorious haven for smugglers; it was almost completely surrounded by American soil, but lay outside the city limits of Ciudad Juárez, a "no-man's land" on the border.[120] According to many patrolmen and other authorities, Cordova Island's topography was enough to offer protection to smugglers, or contrabandistas as they were known in the area. A screen of brush and cottonwoods littered the Mexican side of the one-time riverbed, and the densely packed maze of Mexican homes on the American side gave immediate shelter to smugglers.[121] Moreover, the strip of land belonged to Mexico, and "all Mexicans had to do was cross the river and they were still in their own territory" and safe from US law enforcement and soldiers.[122] The geography and infrastructure of the El Paso–Ciudad Juárez borderlands offered little in protection for border agents. In the early 1930s, the boundary was marked by nothing more than a crudely constructed wire fence in some areas. Smugglers often cut the fence or dug beneath it to allow both humans and contraband to cross back and forth.[123]

Rumrunners used a rather simple but effective method to smuggle cargo and avoid detection by Border Patrol and other agents. According to El Paso residents who lived near a contraband crossing point, smugglers would cross the border and race past their doors, which were on the edge of the river. They were often in groups of five or six with one lookout man in front. The lookout man always carried a .30 caliber rifle or carbine, a .45 in his holster, and "every rumrunner had a .45 in his hand." Others in the group stored the liquor load in five-gallon square tin cans, placed them in gunnysacks, tied them together, and carried them on their shoulders. The lookout traveled first across the river, reached a high point like a small hill located in the heart of Segundo Barrio, and checked for the location of the border patrolmen. If he did not see the agents, he would signal his men to come across to the lookout's location. At that point, the lookout would race down a bit farther and repeat the process until the group reached a stash house located near present-day Chamizal National Park. The tactic was similar to an infantry maneuver some residents had learned from their days in the United

States military. Sometimes the Border Patrol would get word of a smuggling operation and would set up to intercept them. They too would approach in a military-style fashion by hiding around a few houses; they set up machine guns to capture the men in cross fire. Few safety measures were taken to protect civilians; one El Paso resident who lived in the area recalled that his house walls were "all full of bullet holes."[124]

Among border patrolmen and customs agents, Cordova Island was the worst smuggling point for agents. The Border Patrol chief, H. C. Horseley, said, "there is not another section of the El Paso immigration district I hate worse to send my men into. Cordova Island is the most dangerous sector of my district, and when I send men in there I realize I may receive information at any moment of a casualty among them."[125] Murders and gun battles became so frequent that storylines in daily newspapers reporting the events were hardly noticed.[126] Between 1926 and 1930, at least seventeen border patrol officers were killed on the border, which at the time was more than one-third as many men who were killed by mounted customs officers in fifteen years of patrolling the 850 miles of border.[127] Rough estimates made by customs and immigration officials in 1930 speculated that the number of officers and smugglers killed since 1920 was approximately fifty men. Records were not kept on the number of smugglers or Mexican civilians killed, thus resulting in an inaccurate estimate.[128]

Border patrolmen considered other areas around downtown El Paso as "hot spots," as the following interview with a former border patrolman indicates:

> You know, you'd maybe go into Eighth and Ninth Street . . . and they'd start shooting at you. You'd crawl on your belly so you could return the fire. I've had bullets throw gravel in my face; they've come pretty close.[129]

Violence, in fact, became commonplace as customs agents and the Border Patrol sought smugglers. Newspaper reports from February 1927, for example, suggest that not one twenty-four-hour period passed without a report of gunfire along the border between Fort Hancock and Anapra, a seventy-mile stretch extending east and west of El Paso's city limits.[130] Thirty-two gun battles were also reported that same year.[131] One El Paso resident who was in his late teens and early twenties during Prohibition recalled that the intensity of the gun battles was similar to that of full-blown war: "one of my friends was in that bunch, and he told me afterwards that he was never in such a tight place in his life. He had been through World War I, and he hadn't seen anything like that down there. They was all around them, and it seemed that they was shooting at them from three or four feet away sometimes."[132] An older resident of El Paso who had emigrated from Mexico once recounted that "every night people would get caught in the crossfire and both Mexicans and Americans died."[133]

According to a patrolman, the passing of the prohibition laws in West Texas increased the lawlessness.[134] Rumrunners were especially violent and were considered ready to fight at the "drop of a hat." Famed border patrolmen E. A. "Dogie" Wright added, "there was much public sentiment against those officers who enforced the law."[135] On numerous occasions, the smugglers would drop their cargo at the point of possible apprehension and flee back to Mexico. Once near or on the Mexican side of the boundary, smugglers would often fire on the border patrolmen. Another border patrolman described one such encounter:

> When challenged to halt the smugglers dropped their loads and ran through the Box Factory Fence. When one of the smugglers reached the Box Factory platform he turned and fired two shots at our officers and further when the smugglers were making good their escape into the settlement.[136]

The isolated episodes of seemingly spiteful acts against the Border Patrol emphasize the wide range of violence that existed in West Texas. More importantly, they underscore the raging animosity that persisted between Anglo authority and a resistant Mexican community.

Battles between smugglers and border guards occurred over a variety of legal infractions. Although liquor and immigrants were the principle commodities smuggled across the border, smugglers fiercely protected other contraband as well. In one case, ammunition was smuggled into Ciudad Juárez from El Paso near the downtown Santa Fe Bridge. The smugglers were attempting to carry two cases of ammunition across the river when they were spotted and ordered to halt by US soldiers who were on guard at the bridge. The smugglers dropped the cases of ammunition and fled to Ciudad Juárez under a cover of gunfire for protection, prompting the soldiers to seek shelter behind a pile of adobe bricks. Customs and border agents telephoned El Paso police, and Captain Bill Simpson answered the call. He made an attempt to recover the abandoned cases of ammunition but was fired upon; the soldiers and smugglers continued to exchange gunfire for several minutes until the Mexican cavalry appeared on the scene. Captain Simpson, who spoke fluent Spanish, communicated to the Mexican officer that he needed to get to the cases of ammunition, to which the officer agreed, and the incident was over without any reported deaths or injuries.[137] El Paso presented major difficulties to the Border Patrol, especially since cooperative measures once utilized by other law enforcement agencies rarely existed.

The difficult conditions on the border involved Mexican officials. Mexican fiscal guards, or *fiscales*, worked closely with smugglers and persons interested in immigrating illegally to the United States. The cooperation of earlier times was no longer evident. Both groups promoted official policies that sought peaceful relations. The *fiscales*, however, generally supported illegal border crossers much like the Border Patrol looked the other way when farmers recruited Mexicans on both sides of the border.

The fiscal guards would often position themselves in areas where known smugglers would congregate and force them to pay a nominal fee to guarantee free and safe passage. According to at least one apprehended smuggler, *fiscales* were a prominent fixture in the contraband business:

> There have been some Fiscal Guards on the levee as they usually come down for the purpose of collecting fees from "Cucho" for allowing him to run

107

liquor over the river. One "fiscal" came down tonight and made "cucho" pay him five pesos for each of the eight loads which we were to bring across. I know that money is turned to the Fiscal Guards for passing liquor.[138]

It has been suggested that as long as smuggling retained considerable value, Mexican *fiscales* stood to benefit economically and therefore resisted cooperation with the Border Patrol. The combined efforts of residents and officials to resist prohibition policy further isolated the Border Patrol from the community.

Cordoba Island and the border's bloody chapter came to an end in May 1940 when a mile-long fence was erected surrounding the notorious hot spot. The fence was six feet high, of wire mesh on concrete posts, and the completed project would extend to approximately four miles around the disputed land. It was a bilateral initiative that included both Mexican and American engineers and political officials.[139] The building of the fence along El Paso's most notorious smuggling hot spot was but a small step in taming the border. Five years prior, a group of border patrolmen and an investigative reporter noted: "The personnel of the Border Patrol is all-too-limited and it would take a virtual army to patrol the entire river with 100 per cent efficiency."[140] It didn't take long into the reporter's assessment to identify who the virtual army's enemy was: the Mexican. In a follow-up article, the newspaper reporter grouped "Mexican residents just over the line" in downtown El Paso and the smugglers as the common enemy.[141]

The US Border Patrol experienced major changes in the early 1930s. In 1933, just a few months after President Franklin D. Roosevelt took office, the US Congress at his urging moved to modify the prohibition laws enacted with the Eighteenth Amendment. The Blaine Act of 1933 passed through Congress in February and for the Border Patrol, "large scale liquor smuggling came to an end, and with the end of the smuggling came an end to the violent battles on the border." In 1934, Camp Chigas and the Border Patrol transferred from the Department of Labor to the Justice Department, marking a significant militarized shift in the agency. At the dawn of World War II and with the renewed emphasis on border security, the Border Patrol agents were ordered to guard detention camps and protect the interior from Axis saboteurs. However, the agency's role in labor management did not disappear. The Bracero Program in 1942 supplied America's farms and factories with thousands of Mexican workers; the Border Patrol believed the program possessed the potential to "add to the vast pool of knowledge of routes and employment for the illegal alien."[142]

Conclusion

The history of the Border Patrol, especially in West Texas, reveals that border work involved changing responsibilities that reflected important political and economic trends, including immigrant flows that corresponded to distinct phases in the industrialization of the southwestern economy and a spirited national discourse over immigration policy that followed the up-and-down motion of the economy. The Border Patrol and its predecessors helped mediate growers' demands for foreign-born labor and the demands by restrictionists for stricter immigration controls. Growers and federal officers worked jointly in regulating the flow and distribution of labor by systematically monitoring immigrants and assigning them to low-wage jobs. The added responsibility of enforcing prohibition complicated the Border Patrol's ability to do its job. The lack of cooperation with Mexican officials made it even more difficult for the federal agency to enforce the law.

The ambiguous enforcement of immigration policy in the mid-1910s affected the incorporation of the Mexican into American society. The relaxation of the immigration laws of 1917, for instance, allowed Mexican laborers to avoid various restrictions.[143] Greater accessibility to the United States, however, did not necessarily mean that the workers could travel freely and obtain jobs according to their training and experience. The immigrants were mostly channeled to work in low-wage and low-skilled jobs in agriculture. Recruiters representing various southwestern industries regulated their movement. These recruiters often worked together and in collaboration with government agencies like the Border Patrol. The idea was to guarantee agriculturalists the workers they needed, especially during harvest time.

The Border Patrol assisted in these recruitment and distribution activities on the border mostly by looking the other way when immigrants crossed and recruiters enticed them to different farming areas. The agency was able to fulfill its official responsibilities by conducting raids in urban areas and stepping up arrests after the harvest was completed. The ambiguous nature of enforcement spoke only to this seeming contradiction. Immigration enforcement, however, responded to a certain logic of labor control: that is, immigration policy could be applied in a flexible manner to accommodate southwestern employers.

Enforcing prohibition was less ambiguous, although it complicated the job of border patrolmen, many of whom described the 1920s as the most violent years in the history of the Border Patrol.[144] The added responsibility of patrolling for contraband liquor was enough to challenge the ability of the Border Patrol to effectively guard the border. Violence, abetted partly by Mexican officials, complicated matters further. In the process of enforcing prohibition laws, the Border Patrol further antagonized local residents. Mexican immigrants were already chafing under the watchful eye of border patrolmen. Their action against liquor smugglers, most of whom were Mexicans, and the violence that accompanied this enforcement activity, alienated the Mexican community more. Anglo businessmen and consumers who supported the illicit trade also reacted to the work of the Border Patrol. The Mexican community, however, came out of this story the greatest loser, because they endured the inconsistent enforcement of immigration policy as well as the negative image of law-breaking foreigners who threatened to depress wages, displace US workers, and ruin the moral fabric of American communities.

Conclusion

THIS STUDY EXAMINED THE HISTORY OF WEST TEXAS AND
northern Mexico between 1893 and 1933 with a special focus on the establishment of US militarization and its connection to racialized social relations. West Texas as a border region provided a transnational perspective
from which to analyze localized and national histories. Varying events and
authority figures throughout the period demonstrate how militarization of
the region as a pacifier, protector, and modernizing initiative incorporated
the area into the political and cultural fabric of the United States. American
authority was established during the late nineteenth century and the early
twentieth century, despite challenges that included a general state of lawlessness, great distance from centers of power in Austin and Washington, DC,
and the use of Mexico as a safe haven for clandestine behavior and a staging
area for violent depredations into Texas. Establishing authority proved to be
complicated and laden with problems, as many West Texas residents often
reacted to the imposition of outside authority and order. Personal stories,
policies, progressive reform, the Mexican Revolution, racial conflict, and immigration contributed to a construct of collaboration and collusion.

West Texas was a transnational commercial and political staging point
throughout the period. El Paso and Ciudad Juárez experienced booming
population growth and significant economic development with the introduction of the railroad and modernization. Consistent immigrant flow through
El Paso and Juárez reflected and reinforced the region's development into a
bustling port of trade and commerce between the United States and Mexico.

This study focused on the years 1893–1933 in order to measure change
in the early development of the border region's authority structure. Military efforts to pacify the region and civic efforts to establish basic American
institutions such as schools, banks, and commercial enterprises characterized the last half of the nineteenth century. Pacification followed a period of wars—the Texas war for independence and the Mexican-American
War—and the persistence of violence that often took the form of racial and
international conflict. The turn of the century and the early 1900s, on the
other hand, witnessed the establishment of American rule, although conflict
continued largely as a result of efforts to turn the region into an American
cultural enclave.

A review of the events at the turn of the twentieth century underscores
how important the state, regional, and local authorities were in the incorporation of the region into the American social economy. The process of
pacifying the area and building key American institutions continued on into
the early 1900s partly because of the difficulties involved in establishing authority over the great distance separating the region from centers of power.
Unresolved issues of local and international natures and the persistent prob-

lem of racial tension that militarization reinforced also contributed to the slow process of establishing US authority in the region.

The period from 1893 to 1933 saw the transformation of the border region. Along with the economic and commercial changes caused by modernization, social and political shifts served as a backdrop to the story of authority-building in West Texas. The reformist agendas that swept across the state with the election of Governor Charles A. Culberson in the mid-1890s, for instance, influenced the efforts to pacify the region and incorporate it into the cultural and political world of the United States. The governor mobilized the Texas Rangers to enforce the new policy against "vice," especially prizefighting and gambling, in West Texas. True to the independent spirit that had developed, local officials in West Texas garnered popular support for effectively challenging the Rangers. At the turn of the twentieth century, larger issues of an international nature, including immigration and the Mexican Revolution, often brought local authorities in line with state policies that were redefining relations between Mexico and the United States.

While the early efforts at pacifying the region and in securing American rule resulted in major conflicts, a number of new factors further complicated the process of building a new society. The Mexican Revolution, for example, had a significant impact on Texas, not merely in terms of armed conflicts along the Rio Grande, but also because revolutionary thought influenced Mexicans along the border to adopt critical views toward racial discrimination and their perceived condition as a socially dominated group. Others were less ideologically inclined and joined the international movement because of personal grievances or as a matter of survival. The sweeping changes revealed the unavoidable ties between the two countries; as a result, the protection of American lives and property emerged as a serious concern for US government officials and residents living along the border and in Mexico.

The Mexican Revolution threatened and disrupted American economic investments in Mexico, especially in northern Mexico, where US investors owned most of the mines and other industries. Diplomatic uncertainty over the protection of private property and citizens was a critical problem for American investors and the US government. The violence of the revolution also added untold numbers to the already large immigrant flow. The political exiles that joined the migration raised security concerns that complicated the incorporation of Mexicans into American society.

Increased immigration from Mexico, primarily a response to the industrialization of the regional economy of the Southwest and the violence associated with the revolution that overflowed into Texas, frayed social relations. Opposition to immigration also involved nativist groups who claimed that the unregulated flow was increasing the population of Mexicans in the cities. They made xenophobic arguments of racial, cultural, and economic vulnerability. Restrictionist groups argued that Mexicans were not staying on the farms, but traveling to the towns and cities where they depressed wages and displaced Anglo workers. Moreover, Mexican migrants were racially indistinguishable from bandits and revolutionary fighters identified as threats to American national security and neutrality.

The large-scale introduction of Mexican workers and migrants eventually gave rise to a formidable restrictionist campaign. Law enforcement agencies such as the Texas Rangers and the Border Patrol were caught in the middle of the debate over immigration and often found themselves walking the fine line of negotiating different worldviews represented by restrictionists and growers. The challenge of mediating differences between growers and their critics was also part of the story of authority-building in West Texas.

Comprehensive legislation passed in 1924 attempted to bridge the differences between restrictionists and growers. Immigration policies, such as the immigration acts of 1917 and 1924, became more restrictive, and enforcement practices became stricter. The policy greatly reduced immigration from Europe by lowering quota numbers, and it established a permanent federal agency, the United States Border Patrol, to enforce the nation's immigration laws. The Border Patrol established its headquarters in El Paso, Texas, and originally only policed the US-Mexican border. El Paso's role as the "only real labor depot" on the border reflected its significance as a point of convergence for immigrants and employers. This explains its selection as a central headquarters for the Border Patrol. Moreover, the pairing of El Paso and the Border Patrol positioned the agency to broker the labor demands by agriculturalists in the region. Border patrolmen enforced the law but made sure that area growers had all the workers they needed at harvest time.

Problems associated with enforcing the National Prohibition Act of 1919 overshadowed the challenges immigration posed. The insatiable thirst for contraband liquor inspired the illegal flow of alcoholic products from Mexico, especially in places like El Paso. Moreover, the popular taste for liquor and liquor's prohibition created situations that challenged authority in very unique ways. Local authorities and otherwise law-abiding citizens from the border cities, for example, engaged in large-scale alcohol smuggling. The smugglers, though, were mostly Mexicans. Mexican authorities also joined the illicit trade by serving as scouts and hired guns to protect the illegal cargo. The association of the trade with Mexicans, as well as the violence that often erupted between US law enforcement officials and the smugglers, complicated matters even more by reinforcing the idea of the Mexican as a criminal. The increased vigilance that accompanied Prohibition between 1919 and 1933 also bred discontent among Mexicans, including local and federal officials, who often claimed that law enforcement officials violated their rights.

This study pays special attention to race relations between Mexicans and Anglos as well as between Mexico and the United States. The story of establishing order and building a border society included race as a means for defining social relations in West Texas and intergovernmental relations across the international border. Isolated events, such as the Santa Ysabel massacre, antagonized the Mexican community on both sides of the border and prompted violent responses from Anglos and local authorities. Law enforcement agencies reflected and reinforced local prejudice, some of which originated during the period of the Mexican-American War, the San Elizario Salt War, and the Mexican Revolution. Increased militarization of the US-Mexico border furthered established Mexicans' position as an enemy of the state. Mexican castigation coupled with a highly militarized authority structure gave rise to not only a racialized Mexican "other" but also to the ethnic Mexican as a nemesis of the state and local communities.

During the tumultuous years of the Mexican Revolution, law enforcement agencies and the military allowed their racial antipathies to influence their relationship with the Mexican community of West Texas. Battles with suspected bandits evolved from personal vendettas to indiscriminate violence toward innocent Mexican residents. The wholesale murder of innocent Mexican men at Porvenir reflected the categorization of the Mexican as the subject "other" and enemy of the state.

Race became even more important in defining social relations when authorities treated Mexicans as a defeated minority while ostensibly meting out justice in an impartial way. In the El Paso race riot of 1916, for instance, the US Army reinforced segregation between Mexican residents in Chihuahuita and the rest of El Paso with the use of martial law and "dead lines." Army officials intended to use the "dead line" to put down the riot and isolate El Paso's vice industry within the Mexican district. The Mexican community, however, emerged as the culpable party to the atrocities that occurred. As the military's responsibility as a law enforcement entity in pacification of local disturbances grew, so did the categorical criminalization of ethnic Mexicans.

A case study approach here allows the reader to grasp the important role that selected law enforcement bodies played in the development of a border society. As the state's primary police force throughout the late nineteenth and early twentieth centuries, the Texas Rangers carried out state initiatives in the region. The US Army, on the other hand, enforced national policies regarding neutrality and sovereignty while bolstering defenses along the border. Military policies also involved one important intervention in Mexico with General Pershing's Punitive Expedition in 1916. This left the National Guard to assume a greater role in peacemaking along the American side of the border. Militarization also involved the Border Patrol, a permanent federal agency responsible for enforcing immigration and prohibition policies enacted during the time period. Alas, we cannot ignore the role of the civilian sector; many private citizens were deputized or independently enforced punitive measures upon ethnic Mexicans.

Events such as the Chico Cano case, the race riot, the jailhouse holocaust, the mobilization of the National Guard, and Prohibition presented special challenges to the different law enforcement agencies that sought to pacify West Texas and incorporate it into American society. These events represent specific experiences in the history of the Rangers, the US Army, the National Guard, the Border Patrol, and local officials. They also reveal interchanges with the local population as official initiative triggered varied responses. A great disconnect between authority and the local population emerges and complicates the region's incorporation into the American socioeconomic enclave.

The Texas Rangers played a critical role in the establishing authority in West Texas. The Rangers were first entrusted with removing Native Americans from the state. Later, they assumed the responsibility of suppressing violence and disciplining the Mexican community. The Frontier Battalion and Special Ranger Force led the way beginning in the late nineteenth century. Both forces had the distinct responsibility of protecting westward settlement from Indian depredations and suppressing suspected banditry along the Mexican border. The Rangers continued to act as the state's primary police force during the early part of the twentieth century. One of its primary responsibilities was to suppress political activity among Mexicans and to act on the increasing number of raids planned on Mexican soil. Their overzealous activities earned the Rangers a reputation for being a violent police force that victimized Mexicans in Texas.

The Rangers in West Texas confronted unique circumstances that saw their relationship with locals change by end of the nineteenth century. As a representative of the state, the Rangers began to enforce the state's temperance initiatives, which conflicted with local custom and practice. In the mid-1890s, Governor Charles A. Culberson initiated his progressive reform that included the banning of prizefighting and gambling in the state. The governor mobilized the Rangers to enforce the state's antiprizefight legislation in El Paso. Since most El Paso residents were invested in the entertainment industry, progressive reform disrupted the region's way of life. Moreover, local law enforcement officials generally perceived the presence of the Texas Rangers as an affront to their abilities. However, as the political landscape shifted toward a more progressive-minded polity in 1903, so did the Rangers' role in the region. Problems associated with Mexican immigration and the Mexican Revolution changed the relationship of the Texas Rangers with local officials and West Texas residents. Increasingly, local Anglos came to see the Rangers as a necessary bulwark against violence associated with the Mexican Revolution.

The appearance of Captain John Hughes as the new head of Company D marked a shift in the local perception of the Texas Rangers in the region. Although concerns over border violence were foremost in the minds of many residents, the Rangers also influenced them by seeking more collaborative relationships with Anglos, as well as with Mexicans. Hughes was able to nurture cooperative relationships with many of the authorities and ranchers in West Texas and Ciudad Juárez. For example, Hughes, along with other Ranger officers like Joe Sitters, developed a rapport with Francisco "Pancho" Villa. Hughes was also instrumental in building positive relationships with local Mexicans by working closely with many of them and by learning some Spanish. Hughes did this because he understood that the Mexican population in West Texas greatly outnumbered Anglos and often challenged local Anglo-American authority.

Increasing violence threatened any hope of lasting racial peace and over-shadowed friendly relations that Rangers like Hughes were able to develop. Livestock thefts and border raids, in particular, plagued ranchers living in remote areas, and they became increasingly suspicious of Mexicans in the area. So-called bandit gangs were driven by two compelling motivations. They ransacked ranch properties to advance their financial interests and to obtain retribution for the injustices Anglos had inflicted upon the Mexican population. Their actions, coupled with a popular disposition to see Mexicans in negative terms, encouraged Anglo ranchers and the larger society to believe that criminality was synonymous with being Mexican. The Rangers' treatment of Mexicans became harsher and more indiscriminate.

Many Rangers utilized humiliating and brutal tactics to deter banditry in the area. They had developed a reputation for killing Mexicans on trumped-up charges and for attempting to "escape" before they reached the local jail. The harsh treatment exercised by the Rangers reinforced the violent relationships between Mexicans and Anglos.

Anglos generally categorized Mexicans as potential bandits or bandit supporters, primarily because their communities at times housed or supported bandits. Some of them believed that Mexicans could not be trusted because they could not distinguish a "friendly" Mexican from a bandit. The massacre at Porvenir demonstrated the inconsiderate and even contemptuous view of Mexicans that characterized the work of the Rangers. The Rangers' treatment of the Mexican community reflected long-standing distrust between Mexicans and Anglos in West Texas.

The Mexican Revolution was an important backdrop to the tenuous relationship between Anglos and Mexicans in West Texas. Several contributing factors emerged throughout the conflict that deepened the divisions between the two communities. Villa's subsequent anti-American tirade fanned fears that many Anglos had been harboring since the outbreak of the revolution. Moreover, many Anglo ranchers and residents in West Texas feared reprisals from local Mexicans. This was evident throughout the revolutionary period and especially in 1916, following the series of events that included the Santa Ysabel massacre, the El Paso race riot, the jailhouse holocaust, and Villa's raid on Columbus. Anglos and Mexicans at times took the law into their own hands to exact revenge on each other. Army troops and National Guard soldiers also reacted. They took to the streets of Chihuahuita in what the mayor called a "precautionary" effort because of rumors of an uprising. The feared uprising did not occur. Nevertheless, soldiers entered Chihuahuita and began to institute order in the district by declaring martial law.

Following the El Paso race riot in January 1916, General John Pershing resurrected a Civil War prison guard tactic by imposing a "dead line." A perimeter was outlined and patrolled by the soldiers to keep Mexicans contained in their neighborhood. The military-enforced "dead line" was full of meaning. First, Mexicans were to remain in their place under threat of violence, both from angry Anglos and US soldiers. Second, concerned military officials and the policy carried the meanings of segregation and containment. Last, the "dead line" imposed the notion that ethnic Mexicans on both sides of the border were responsible for the atrocities committed on American citizens. In what became a highly militarized scenario with the use of military tactics, personnel, and rhetoric, Mexicans were treated as enemies of the state.

The Columbus Raid raised the stakes even higher. It led the federal government to further militarize the border by mobilizing the National Guard. Congress passed the National Defense Act in 1916, which federalized all state militias and placed them under the command of the US army. Their principle responsibilities were to protect property owners from ranch raids, enforce the country's neutrality policies, and organize surveillance networks to anticipate any incursions that might occur from enemy Mexicans on both sides of the river.

This buildup, however, once again demonstrated that it was difficult for authorities to establish order on the West Texas border. The vast space, rough terrain, and limited manpower, the same obstacles that hampered the work of the Texas Rangers, limited the effectiveness of the National Guard. National Guard officers responded much like the Texas Rangers, that is, they organized civilian groups known as Home Guards to report suspected illegal activity or potential ranch raids. The National Guard, like the Texas Rangers, also treated Mexicans as potential threats, and in that way contributed to the anti-Mexican feelings and vilification of ethnic Mexicans that dominated the border region.

The Border Patrol, like the National Guard, also faced difficulties on the border. Many of its problems stemmed from the fact that the agency assumed two major responsibilities in the border region. It was responsible for enforcing immigration law, and after the passage of the Prohibition Act, the smuggling of contraband liquor. The initial responsibility of the Border Patrol was to enforce the provisions of the Immigration Act of 1924 that included the restriction of immigrants from Europe, Asia, and the Middle East. However, the quota did little to affect the Mexican immigrant flow. Immigrants from Mexico were excluded from the restrictive rolls but were subject to fees, literacy tests, taxes, and medical examinations. Despite increased restrictions on immigration, the immensity of the immigrant flow coming into the United States overwhelmed the Border Patrol.

In the early years of the Border Patrol, full attention could not be paid to illegal Mexican immigration since customs regulations and prohibition laws were vehemently undermined. American Prohibition was in full swing and much attention was given to it. Alcohol and alien smuggling was a lucrative business, and many were willing to go to any extent to protect their cargo. Violence resulted from this stubborn will and economic payoff. The insatiable appetite for contraband liquor in the United States and Mexico's willingness to supply it created an added obstacle to fully establish authority in West Texas. Although the liquor trade detracted the Border Patrol from its primary responsibility in the area of immigration, it continued to play an important role in both insuring that farmers had the workers they needed and in responding to the restrictionist calls for tighter immigration controls.

Border patrolmen walked a fine line when it came to enforcing immigration laws and distributing labor to US farmers. Employers, such as railroad companies and growers, worked in tandem with the Border Patrol to satisfy their labor needs and regulate the workers' movement. Amendments made to restrictive immigration policies that allowed for Mexican immigrant contract labor satisfied the growers' needs. However, Mexican mobility was regulated, since employers and immigration officials made sure laborers stayed on specified sites and returned to their homeland when their contracts expired. This reflected how the Border Patrol facilitated labor distribution while enforcing immigration policy.

West Texas became a major supply route for much of the United States' agricultural and industrial needs. The border region boasted the highest concentration of Mexicans in the Southwest. Moreover, El Paso's proximity to a large pool of Mexican labor allowed American corporations to recruit directly in El Paso without the help of intermediary labor agents. Industrial and agricultural industries tapped into El Paso's labor supply throughout the 1910s and 1920s. The establishment of the Border Patrol as a labor facilitator and its officers as immigration enforcers reflected the mediating role the agency had in placing the Mexican within the socioeconomic enclave of the United States.

The overall relationship between law enforcement agencies and local communities contributed to the establishment of racially divided communities. Singly and collectively, the agencies reinforced these divisions at the same time that they established authority and helped incorporate the region into the US social economy. At the same time, however, they reinforced problems, particularly the racialization of social relations in West Texas. The divisions between Mexicans and Anglos were, in part, militarily enforced. General Pershing's declaration of martial law and "dead lines" reinforced a policy of segregation that isolated and castigated the Mexicans in Chihuahuita. The extended uses of the "dead line" policy to contain El Paso's vice industry near the Mexican sector and restrict the military's patronage further hampered the integration of the community into the larger socioeconomic fabric of the region.

The Rangers, on the other hand, introduced even harsher law enforcement. Their wholesale murders of innocent civilians at Porvenir and the use of crude justice are cases in point. In the early years of the twentieth century, the skirmishes between the Texas Rangers and the alleged Mexican bandits were especially important in suggesting that the Mexican community was given to criminal behavior to a greater extent than the rest of the population in West Texas. Anglo residents in West Texas were thus encouraged to consider all Mexicans as potential bandits or enemies of the state.

Immigration policy also marginalized the Mexican. Congress, on the one hand, exempted Mexicans from the restrictive policies of the twentieth century and flooded the Southwest and other parts of the country with labor supplies that often exceeded actual labor needs. The labor surplus mostly benefited growers. Immigration policy did not address what happened to the workers who were arriving by the hundreds of thousands. Employers, especially southwestern farmers, consistently assigned them the lower-paying and lower-skilled jobs regardless of prior training or experience. Government agencies like the Border Patrol actually participated in this process by allowing immigrants to cross relatively undisturbed during the harvest season. The Border Patrol also promoted the idea that the government was responsive to the pleas of the restrictionists by occasionally conducting raids or by stepping up their apprehension activities. The exercise of authority in West Texas, in other words, reinforced social divisions between Mexicans and Anglos, contributed to the racialization of Mexicans as a subject "other," and categorically labeled Mexicans as an enemy of the state.

The emergence of the Mexican nemesis is placed within a historical context. Immigration policy aimed at both growers and restrictionist groups marginalized the Mexican. On one hand, the Mexican laborer is exempted from the restrictive policies passed in the early part of the twentieth century to satisfy the labor demands of growers and industries throughout the southwest. However, their status remained largely at the lower-paying echelons of labor, inhibiting their social upward mobility. On the other hand, the influx of Mexican immigrants threatened the cultural homogeneity preserved by nativist groups. Restrictive policies such as head taxes and medical evaluations coupled with the enforcement powers of the United States Border Patrol were thought to preserve Anglo cultural homogeneity. The racialized Mexican as neither black nor white complicated the racial hierarchy of American society.[1] Their increasing population numbers alarmed the Anglo community, which projected its fears by vilifying Mexicans as the cause for social decay and degeneracy. Full incorporation of the Mexican into the American cultural enclave was disrupted by intense moments of crisis and fear of American power displacement by the threat Mexicans posed.

Nevertheless, the series of events, the militarization of the region, and the reaction by its residents underscore that West Texas and El Paso offer a unique challenge to militarization and the development of authority. This study offers a framework that takes account of local experience and the larger political world beyond. It looks at how agencies affected social relations and how larger events impacted the way the agencies behaved. In addition, the larger context is couched into a localized study that adds another perspective on changing social relations. A full appreciation of immigration, the Mexican Revolution, and Prohibition cannot be achieved without understanding the ongoing activities that defied authority at the local level and resulted in lasting racialized impressions that affect both Anglos and Mexicans in the borderlands.

The long-running process of militarization and conflict in the region provides another look at the complexity of social and political relationships along the border. An examination of each border institution underscores that unique and varied approaches were taken to incorporate and pacify the region. In addition, the continued conflict associated with the militarization took on an ethnic and international nature. As a result of this process, social relations between Anglos and Mexicans became far more complex and varied across time and circumstance. The coupling of an intense time period and militarization of the US-Mexico border helped define racial and ethnic relations in a context heavily influenced by military rhetoric and practice, thus giving rise to the Mexican as an enemy of the state. Moreover, the incorporation of Mexicans during times of crisis and reinforced militarization was complicated as events such as the Mexican Revolution increased political and criminal activity and national security issues became a concern for the United States. The difficulty in establishing an effective authority consequently defined Mexicans as the focused enemy of a militarized authority apparatus. Each institution of authority and vigilante group discussed in this study reinforced and widened the gap between Anglos and Mexicans in West Texas. Scholars, such as David Montejano, have argued that changes in the economic and political structure in Texas molded race relations between Anglos and Mexicans.[2] However, by peering through a narrow lens of individual authority figures entrusted with the responsibility of enforcing policies and castigation, we are able to understand how segregation and stigmatization of the ethnic Mexican along the border was reinforced. Militarization gave way not only to a racialized Mexican that is excluded socially, politically, and economically from the main fabric of American society, but it also identified the Mexican as an enemy of the state, a threat to the homogenous society fiercely protected and defined by xenophobic and nativist activists at the turn of the twentieth century.

Epilogue
"Where the Bad Guys Are"

IN NOVEMBER 1989, PRESIDENT GEORGE H. W. BUSH sup-
ported General Colin Powell's order to establish Joint Task Force 6 (JTF-6)
at Fort Bliss, Texas.[1] The task force's original mission was to "to serve as the
planning and coordinating operational headquarters to support local, state,
and federal law enforcement agencies within the Southwest border region
to counter the flow of illegal drugs into the United States."[2] JTF-6's original
area of operations consisted of the four border states of California, Arizona,
New Mexico, and Texas. In February 1995, by directive of the commanding
general of US Army Forces Command, JTF-6's area of responsibility was expanded to include the entire continental United States, Puerto Rico, and the
Virgin Islands. In June 1997, responsibility for Puerto Rico and the US Virgin
Islands transferred to US Southern Command.[3] JTF-6 was created amid a
flurry of protests by political and civic groups who felt that the military outfit
violated the law of *posse comitatus*, which forbade the use of the military for
law enforcement activities. By restricting the military's role to surveillance
and technical backup, legal consistency prevailed.[4] Nevertheless, social and
political pressure to win the "War on Drugs" in the late 1980s and early 1990s
encouraged President Bush to form JTF-6 and expand governmental role in
law enforcement.[5]

In 1991, at least six hundred troops from the Army's Seventh Infantry
Division conducted Operation Block It in the southwestern corner of New
Mexico in Hidalgo County.[6] At the same time, a contingent of US Marines as-
sisted Doña Ana County officers with the arrest of drug smugglers in south-
ern New Mexico.[7] In 1997, JTF-6 would see their services called to Redford,
Texas, a small border town of roughly one hundred inhabitants in Presidio
County that the United States Border Patrol had identified as a major drug
corridor.[8]

On the evening of May 20, 1997, seventeen-year-old Esequiel Hernández Jr. of Redford, Texas, took his modest herd of goats out to the Rio
Grande. Hernández took along with him a World War I–era .22 caliber rifle
because some wild dogs had harassed the goats on a previous occasion. At
some point while the goats grazed, Hernández fired two shots. Although it
is not clear why Hernández fired into the desert bushes, the consequences
were severe.[9] Unbeknownst to the young man, Hernández had fired in the
direction of US Marines from JTF-6 who were in their third day of a reconnaissance mission in the area and were heavily camouflaged and largely
undetectable to the common civilian.[10] The soldiers were each wearing
clothing that rendered their presence "unclear whether they were shrouded
by land bunkers or vegetation cover."[11] Marine Corporal Clemente Banuelos
interpreted Hernández's inadvertent fire as an aggressive attack against his

company by a suspected drug trafficker and responded with a single shot, striking Hernández's chest. The four densely camouflaged United States Marines approached their target only to find seventeen-year-old Esequiel Hernández Jr.'s dangling feet; he had fallen into a well after being shot. They soon discovered that the man they believed to be a menacing drug trafficker was in fact a young American high school student, tending to his goats and shooting at what many law enforcement and military experts concluded were wild dogs or the vacant desert breeze.[12]

Hernández's family heard the helicopters and sirens wailing near their property. Esequiel's father hopped in his truck and searched for his son, unaware that he had been killed. A deputy informed Mr. Hernández that Esequiel died of a gunshot wound after having been fired on by US Marines. An investigation by the Texas Rangers, Department of Defense, and local law enforcement ensued, raising several questions including the justification for the shooting. For example, at the time of the shooting, Corporal Banuelos and the three other privates in the patrol never identified themselves to Hernández. However, Marine Colonel Thomas Kelly said later that the Marines responded within the Joint Chiefs of Staff's peacetime rules of military engagement.[13]

The Department of Defense and military officials quickly went on the defensive following the incident. Local, state, and national media outlets descended upon the small border town of Redford, causing a hailstorm of criticism throughout the Southwest and beyond. Public outcry and an official "review" of the military's role in border patrol activities forced JTF-6 to suspend all operations in the Marfa sector and, eventually, all along the US-Mexico border.[14] Corporal Banuelos and his Marine comrades were subject to a grand jury investigation to determine the legality of the shooting. After an exhaustive process, the Texas grand jury cleared the Marines of any wrongdoing in August 1997.[15] Not long after Esequiel Hernández Jr. was gunned down by US Marines, in May 1998, the US House of Representatives voted and authorized enlisting the military to help patrol US borders in the war against drug smuggling and illegal immigration.[16] The federal government would continue the policy of militarizing the border in the fight against drug trafficking well into the twenty-first century.

It is not the objective of this book to provide a detailed account of the contemporary militarization of the US-Mexico border. Rather, the consequences of border militarization are most revealing. Jack Zimmerman, the defense attorney for Corporal Banuelos, stated that "an armed man on foot, walking behind a herd of goats" fit the profile of a drug trafficker, a threatening figure that undermined the country's efforts in the "War on Drugs" and the enforcement of federal immigration policies.[17] In other words, a young man of Mexican descent along the US-Mexico border with a .22-caliber rifle, tending to his goats, "fit the profile" of the enemy the military, law enforcement, and politicians sought in their "War on Drugs" campaign. The Esequiel Hernández murder in May 1997 served as a climactic event that epitomized the conflictive and complicated legacy of militarization efforts along the US-Mexico border that started in the late nineteenth century.

The Hernández murder suggests that ethnic Mexicans continue to be categorized as an enemy and threat to United States society regardless of their citizenship or social standing. Not only did Zimmerman's description of Esequiel Hernández Jr. paint a picture of an enemy combatant, but also the intelligence the Border Patrol provided that portrayed Redford as a center for drug traffickers with 70 to 75 percent of the population involved in the illicit trade, framed the "criminal portrait" perfectly.[18] Criminalizing members of Redford's mostly Mexican population categorically labeled them as enemies of the state. Or, as borderlands scholar Joseph Nevins contends:

> Seen from Washington, the border region—Redford included—is to a highly significant degree an area of existential threats to the larger national body, an area that needs to be secured—whether against "illegal" migrants crossing the boundary to "steal" jobs, drug cartels, or would-be terrorists.[19]

Ethnic Mexicans residing in the United States, regardless of status, are guilty by association and, because of border militarization, are identified as enemies of the state. Since the establishment of JTF-6, the US-Mexico border has experienced a continuing and expanding presence of military personnel. The increased militarization of state and local law enforcement further complicates ethnic Mexican integration into the larger socioeconomic fold. In other words, the militarization of local authority and the expansion of its powers to enforce federal law draw in the marginal borders to the center of policy and social debate. The once "existential threat" is assumed a mainstream reality, especially in the post-9/11 era.[20]

In September 2009, Texas Governor Rick Perry dispatched a team of specially trained Texas Rangers, called Recon Rangers, to the "hostile border wilderness near the Río Grande to maintain a constant vigil for 'bad guys' from Mexico."[21] According to newspaper reports, the Recon Rangers resembled more a "military-style commando unit in a foreign war zone."[22] Members of the recon force, who trained at Texas military bases and were taught advanced military skill sets, were sent to the "foreign war zones" of West and South Texas where desolate areas were difficult for undermanned sheriff's departments to patrol.[23] The Texas Department of Public Safety (DPS), the umbrella agency of the Texas Rangers, reported that the entire Ranger force consisted of only 144 officers, and Governor Perry was not clear on how many of those would patrol the 1,254-mile Texas-Mexico border.[24] Governor Perry's mobilization of the Rangers for border duty would evoke a mythical past that would garner the political support he so desired in a hotly contested primary race for the Republican nomination for governor with Senator Kay Bailey Hutchinson.[25] However, for some in the Mexican community, mobilization of the Rangers brought back the vividly horrid memories of lynchings, violence, terrorism, and marginalization represented by the iconic agency and its civilian supporters in the early decades of the twentieth century.[26] Governor Perry's politicization of the international boundary was a page out of the old political book; however, the organization of a special Ranger team did more than win Perry a few votes. Perry's border security campaign mobilized the civilian sector in a manner reminiscent of the old

Home Guard of the 1910s and eerily foreshadowed by the Arizona "Minute-men" project.

Perry's border security campaign explicitly sought and encouraged civilian involvement. In addition to Rangers patrolling the border, the governor authorized the "Virtual Border Watch Program." It was a hi-tech system of cameras placed along the border that created a virtual online patrol presence and allowed the public to view and report suspicious activity to law enforcement. Members of the public were encouraged to assist law enforcement and register with the Virtual Border Watch program online.[27] The governor's recruitment of the public in assisting law enforcement followed a relatively popular wave of vigilantism that began in Arizona in 2005 and spread to neighboring border states.

Perry's program of civilian "activism" runs parallel in 2005 when civilian participation in the militarization of the international boundary line came to a head in Arizona. In April 2005, James Gilchrist of California and Chris Simcox formed "The Minuteman Project" to "get a neglectful US government to simply enforce existing immigration laws."[28] They soon splintered into two separate groups. The group Simcox led hoped to "embarrass the government" into action by keeping watch on the Arizona-Sonora (Mexico) border with hundreds of armed and unarmed volunteers.[29] In response to growing public and political pressure, President George W. Bush ordered nearly six thousand National Guard troops to the US-Mexico border in May 2006 under Operation Jump Start to provide intelligence, surveillance, and other support.[30] Under the order, National Guard troops provided mobile communications, transportation, logistics, training, and construction support to the US Border Patrol for a security fence along the southern border.[31] After two years and millions of dollars in drug seizures and thousands of apprehended illegal immigrants, Operation Jump Start ended on July 15, 2008.[32] Although Operation Jump Start was politically popular, according to border scholar Timothy Dunn, "the rate of return on the use of the National Guard in immigration enforcement [was] not spectacular and costs appear high."[33] Initial forecasts believed it would take up to one-third of the National Guard's total force to staff the border. A great undertaking and burden, according to Dunn, for a force already spread thinly in Afghanistan and Iraq. In addition, he argues that increased numbers do not necessarily result in more apprehensions or reduction in illegal crossings.[34] Despite data suggesting that increased militarization is too costly and largely ineffective, in May 2010, President Barack Obama announced the deployment of at least 1,200 National Guard troops to the southern border, again, amid public and political pressure stemming from unprecedented drug violence in northern Mexico, illegal immigration flow into the United States, and state governments, like Arizona, challenging federal border policy.[35]

In April 2010, Arizona Governor Jan Brewer signed Senate Bill 1070, also known as the "Support Our Law Enforcement and Safe Neighborhoods Act," into law.[36] For any lawful contact made by a law enforcement official of the State of Arizona where a "reasonable suspicion exists that the person is an alien who is unlawfully present in the United States, a reasonable attempt shall be made . . . to determine the immigration status of that person."[37] Local police wielded broader power to detain anyone suspected of being in the United States illegally. Opponents of Senate Bill 1070 argued that vague wording, such as "reasonable suspicion" and "reasonable attempt," provided an open invitation for harassment and discrimination against Latinos, particularly against Mexican Americans, regardless of their citizenship status.[38] Moreover, the law served to further marginalize ethnic Mexicans as the very presence of ethnic Mexicans became questionable, indeed, virtually and practically vilified. In her press conference following the bill signing, Governor Brewer categorically linked all criminal activity to immigrants simply by emphasizing that the bill, "protects all of us, every Arizona citizen and everyone here in our state lawfully. . . . Border-related violence and crime due to illegal immigration are critically important issues to the people of [Arizona]."[39] Governor Brewer obviously did not refer to immigrants from Europe, Asia, or Africa in these border issues. Criminal activities and illegal immigration were inextricably understood to refer to ethnic Mexicans and Mexico.

Ironically, the 2009 crime data report published by the Federal Bureau of Investigation showed that violent crime in Arizona declined dramatically in the pervious two years; the crime rate was significantly lower than average crime rates across the United States.[40] Despite contradictory evidence that clearly dismisses Governor Brewer's claims of increased crime rates because of illegal immigration, the governor understood the power of xenophobia and the historical deep-seated racism that would make immigration and the politicization of the border discourse into election-winning rhetoric. The broadening of federal policing powers to include city police suggests a dire set of circumstances unfulfilled by federal agencies, including the Border Patrol and military. The apparent desperate state of affairs attributed to the border thus requires full protection from an outward threat, the ethnic Mexican. Again, the combination of harsh social and political rhetoric as well as stricter immigration enforcement further criminalizes not only migrants but also their ethnic brethren and communities.

Border militarization finds itself center stage one hundred years after the Mexican Revolution. New multiagency and military operations continue under the tutelage of President Barack Obama. The lingering effects of border militarization and the role it plays on the social stratification of ethnic Mexicans in the United States continue to render identity formation a fragile and precarious process. "¡Pobre México! Tan lejos de Díos, tan cerca a los Estados Unidos (Poor Mexico! So far from God, so close to the United States), the classic Mexican proverb rings ever more true today.[41] A reinterpretation of the phrase could just as well be applied to the borderlands, a region so far from Washington, DC, so close to Mexico. People in political and economic centers of power, such as Washington DC, Phoenix, Austin, and such, view the border as an "area of existential threat to the larger national body, an area that needs to be secured."[42] As Joseph Nevins argues:

> The U.S.-Mexico borderlands has increasingly become a society comprised substantially of "police and thieves" . . . one in which civil and human rights

are effectively less than they are elsewhere in the United States, making it a zone of exception . . . a site in which the state acts in a manner outside of normal constraints and takes extreme measures for the declared safe of security. In doing so, the federal [and state] government has normalized various forms or violence in the name of fighting threats . . . thus requiring mobilization of U.S. society as a whole.[43]

Because of the proliferation of security measures along the border since 9/11, ethnic Mexicans have emerged as criminals of the state due to persistent concerns over illegal immigration and drug smuggling. National security concerns naturally assumed the highest priority after 2001. A narrowed focus toward a porous border consequently positioned migrants from Mexico and ethnic Mexicans residing in the United States as potential terrorists.[44] Militarization efforts along the United States' southern border contribute to Mexican otherness and more specifically to Mexicans' criminalization despite citizenship or social standing.[45]

The United States' approach to border enforcement follows a well-established modus operandi that includes reactive policies to social, economic, and political pressures. These restrictive policies are then followed by enforcement details that are ineffective due to topographical obstacles, lack of manpower and financial resources, and economic demands that require looser enforcement. Moreover, the impetus for such policies falls short of long-term objectives. Why? According to political scientist and borderlands scholar Peter Andreas, federal and state governments continue to perform an "audience-directed" nature of border enforcement:

Audience-directed border enforcement draws from sociological insights about the role of images and symbols in public interaction . . . the border as a political stage, state actors continuously engage in 'face work' and the 'art of impression management.'"[46]

Law enforcement officials and politicians are engaged in what Andreas calls a "double performance," having to assure the populace that the border is open to legal commercial trade while reassuring others that the border is sufficiently closed to illegal flows. An inherent contradiction exists within the infrastructure of border enforcement. Those entrusted with its integrity are forced to concede to the undermining demands of the border's major actors, employers' dependency on cheap migrant labor, and the populace's demand for illicit drugs.[47] However, the consequence of this melodrama has real effects on ethnic Mexicans on both sides of the border. Like with any classic narrative, actors are categorized as protagonists and antagonists. Border militarization defines these roles, and ethnic Mexicans are typecast as "those bad guys." The never-ending cycle of identifying the villain that hails from the US-Mexico borderlands and retaliating with militarization reinforces the categorization of ethnic Mexicans as the enemy. With every passing decade ethnic Mexicans struggle to find their place in the American social, political, and economic mainstream.

In 2008, General Motors aired a series of television commercials for its Chevrolet brand titled, "This Is Our Country," promoting their Silverado truck line. The commercials are laden with iconic "Americana": images of farming communities, rock 'n' roll, firemen, cowboys, and other iconic symbols. Included in the string of images are photographs of Rosa Parks, Muhammad Ali, and a clip of Dr. Martin Luther King's "I Have a Dream" speech. The basic racial binary of white and black flashes across the screen, symbolizing the face of America. In this idyllic postracial America, African Americans are, too, the face of America. Noticeably absent in most of the commercials is the Latino. In a separate commercial but still part of the "This Is Our Country" series is the "My Truck" advertisement. In this short piece, various men give a short anecdote about their Chevrolet trucks and how the trucks either represent them or help them improve their communities. One of the featured men is a Spanish-speaking man whose grandsons explain that their Chevy has been passed down from generation to generation. In the last ten to fifteen seconds of the commercial each featured speaker states, "This is my truck," except for the Spanish-speaking man. He proudly states, "esta es mi troca/this is my truck."[48]

The Chevy commercial series "This Is Our Country" reveals a vivid and homogenous image of what "our country" should look like in the twenty-first century. In three of the four commercials the vast majority of images that depict America are largely of white males and children, while only a handful of images are of African Americans. Latinos are visibly absent from the commercial series, with the sole exception of the "my truck" commercial. The commercial that specifically spoke to brand loyalty featured the only obvious Spanish-speaking customer. A serious disconnect emerges out of this commercial series. "Our country" is made of whites, mostly male, with a sprinkling of African Americans. Latinos are absent, nonexistent, not members of "our country," but are welcomed as consumers. Are ethnic Mexicans a part of "our country?" Can they be the face of "America?" The multipronged authority structure that includes federal, state, and local law enforcement, xenophobic legislation, increased militarization along the US-Mexico border, and organized civilian resistance suggests that ethnic Mexicans are not a part of "our country." If they are not a part of the United States, are they in turn an enemy of America? Perhaps. A comprehensive review of the history of ethnic Mexicans in the United States suggests that their full inclusion in the American sociopolitical fabric has not been fully realized. As one observer of Texas race relations once said, "It is difficult to convince these people that a Mexican is a human being. He seems to be the Texan's natural enemy."[49] The struggle continues.

APPENDIX 1

Post Returns for Fort Bliss, 1910–16

Table A.1. Fort Bliss Post Returns for 1910

Month and Year	Number of Soldiers Listed in Fort Bliss	Corresponding Event
January 1910	62 (December 1909, 352)	The F.S. and Band and 1 "Bat" 19th Inf. left Post at noon January 31, 1910 en route to Phil Islands for station.
February 1910	57	
March 1910	57	
April 1910	381	Headquarters, band, Co's E, F, G, X, V, M Platoon 92nd Infantry arrived at Post April 24, 1910.
May 1910	340	
June 1910	336	
July 1910	338	
August 1910	329	
September 1910	328	
October 1910	304	
November 1910	307	Francisco I. Madero calls for an uprising and the Mexican Revolution begins with several insurrections taking place across the country including Chihuahua.
December 1910	254	

Source: Fort Bliss Post Return 1910, Fort Bliss Archives and Museum, El Paso, Texas, data compiled by Angie Chávez and Jennifer Nielsen; "Mexican Revolution Timeline," *México, 1810/1910 UTEP 2010*, University of Texas at El Paso, http://academics.utep.edu/Portals/1719/Publications/MexicanRevolutionTimeline.pdf.

Table A.2. Fort Bliss Post Returns for 1911

Month and Year	Number of Soldiers Listed in Fort Bliss	Corresponding Event
January 1911	275	Madero establishes his headquarters in Caples Building in El Paso, Texas.
February 1911	336	
March 1911	57	
April 1911	381	Madero establishes provisional capital of Mexico in an adobe building near Monument Marker #1 in El Paso, Texas near the ASARCO plant.
May 1911	340	Battle of Juárez; Madero is made interim president of Mexico.
June 1911	336	
July 1911	338	
August 1911	329	
September 1911	328	
October 1911	304	Madero elected president of Mexico.
November 1911	307	
December 1911	254	

Source: Fort Bliss Post Return 1911, Fort Bliss Archives and Museum, El Paso, Texas, data compiled by Angie Chávez and Jennifer Nielsen; "Mexican Revolution Timeline," *México, 1810/1910 UTEP 2010*, University of Texas at El Paso, http://academics.utep.edu/Portals/1719/Publications/MexicanRevolutionTimeline.pdf.

Table A.3. Fort Bliss Post Returns for 1912

Month and Year	Number of Soldiers Listed in Fort Bliss	Corresponding Event
January 1912	352	Federal troops in Juárez mutiny. American troops sent to Fort Bliss.
February 1912	367	
March 1912	360	Pascual Orozco breaks from Madero and leads new revolt against Madero and his forces. Taft administration announces embargo on arms to Orozco.
April 1912	352	Several hundred if not thousands of Juárez residents move to El Paso as refugees.
May 1912	353	
June 1912	792	Fort Bliss becomes a regimental post for the first time.
July 1912	928	European refugees fled Chihuahua for El Paso escaping anti-Americanism sweeping northern Mexico.
August 1912	909	
September 1912	869	Villa bribes his way out of prison and flees to El Paso.
October 1912	849	
November 1912	824	
December 1912	846	

Source: Fort Bliss Post Return 1912, Fort Bliss Archives and Museum, El Paso, Texas, data compiled by Angie Chávez and Jennifer Nielsen; Leon Metz, *El Paso Chronicles: A Record of Historical Events in El Paso, Texas* (El Paso: Mangan Books, 1993).

Table A.4. Fort Bliss Post Returns for 1914

Month and Year	Number of Soldiers Listed in Fort Bliss	Corresponding Event
January 1913	846	
February 1913	1,046	Victoriano Huerta breaks from Madero and leads a coup d'état against him. Madero is assassinated and Huerta assumes power but is not recognized by US president Woodrow Wilson.
		Fort Bliss receives the 22nd Inf. Reg., the 2nd and 13th Cav. Reg., a battery of artillery and a company of Signal Corps, thus converting the base into a full regimental cavalry post.
March 1913	1043	
April 1913	1037	
May 1913	978	
June 1913	960	
July 1913	933	
August 1913	1,025	Mexican refugees cross border at Columbus, NM and make their way to El Paso.
September 1913	1,006	
October 1913	1,069	
November 1913	1,132	
December 1913	1,101	

Source: Fort Bliss Post Return 1913, Fort Bliss Archives and Museum, El Paso, Texas, data compiled by Angie Chávez and Jennifer Nielsen, Texas; Leon Metz, *El Paso Chronicles: A Record of Historical Events in El Paso, Texas* (El Paso: Mangan Books, 1993); "Mexican Revolution Timeline," *México, 1810/1910 UTEP 2010*, University of Texas at El Paso, http://academics.utep.edu/Portals/1719/Publications/MexicanRevolutionTimeline.pdf.

Table A.5. Fort Bliss Post Returns for 1914

Month and Year	Number of Soldiers Listed in Fort Bliss	Corresponding Event
January 1914	1,118	Nearly 3,000 Mexican refugees at Presidio, TX are taken by train to El Paso and incarcerated by the US Army at Fort Bliss.
February 1914	1,159	
March 1914	1,141	Troops assigned to border patrol duty at the Sierra Blanca-Fabens-Clint patrol district.
April 1914	1,143	The Army has a full division at Fort Bliss and place two regiments near downtown El Paso. Brig. Gen. John J. Pershing assumes command at Fort Bliss. Wilson sends troops to occupy Veracruz. Georgia National Guard patrol downtown. 500 citizens volunteer their services to El Paso police chief and assigned to patrol the south end of the city (Chihuahuita).
May 1914	1,132	
June 1914	1,104	
July 1914	1,150	
August 1914	1,028	Gen. Pershing escorts Gen. Villa across the Santa Fe International Bridge for reception and review at Fort Bliss.
September 1914	1,066	
October 1914	1,124	
November 1914	1,175	
December 1914	1,219	

Source: Fort Bliss Post Return 1914, Fort Bliss Archives and Museum, El Paso, Texas, data compiled by Angie Chávez and Jennifer Nielsen; Leon Metz, *El Paso Chronicles: A Record of Historical Events in El Paso, Texas* (El Paso: Mangan Books, 1993); "Mexican Revolution Timeline," *México, 1810/1910 UTEPw 2010*, University of Texas at El Paso, http://academics.utep.edu/Portals/1719/Publications/MexicanRevolutionTimeline.pdf.

Table A.6. Fort Bliss Post Returns for 1915

Month and Year	Number of Soldiers Listed in Fort Bliss	Corresponding Event
January 1915	1,189	Gen. Hugh Scott and Gen. Villa meet at the customs house in Ciudad Juárez.
February 1915	1,168	
March 1915	1,158	
April 1915	1,155	Gen. Villa is defeated by *carrancista* general Alvaro Obregón at the Battle of Celaya.
May 1915	1,144	
June 1915	1,201	Huerta and Orozco are arrested in Newman, NM and placed under house arrest in El Paso.
July 1915	1,186	Orozco escapes house arrest and Huerta is placed under barracks arrest at Fort Bliss.
August 1915	1,142	Orozco is killed by American authorities and interred at Concordia Cemetery in El Paso.
September 1915	1,141	
October 1915	1,230	The Wilson administration formally extends presidential de facto recognition to Carranza.
November 1915	1,208	Troop I, 8th Cavalry left post patrolling to Noria, NM for the purpose of guarding the movement of Carranza troops through the United States.
		Battle of Agua Prieta. Villa troops defeated by *carrancistas*.
December 1915	1,078	

Source: Fort Bliss Post Return 1915, Fort Bliss Archives and Museum, El Paso, Texas, data compiled by Angie Chávez and Jennifer Nielsen; Leon Metz, *El Paso Chronicles: A Record of Historical Events in El Paso, Texas* (El Paso: Mangan Books, 1993); "Mexican Revolution Timeline," *México, 1810/1910 UTEP 2010*, University of Texas at El Paso, http://academics.utep.edu/Portals/1719/Publications/MexicanRevolutionTimeline.pdf.

Table A.7. Fort Bliss Post Returns for 1916

Month and Year	Number of Soldiers Listed in Fort Bliss	Corresponding Event
January 1916	1,108	Santa Ysabel massacre and El Paso race riot; Huerta dies of cirrhosis in El Paso.
February 1916	1,080	
March 1916	1,074	El Paso city jail holocaust; Columbus, NM attack by Pancho Villa; Pershing marches with several thousand troops into Mexico in search of Villa.
April 1916	1,126	
May 1916	1,427	TX, NM, AZ, and other state militias are mobilized for border duty.
June 1916	1,427	
July 1916	2,201	17th Cavalry organized at Ft. Bliss by Act of Congress. 180 recruits joined post, 134 reservists reported as well.
July 1916(*)	2,396	Field Artillery Brigade organized under instruction of commanding general.
August 1916	2,592	
September 1916	2,617	
October 1916	2,618	Additional 894 labeled 20th Infantry Camp Fort Bliss.
November 1916	2,622	
December 1916	2,668	

Source: Fort Bliss Post Return 1916, Fort Bliss Archives and Museum, El Paso, Texas, data compiled by Angie Chávez and Jennifer Nielsen; Leon Metz, *El Paso Chronicles: A Record of Historical Events in El Paso, Texas* (El Paso: Mangan Books, 1993); "Mexican Revolution Timeline," *México, 1810/1910 UTEP 2010*, University of Texas at El Paso, http://academics.utep.edu/Portals/1719/ Publications/MexicanRevolutionTimeline.pdf.

Demographic Growth in El Paso County and City, 1880–1930

Table B.1. Population growth for El Paso County, 1880–1930

POPULATION— EL PASO COUNTY	1880	1890	1900	1910	1920	1930
White*	3,598	14,996	24,886	50,729	99,845	51,831
Black/Colored**	47	622	N/A	1,562	1,548	1970
Mexicans***	N/A	N/A	N/A	N/A	N/A	77,389
Total Pop.	3,845	15,678	24,886	52,599	101,877	131,597

Source: United States Department of the Interior, Census Office, *Statistics of the Population of the United States,* Tenth Census, June 1, 1880 (Washington, DC: GPO, 1882); United States Department of the Interior, Census Office, *Report on Population of the United States,* Eleventh Census, 1890 (Washington, DC: GPO, 1895); United States Department of the Interior, Census Office, *Census Reports, Volume I: Population of the United States,* Twelfth Census, 1900, prepared under the supervision of William C. Hunt, chief statistician for population (Washington, DC: GPO, 1901); United States Department of Commerce, Bureau of the Census, *Population 1910: General Report and Analysis,* Thirteenth Census, 1910, prepared under the supervision of William C. Hunt, chief statistician for population (Washington, DC: GPO, 1913); United States Department of Commerce, Bureau of the Census, *Population of the United States, Volume I & III,* Fourteenth Census, 1920, prepared under the supervision of William C. Hunt, chief statistician for population (Washington, DC: GPO, 1921, 1922); United States Department of Commerce, Bureau of the Census, *Population of the United States 1930, Volume I & III,* Fifteenth Census, 1930, prepared under the supervision of Leon E. Truesdell, chief statistician for population (Washington, DC: GPO, 1931, 1932).

Table B.2. Population growth for City of El Paso, 1880–1930

POPULATION— EL PASO CITY	1880	1890	1900	1910	1920	1930
White*	N/A	9,767	15,140	23,338	75,804	41,965
Black/Colored**	N/A	511	466	1,452	1,330	1,855
Mexicans***	N/A	N/A	N/A	N/A	N/A	58,291
Total Population	736	10,838	15,906	39,279	77,560	102,421

Table B.3. Native and foreign-born population of El Paso County, 1900–1930

POPULATION— EL PASO COUNTY	1900	1910	1920	1930
Native Born White	15,089	32,388/23,338 (city)	57,540	48,475
Foreign Born White	9,797	18,341/14,504 (city)	42,305	3,356
Born in Mexico	8,368	12,353 (city pop.)	38,625	416

*Ethnic Mexicans were considered "White" until the 1916 Special Census for El Paso, Texas, and later at the federal level for the 1930 US Census. Figures include both "Native White" and "Foreign White."

** For the 1880 and 1890 census "Colored" races included "Negro Descent, Chinese, Japanese, and Civilized Indians." By the 1900 census people of African descent were separated from Chinese, Japanese, and Indians.

*** In the 1930 census "Other Races," which counted Chinese, Japanese, and Indians, was expanded to include ethnic Mexicans. The total number listed for "Other Races" in the 1930 census for the county of El Paso was 77,796, with Mexicans comprising 99 percent of the total "Other" population. In the 1920 census "Other Races" were listed as "Indian (Native American), Chinese, Japanese, and All Other," and the number was 484. The city of El Paso listed "other races" at 58,601 in 1930.

Special Census of the Population of El Paso, Texas, 1916

A special census of the city of El Paso, Texas, began on January 15, 1916, under the supervision of the Bureau of the Census, by order of the president of the United States, issued October 20, 1915, in compliance with a request made by the El Paso Chamber of Commerce.

Many of El Paso's Anglo residents were weary of the increased numbers of Mexicans residing within the city limits. Many suspected that the ethnic Mexican population outnumbered the Anglos in the city. The census validated their suspicions.

The city of El Paso's demographic was relatively diverse. Not enumerated in the total city population were 7,051 Mexican refugees within the city limits or the 1,762 soldiers standing guard within and around the city. Of the 1,762 soldiers enumerated in January 1916 all were white males with the vast majority between the ages of eighteen and twenty years old. Moreover, within the civilian population white adult males over the age of twenty-one outnumbered Mexican adult males of the same age group by nearly three thousand men.

Table C.1. Special census of the population of El Paso, Texas

ETHNIC POPULATION, EL PASO, TEXAS		PERCENT OF TOTAL POPULATION
Total Population	61,898*	100.0
White (excluding Mexican)	27,356	44.2
Mexican (persons of Mexican ancestry regardless of citizenship)	32,724	52.9
Negro	1,526	2.5
Indian	5	—
Chinese	243	0.4
Japanese	44	0.1

Source: United States Department of Commerce, Bureau of the Census, *Special Census of the Population of El Paso, Tex.*, prepared under the supervision of Emmons K. Ellsworth, January 15, 1916 (Washington, DC: GPO, 1916).

Notes

Introduction

1. "U.S. Blockade of Workers Enrages Mexican Town," *New York Times*, October 1, 1993; Timothy Dunn, *Blockading the Border and Human Rights: The El Paso Operation That Remade Immigration Enforcement* (Austin: University of Texas Press, 2009), 51; John L. Martin, "Can We Control the Border? A Look at Recent Efforts in San Diego, El Paso, and Nogales," Center for Immigration Studies, Washington, DC, May 1994.

2. The primary geographic focus of this study is El Paso and Ciudad Juárez. The broad political, social, and commercial significance of the twin border cities during the late nineteenth and early twentieth centuries, however, require a broader geographical setting. This is why I use the term West Texas. It incorporates the various settlements surrounding El Paso, Texas, including the Big Bend and southern New Mexico.

3. I use the terms *Mexicans* and *ethnic Mexicans* to identify all peoples of Mexican origin regardless of citizenship. Citizenship will be noted when necessary to distinguish between Mexican nationals born in Mexico and Mexican Americans born in the United States. I prepared all the translations from Spanish-language sources that appear in the text and notes.

4. Timothy Dunn, *The Militarization of the U.S.-Mexico Border 1978–1992: Low Intensity Conflict Doctrine Comes Home* (Austin: University of Texas Press, 1996), 3.

5. Ibid., 3–4.

6. Although Mexican Americans were legally and politically identified as "white" since the signing of the Treaty of Guadalupe Hidalgo in 1848, the United States Supreme Court case, *Hernández v. State of Texas* (1954), ruled that Mexican Americans in Texas had long been treated as a "class apart." *Hernández v. State of Texas* challenged Jim Crow practice and the Constitution's Fourteenth Amendment that protects groups marked by "differences in race and color," and argued that the "exclusion of a class of persons from jury service on grounds other than race or color may also deprive a defendant who is a member of that class of the constitutional guarantee of equal protection of the laws." Ian Haney López, "Race and Colorblindness after *Hernández* and *Brown*," in *"Colored Men" and "Hombres Aquí,"* ed. Michael A. Olivas (Houston: Arte Público Press, 2006), 42–43. For more on Mexican racial identity see Arnoldo De León, *They Called Them Greasers: Anglo Attitudes toward Mexicans in Texas, 1821–1900* (Austin: University of Texas Press, 1983); David Montejano, *Anglos and Mexicans in the Making of Texas, 1836–1986* (Austin: University of Texas Press, 1987); David Gutiérrez, *Walls and Mirrors: Mexican Americans, Mexican Immigrants, and the Politics of Ethnicity* (Berkeley: University of California Press, 1995); Albert Camarillo, *Chicanos in a Changing Society: From Mexican Pueblos to American Barrios in Santa Barbara and Southern California, 1848–1930* (Cambridge, MA: Harvard University Press, 1979).

7. Elizabeth Benton-Cohen discusses the events leading up to the Bisbee Deportation of 1917 in southern Arizona as a lens into racial and national conflict between Americans and Mexicans. Elizabeth Benton-Cohen, *Borderline Americans: Racial Divisions and Labor War in the Arizona Borderlands* (Cambridge, MA: Harvard University Press, 2009), 6.

8. Ibid., 9; David Montejano, ed., *Chicano Politics and Society in the Late Twentieth Century* (Austin: University of Texas Press, 1999), xvi.

9. Mae Ngai, *Impossible Subjects: Illegal Aliens and the Making of Modern America* (Princeton, NJ: Princeton University Press, 2004), 25.

10. Ibid., 8; The juxtaposition of foreign and "American" is furthered by immigration scholar Erica Lee's study on Chinese immigration during the

137

"Exclusion Era, 1882–1943." Lee argues, "Americans learned to define 'American-ness' by excluding and containing foreign-ness. Through the admission and exclusion of foreigners, the United States both asserted its sovereignty and reinforced its identity as a nation." Erika Lee, *At America's Gates: Chinese Immigration during the Exclusion Era, 1882–1943* (Chapel Hill: University of North Carolina Press, 2003), 22. For more on race formation see Peter Schrag, *Not Fit for Our Society: Nativism and Immigration* (Berkeley: University of California Press, 2010), 84, 139; Michael Omi and Howard Winant, *Racial Formation in the United States: From the 1960s to the 1990s*, 2nd ed. (New York: Routledge, 1994), 55–61; Audrey Smedley, *Race in North America: Origins and Evolution of a Worldview*, 3rd ed. (Boulder, CO: Westview Press, 2007).

11. Lee, *At America's Gates*, 10.

12. Thomas M. Wilson and Hastings Donnan argue that "social identities are shaped by the state and may emerge as a result of, or in response to, the state's attempts to define or redefine its outer limits. Because of their liminal and frequently contested nature, borders tend to be characterized by identities which are shifting and multiple, in ways which are framed by the specific state configurations which encompass them and within which people must attributed meaning to their experience of border life." Thomas M. Wilson and Hastings Donnan, eds., *Border Identities: Nation and State at International Frontiers* (Cambridge: Cambridge University Press, 1998), 12–13.

13. "Americans and Mexicans to Be Segregated New Federal Census Will List Each Race," *El Paso Herald*, January14, 1916, 6; "Special Census of the Population of El Paso, Texas," January 15, 1916, Department of Commerce, Bureau of the Census (Washington, DC: Government Printing Office, 1916).

14. Mexican migration into the United States, especially in the twentieth century, has served as a lens into the intertwined themes of labor, immigration, and race. Economic relations, cultural commonalities, and political maneuvering between Mexico and the United States have contributed to a highly complex web of race, migration, and labor. Several scholars have addressed these themes simultaneously or independently. For more information on labor, immigration, and race along the US-Mexico border, see Gilbert Gonzalez, *Guest Workers or Colonized Labor?: Mexican Labor Migration to the United States* (Boulder, CO: Paradigm Publishers, 2007); Emilio Zamora, *Claiming Rights and Righting Wrongs in Texas: Mexican Workers and Job Politics during World War II* (College Station: Texas A&M University Press, 2009); Deborah Cohen, *Braceros: Migrant Citizens and Transnational Subjects in the Postwar United States and Mexico* (Chapel Hill: University of North Carolina Press, 2011); Mario T. García, *Desert Immigrants: The Mexicans of El Paso, 1880–1920* (New Haven, CT: Yale University Press, 1981); George J. Sánchez, *Becoming Mexican American: Ethnicity, Culture, and Identity in Chicano Los Angeles, 1900–1945* (New York: Oxford University Press, 1995); Albert Camarillo, *Chicanos in a Changing Society: From Mexican Pueblos to American Barrios in Santa Barbara and Southern California, 1848–1930*, 2nd ed. (Dallas: Southern Methodist University Press, 2005).

15. Walter L. Buenger identifies a dramatic shift in racial demography as contributing significantly to racial violence and the lynching of blacks in the town of Paris, Texas. The escalation of the black population in the town contributed to lynching and other gruesome deeds used to intimidate the African American community, Buenger found. By 1890 the African American population had increased 187 percent and now constituted about one-third of the total number of people there. Whites throughout northeast Texas, meanwhile, grew increasingly fearful of newly arriving blacks and "decried the breakdown in black behavior" and condemned those that "no longer knew their place." Whites thus resorted to violent means to control the social and political ambitions of blacks at the turn of the twentieth century. Walter L. Buenger, *The Path to a Modern South: Northeast Texas between Reconstruction and the Great Depression* (Austin: University of Texas Press, 2001), 22–23; borderlands historian Mario T. García emphasizes the anxiety expressed by Anglo residents in El Paso at the turn of the twentieth century when Mexican immigration increased significantly. Several civic groups like the El Paso

Medical Association complained that "unrestricted immigration of Mexican 'peons' had caused a potential health problem for El Paso." Moreover, it was the sheer numbers of Mexicans crossing into El Paso that worried many in the city, especially the labor sector. García, *Desert Immigrants*, 38–39, 102–5.

16. Oscar J. Martínez, *Troublesome Border*, rev. ed. (Tucson: University of Arizona Press, 2006), 3–4, 6.

17. Montejano, *Anglos and Mexicans*, 196.

18. For more on Mexican and Mexican American racial and political identity, see David Gutiérrez, *Walls and Mirrors*; George J. Sánchez, *Becoming Mexican American*; Mae Ngai, *Impossible Subjects*; Emilio Zamora, *Claiming Rights and Righting Wrongs in Texas: Mexican Workers and Job Politics during World War II* (College Station: Texas A&M University Press, 2009); Benjamin Heber Johnson, *Revolution in Texas: How a Forgotten Rebellion and Its Bloody Suppression Turned Mexicans into Americans* (New Haven, CT: Yale University Press, 2005).

19. Wilson and Donnan, *Border Identities*, 26. The thesis that borders are contradictory zones of culture and power is expanded to address a variety of borderland regions across the globe. Scholar Pieter Judson argues that those who inhabited the frontier, or multilingual areas, "often exhibited inexplicable behaviors, identifying themselves with neither nation or with both nations." Pieter M. Judson, *Guardians of the Nation: Activists on the Language Frontiers of Imperial Austria* (Cambridge, MA: Harvard University Press, 2006), 2. For more on the concept of contradictory border zones, see Alexander C. Diener and Joshua Hagen, eds., *Borderlines and Borderlands: Political Oddities at the Edge of the Nation-State* (Lanham, MD: Rowman and Littlefield, 2010), 1–14; Paul Ganster and David E. Lorey, eds., *Borders and Border Politics in a Globalizing World* (Lanham, MD: SR Books, 2005); Andrés Reséndez, *Changing National Identities at the Frontier: Texas and New Mexico, 1800–1850* (Cambridge: Cambridge University Press, 2004); Bobby Byrd and Susannah Mississippi Byrd, eds., *The Late Great Mexican Border: Reports from a Disappearing Line* (El Paso: Cinco Puntos Press, 1996).

20. Oscar J. Martínez, *Border Boom Town: Ciudad Juárez since 1848* (Austin: University of Texas Press, 1975), 4. For more information on El Paso and Ciudad Juárez interdependence and broader border interdependence, see Wilbert H. Timmons, *El Paso: A Borderlands History* (El Paso: Texas Western Press, 1990); Charles Leland Sonnichsen, *Pass of the North* (El Paso: Texas Western Press, 1968); Mario García, *Desert Immigrants*.

21. Oscar J. Martínez, *Troublesome Border* (Tucson: University of Arizona Press, 1988), 2.

22. W. D. Smithers, a soldier and special observer who settled in the El Paso area after military service, called the period from 1916 to the 1930s the "border trouble days." Wilfred Dudley Smithers, "Too Rough for Comfort—The Mexico Border," undated, unpublished essay, W. D. Smithers Collection, Dolph Briscoe Center for American History, University of Texas at Austin.

23. Jim Tuck, "The Mexican Revolution: A Nation in Flux, pt. 1 and pt. 2," mexconnect.com, http://www.mexconnect.com/articles/296-the-revolution -a-nation-in-flux-part-1-1910-20 (accessed April 5, 2011).

24. For more information on the Mexican Revolution of 1910, see John Mason Hart, *Revolutionary Mexico: The Coming and Process of the Mexican Revolution*, 10th ed. (Chapel Hill: University of North Carolina Press, 1997); Adolfo Gilly, *The Mexican Revolution: A People's History* (New York: New Press, 2006); Anita Brenner, *The Wind That Swept Mexico: The History of the Mexican Revolution, 1910–1942* (Austin: University of Texas Press, 1984); William H. Beezley and Colin M. MacLachlan, *Mexicans in Revolution, 1910–1946: An Introduction (The Mexican Experience)* (Lincoln: University of Nebraska Press, 2009).

25. For more on cross-border violence and political intrigue during the Mexican Revolution of 1910, see Benjamin Heber Johnson, *Revolution in Texas*; Charles H. Harris III and Louis R. Sadler, *The Secret War in El Paso: Mexican Revolutionary Intrigue, 1906–1920* (Albuquerque: University of New Mexico Press, 2009); Joseph Stout, *Border Conflict: Villistas, Carrancistas, and the Punitive Expedition, 1915–1920* (Fort Worth: Texas Christian University Press, 1999);

Eileen Welsome, *The General and the Jaguar: Pershing's Hunt for Pancho Villa: A True Story of Revolution and Revenge* (New York: Little, Brown, 2006).

26. Martínez, *Border Boom Town*, 41.

27. Marshall W. Meyer, "Two Authority Structures of Bureaucratic Organization," *Administrative Science Quarterly* 13, no. 2 (1968): 213.

28. Ibid., 214.

29. Martínez, *Troublesome Border*, 3.

30. Ibid., 3–4; Wilson and Donnan, *Border Identities*, 21–26.

31. C. Edward Weber, "The Nature of Authority: Comment," *Journal of the Academy of Management* 4, no. 1 (1961): 62–63.

32. Ana María Alonso, *Thread of Blood: Colonialism, Revolution, and Gender on the Mexican Northern Frontier* (Tucson: University of Arizona Press, 1995), 10.

33. Ibid., 15–17; William D. Carrigan, *The Making of a Lynching Culture: Violence and Vigilantism in Central Texas, 1836–1916* (Urbana: University of Illinois Press, 2006), 26–30.

34. Sebastian de Grazia, "What Authority Is Not," *American Political Science Review* 53, no. 2 (1959): 322.

35. Carrigan, *The Making of a Lynching Culture*, 2–3.

36. Ibid.

37. Martínez, *Troublesome Border*, 4.

38. De Grazia, "What Authority Is Not," 322.

39. Montejano, *Chicano Politics and Society in the Late Twentieth Century*, xvi.

40. Martínez, *Border Boom Town*, 35–36.

41. Sonnichsen, *Pass of the North*, 311.

42. For more on the Plan of San Diego and racial conflict between Anglos and Mexicans in Texas, see Charles H. Harris III and Louis R. Sadler, *The Texas Rangers and the Mexican Revolution: The Bloodiest Decade, 1910–1920* (Albuquerque: University of New Mexico Press, 2004); James A. Sandos, *Rebellion in the Borderlands: Anarchism and the Plan of San Diego, 1904–1923* (Norman: University of Oklahoma Press, 1992); Benjamin Heber Johnson, *Revolution in Texas*; Walter Prescott Webb, *The Texas Rangers: A Century of Frontier Defense* (Austin: University of Texas Press, 1935).

43. Martínez, *Border Boom Town*, 30.

44. The term *Mexican bandit* is complex and projects different meanings. The bandit is generally understood from two separate perspectives. Anglo-American society viewed the Mexican bandit as an outlaw and/or fugitive. Some Mexicans, on the other hand, held a starkly different view of banditry as a struggle of an oppressed people to assert themselves and defend what they felt was rightfully theirs. Pedro Castillo and Albert Camarillo, eds., *Furia y muerte: Los bandidos Chicanos* (Los Angeles: Aztlán Publications, 1973), 3. Castillo and Camarillo apply Eric J. Hobsbawm's definition to Mexican banditry. For Castillo and Camarillo, Mexican social bandits were not lawbreakers, but victims of Anglo invasion and resistant. Furthermore, Mexican banditry was a form of retribution and was for the purpose of survival. For this study it will be understood that the "Mexican bandit" is not just an outlaw or fugitive, but a social actor resistant to Anglo dominance. According to Hobsbawm, "bandits reflect the disruption of an entire society, the rise of new classes and social structures, the resistance of entire communities or people against the destruction of its way of life." Eric J. Hobsbawm, *Bandits* (London: Weidenfeld and Nicolson, 1969), 13.

45. I understand that the use of the term *holocaust* in this chapter's title possibly suggests hyperbole or a misunderstanding of the tragic era of Nazi Germany and the ruling party's mass slaughter of millions of Jews in Germany in the 1930s and 1940s. However, the use of this term does not reflect or echo the tragedy of the Nazi era. Rather, local newspapers used the literal term *holocaust* to describe the horrible accident that killed over two-dozen prisoners in a fire. In order to stay true to the primary sources I adopt the term *holocaust* used by many El Paso newspapers in 1916 to describe the mass murder of El Paso city jail prisoners. There is absolutely not a connection made by

the author or the newspapers between the two very different events. "Grand Jury to Probe Fire: Coroner's Inquest in Progress; Grand Jury Representative is Present: Awful Scenes in Jail Holocaust," El Paso Herald, March 7, 1916, 1; "Searching Investigation of Jail Holocaust Ordered," El Paso Morning Times, March 8, 1916, 1; "Grand Jury Probing Jail Fire; One More Victim Is Identified: Investigation of Holocaust at City Jail is Being Made," El Paso Herald, March 8, 1916, 1, 5; "Indictments May Follow Fire; 3 Die; Now 19 Fatalities: Grand Jury Expected to Return True Bills as Result of the City Jail Holocaust Monday Afternoon," El Paso Herald, March 9, 1916, 4; "Another Jail Holocaust Victim Dies in Jail," El Paso Morning Times, March 14, 1916, 5; "Twenty-Fifth Victim of Jail Holocaust Is Dead," El Paso Morning Times, March 17, 1916, 6; "Mexicans Connect Jail Horror with Columbus Outrage: Miss Houghton of Chihuahua Says Lower Classes Think Holocaust Was Planned," El Paso Morning Times, March 21, 1916, 2; "Fire in City Jail Ignored: Grand Jury Fails to Return Indictments or Make Report on Holocaust," El Paso Herald, March 24, 1916, 13; David Dorado Romo, Ringside Seat to a Revolution: An Underground Cultural History of El Paso and Juárez: 1893–1923 (El Paso: Cinco Punto Press, 2005), 226–27.

CHAPTER 1: COWBOYS AND BANDIDOS

Chapter 1 is a revised version of a previously published essay titled, "Cowboys and Bandidos: Authority and Race in West Texas, 1913–1918," which appeared in the West Texas Historical Association Year Book, vol. 85 (2009): 7–27. The quote in the chapter epigraph is from Tony Cano and Ann Sochat, Bandido: The True Story of Chico Cano, the Last Western Bandit (Canutillo, TX: Reata Publishing, 1997), 51.

1. Gary Clayton Anderson argues that Texans in the nineteenth century endorsed a policy of ethnic cleansing that has as its intentions the "forced removal of certain culturally identified groups from their lands," groups that included Indians and Tejanos. Gary Clayton Anderson, The Conquest of Texas: Ethnic Cleansing in the Promised Land, 1820–1875 (Norman: University of Oklahoma Press, 2005), 7.

2. Julian Samora, Joe Bernal, and Albert Peña, Gunpowder Justice: A Reassessment of the Texas Rangers (Notre Dame, IN: University of Notre Dame Press, 1979), 15.

3. Jack Shipman, "Texas Rangers," undated, Texas Rangers Vertical File, Border Heritage Collection, El Paso Public Library, El Paso, Texas.

4. Robert M. Utley, Lone Star Lawmen: The Second Century of the Texas Rangers (New York: Oxford University Press, 2007), 4.

5. Walter Prescott Webb, The Texas Rangers: A Century of Frontier Defense (Austin: University of Texas Press, 1965), 345; Utley, Lone Star Lawmen, 4–5.

6. Américo Paredes characterized the Lower Rio Grande region in Texas as a "patriarchal system [that] not only made the Border community more cohesive, but emphasizing its clanlike characteristics, but it also minimized outside interference, because it allowed the community to govern itself to a great extent . . . the Border Mexican simply ignored strangers." Américo Paredes, With His Pistol in His Hand: A Border Ballad and Its Hero (Austin: University of Texas Press, 1958), 10, 12–13; also see Oscar J. Martínez, Troublesome Border (Tucson: University of Arizona Press, 1991), 107.

7. Charles H. Harris III and Louis R. Sadler, The Texas Rangers and The Mexican Revolution: The Bloodiest Decade, 1910–1920 (Albuquerque: University of New Mexico Press, 2007), 3–4.

8. Charles H. Harris III and Louis R. Sadler argue in their comprehensive study of the Texas Rangers during the Mexican Revolution that the organization did not operate in a vacuum but rather as a law enforcement agency within a political context, and that it served as the governor's personal police force. They conclude that their activities had an important bearing on the relations between the United States and Mexico. Harris and Sadler, The Texas Rangers and the Mexican Revolution, 7.

9. The quote in the heading comes from "Early Day Rangers," El Paso Times, October 27, 1963.

10. Samora, Bernal, and Peña, *Gunpowder Justice*, 10–12; Anderson, *The Conquest of Texas*, 7–9.

11. Webb, *The Texas Rangers*, 307–18; Robert M. Utley, *Lone Star Justice: The First Century of the Texas Rangers* (New York: Oxford University Press, 2002), 143–77; Samora, Bernal, and Peña, *Gunpowder Justice*, 53–56; Arnoldo De León, *They Called Them Greasers: Anglo Attitudes toward Mexicans in Texas, 1821–1900* (Austin: University of Texas Press, 1983), 87–102.

12. Webb, *The Texas Rangers*, 425.

13. Utley, *Lone Star Justice*, 161.

14. Webb, *The Texas Rangers*, 425; De León, *They Called Them Greasers*, 87–88; Utley, *Lone Star Justice*, 160–64.

15. Samora, Bernal, and Peña, *Gunpowder Justice*, 47–53; De León, *They Called Them Greasers*, 87–102; Carlysle Graham Raht, *Romance of Davis Mountains and Big Bend Country: A History* (Odessa, TX: Rahtbooks, 1963), 225–29, 257–360, 308–12, 377; Ronnie Tyler, *The Big Bend* (Washington, DC: Office of Publications, 1975), 157–58; Webb, *The Texas Rangers*, 425–27, 437–38, 446–47; Michael L. Collins, *Texas Devils: Rangers and Regulars on the Lower Rio Grande, 1846–1861* (Norman: University of Oklahoma Press, 2008), 5.

16. Webb, *The Texas Rangers*, 452.

17. Corrupt officers were, at times, allowed to practice law enforcement despite known criminal behavior. The enlistment of corrupt officers contributed to dissatisfaction toward the Rangers by residents. For example, in his memoirs, Ranger James B. Gillett describes an incident with a Ranger that was on the "fugitive list" issued by the adjutant general. He was charged with assault with intent to kill. Gillett revealed this discovery to Captain George W. Baylor, who quickly condoned the Ranger's actions by stating that "maybe the darned fellow needed killing." James B. Gillett, *Six Years with the Texas Rangers, 1875–1881* (New Haven, CT: Yale University Press, 1925), 191.

18. Adjutant General Thomas Scurry, General Order No. 62, July 3, 1901, Frontier Battalion records, Ranger records, Texas Adjutant General's Department. Archives and Information Services Division, Texas State Library and Archives Commission; "Organization of the Ranger Force, 1901," Texas State House Bill (HB) no. 52, 27th Legislature, Austin, Texas, 1901; Webb, *The Texas Rangers*, 457.

19. For more on the El Paso Salt War see C. L. Sonnichsen, *The El Paso Salt War* (El Paso: Hertzog, 1961); Paul Cool, *Salt Warriors: Insurgency in the Rio Grande* (College Station: Texas A&M University Press, 2008); Webb, *The Texas Rangers*; De León, *They Called Them Greasers*, 99–101; Manuel Callahan, "Mexican Border Troubles: Social War, Settler Colonialism, and the Production of Frontier Discourses, 1848–1880" (PhD diss., University of Texas at Austin, 2003).

20. Callahan, "Mexican Border Troubles," 204.

21. The *Mesilla Valley Independent* claimed that at least two hundred men arrested the García brothers; however, other accounts claim that as many as four hundred men were after Howard. "Mob Law in El Paso County," *Mesilla Valley Independent*, Mesilla, New Mexico, October 6, 1877, no. 16, 2; "El Paso County Troubles," *Mesilla Valley Independent*, Mesilla, New Mexico, October 13, 1877, no. 17, 2; University of Texas at El Paso, Main Library.

22. US Congress. House, *El Paso Troubles in Texas*, 45th Cong., 2nd Sess., Ex. Doc. 93, pp. 73; 142; Callahan, "Mexican Border Troubles," 205.

23. Telegram sent to General Edward Hatch, US Army, commander of the Department of New Mexico, by S. Shutz and Bro. and all citizens of Franklin, Texas, on October 10, 1877. The telegram was reprinted in "A Lone Ranger Rides Troubled El Paso Trails," *El Paso Times*, September 27, 1959.

24. Paul Cool, "El Paso's First Real Lawman, Texas Ranger Mark (Marcus) Ludwick," *Quarterly of the National Association for Outlaw and Lawman History, Inc.* 25, no. 4 (2001).

25. Ibid.

26. "The El Paso County Troubles," *Mesilla Valley Independent*, October 6, 1877, no. 16, 2.

27. Manuel Callahan identifies at least two incidences of murder by the Anglo outfit against Mexican residents who were not directly involved with the Salt War affair. Callahan, "Mexican Border Troubles," 229–30; Cool, *Salt Warriors*, 216–26.

28. Cool, *Salt Warriors*, 227–40.

29. Ibid., 262–64; W. H. Timmons, *El Paso: A Borderlands History* (El Paso: Texas Western Press, 1990), 196.

30. Cool, *Salt Warriors*, 216–23.

31. The prizefight took place on the Mexican side of the river across from a small town called Langtry, Texas, in the Big Bend region. Jack Martin, *Border Boss: Captain John R. Hughes, Texas Ranger* (Austin: State House Press, 1990), 163.

32. "Fighting the Gamblers in the Early Days, Rangers Sent Here Twice against Protest," *Pioneer News Observer*, August 1970, 4, "Texas Rangers" Vertical File, Border Heritage Center, El Paso Public Library, El Paso, Texas (hereafter cited as BHC-EPPL).

33. Ibid.

34. "When the Santa Fe Windows Were Shot Out, Rangers and Citizens Battle in the Street," *El Paso Times*, December 5, 1920, "Texas Rangers" Vertical File, BHC-EPPL.

35. "Battle of Tres Jacales, 25 Years Ago Recalled, Rangers to Ride into Trap and Leader Is Killed," *El Paso Times*, date unknown, "Texas Rangers" Vertical File, BHC-EPPL

36. Paul Cool, "El Paso's First Real Lawman, Texas Ranger Mark (Marcus) Ludwick"; "Texas Rangers" Vertical File, BHC-EPPL.

37. "Grave of Capt. Frank Jones, Texas Ranger Killed in Bandit Battle, Marked 44 Years by Lone Tree," *El Paso Times*, July 18, 1937, "Texas Rangers" Vertical File, BHC-EPPL; Manuel Callahan identifies at least two incidences of murder by the Anglo outfit against Mexican residents who were not directly involved with the Salt War affair. Callahan, "Mexican Border Troubles," 229–30; Cool, *Salt Warriors*, 216–26.

38. "Grave of Capt. Frank Jones, Texas Ranger Killed in Bandit Battle, Marked 44 Years by Lone Tree," *El Paso Times*, July 18, 1937, "Texas Rangers" Vertical File, BHC-EPPL.

39. "Battle of Tres Jacales 25 Years Ago Recalled Rangers Ride into Trap and Leader Is Killed," newspaper and date unknown, "Texas Rangers" Vertical File, BHC-EPPL.

40. Ibid.; Eugene Cunningham, *Triggernometry: A Gallery of Gunfighters* (Caldwell, ID: Caxton Printers, 1958), 223–24.

41. Captain Jim M. Fox of Marfa, Texas, befriended Villa and utilized his services on several occasions to apprehend Mexicans suspected of a variety of crimes in the area. According to Fox, several Rangers chased after three Mexicans suspected of thievery in 1915. One of the Rangers was shot dead. Across the river near the scene of the shooting was a battalion of Villista troops. Fox arranged a meeting with General Villa in Ciudad Juárez regarding the apprehension of the men who killed the Ranger. Villa agreed to have the men captured and executed. When Fox returned to Marfa he received word that Villa had apprehended the men and asked if the Rangers cared to be present during the execution. Ranger medical officer, Dr. Goodwin, witnessed the execution in Ciudad Juárez and gave the spent cartridges to Captain Fox as proof of their execution. Claude Leroy Douglas, *The Gentlemen in the White Hats: Dramatic Episodes in the History of the Texas Rangers* (Dallas: Southwest Press, 1934), 165–66, 168.

42. Dane Coolidge, *Fighting Men of the West* (New York: Bantam, 1952), 148.

43. Mario T. García, *Desert Immigrants: The Mexicans of El Paso, 1880–1920* (New Haven, CT: Yale University Press, 1981), 172.

44. Glenn Justice, *Revolution on the Rio Grande: Mexican Raids and Army Pursuits, 1916–1919* (El Paso: Texas Western Press, 1992), 6.

45. "Scout Reports: Company 'D,' 1907–1908," no. 1188–3, November 1908, Ranger Force records, Ranger records, Texas Adjutant General's Depart-

ment, Archives and Information Services Division, Texas State Library and Archives Commission (hereafter cited as Ranger Force records of the TSLAC).

46. Ibid.; "Revolutionists All Gone?" newspaper unknown, 1911, "Wright, Dogie" Vertical File, Center for American History, University of Texas at Austin; "El Paso without Rangers for More Than 20 Years: Old Timers Recall When They Were Removed after Searching Automobiles in Valley," El Paso Herald-Post, March 20, 1935, "Texas Rangers" Vertical File, BHC-EPPL.

47. Captain John R. Hughes, "Monthly Returns: Company 'D,' November 30, 1908," Ranger Force records of the TSLC.

48. According to Texas Ranger records, Jeff E. Vaughn would later serve as captain of Company A in 1933. "Partial List of Texas Ranger Company and Unit Commanders," http://www.texasranger.org/ReCenter/Captains.pdf, Texas Ranger Research Center, Waco, Texas (accessed June 7, 2007).

49. "Ranger Correspondence, 1917," (1183–15) Ranger Force records of the TSLC.

50. Ibid.

51. Pedro Castillo and Albert Camarillo, eds., Furia y muerte: Los bandidos chicanos (Los Angeles: Aztlán Publications, 1973), 2.

52. Tony Cano (great-nephew of Chico Cano), in discussion with the author, March 18, 2008.

53. Tony Cano and Ann Sochat, Bandido: The True Story of Chico Cano, the Last Western Bandit (Canutillo, TX: Reata Publishing, 1997), 52–53.

54. "Human Rights along the Mexican Border; Shields Other Side," Houston Chronicle, November 15, 1915.

55. Several scholars have discussed that the practice of stealing cattle was a prominent activity not dominated by one particular group but exercised by all. Anglo ranchers stole from each other and, in this example, elicited the help of Mexican "bandit gangs" to retrieve cattle. For more, see Cano and Sochat, Bandido, 48–49; Samora, Bernal, and Peña, Gunpowder Justice, 48–53.

56. Cano and Sochat, Bandido, 49.

57. An interview with Mrs. Mattie Baca, daughter of Texas Ranger Joe Sitters of West Texas, was conducted by El Paso Times writer Dorothea Magadalene Fox in 1963. In her interview she recounts some of her father's exploits prior to his death at the hands of bandit Chico Cano and outlines the conditions experienced by the rangers in West Texas during the mid-1910s. Dorothea Magadalene Fox, "Early Day Rangers, Figured Pretty Good," El Paso Times, October 27, 1963, "Texas Rangers" Vertical File, BHC-EPPL.

58. For more on the "Bandit Wars," see Harris and Sadler, Texas Rangers and the Mexican Revolution, 248–97; Rodolfo Rocha, "The Influence of the Mexican Revolution on the Mexico-Texas Border, 1910–1916" (PhD diss., Texas Tech University, 1981); Utley, Lone Star Lawmen, 26–47.

59. Douglas, The Gentlemen in the White Hats, 166.

60. Personal correspondence, Elmer Kelton to Tony Cano, November 12, 1997, Personal Notes and Archives of Mr. Tony Cano, Canutillo, Texas.

61. Cano and Sochat, Bandido, 55.

62. "Early Day Rangers, Figured Pretty Good," El Paso Times, October 27, 1963, "Texas Rangers" Vertical File, BHC-EPPL.

63. Cano and Sochat, Bandido, 56–57.

64. Ibid., 59–60.

65. According to an interview given by Joe Sitters's daughter, Mattie Baca, Sitters was a personal friend of Pancho Villa. They had exchanged pleasantries on numerous occasions and even exchanged gifts. Baca stated that Sitters had a tremendous amount of respect for Villa and felt that he was a good leader for his people. "Early Day Rangers, Figured Pretty Good," El Paso Times, October 27, 1963, "Texas Rangers" Vertical File, BHC-EPPL.

66. "River Guard and Ranger Killed," El Paso Herald, May 27, 1915, "Texas Rangers" Vertical File, BHC-EPPL.

67. One of the soldiers of the Eighth Cavalry stationed at Camp Evetts remarked that the Rangers who met with Captain Anderson to organize an attack on Porvenir "acted so tough and look[ed] so scared." Robert Keil, *Bosque Bonito: Violent Times along the Borderland during the Mexican Revolution* (Alpine, TX: Center for Big Bend Studies, Sul Ross State University, 2002), 29.

68. Senate Committee on the Investigation of Mexican Affairs, Subcommittee of the Committee on Foreign Relations, *Partial Report of Committee*, report by Senators Albert B. Fall, Frank B. Brandegee, and Marcus A. Smith, 66th Cong., 2nd sess., 1920, S. Res. 106, 3382.

69. Ranch foreman Van Neill had some family members staying at the ranch for the Christmas holiday. His nieces Dorothy Messey and her sisters were at Brite Ranch during the raid and claimed that "Uncle Sam," Van Neill's father, fired the first shot as the bandits approached the ranch headquarters. Dorothy Messey, Oral History Interview, September 23, 1982, Southwest Collection/Special Collections, Texas Tech University; Glenn Justice, *Little Known History of the Texas Big Bend: Documented Chronicles From Cabeza de Vaca to the Era of Pancho Villa* (Odessa, TX: Rimrock Press, 2001), 130–33.

70. For a detailed account of the "Brite Ranch Raid," see Justice, *Little Known History of the Texas Big Bend*; Cano and Sochat, *Bandido*; Keil, *Bosque Bonito*; Roger Batchelder, *Watching and Waiting on the Border* (Boston: Houghton Mifflin, 1917).

71. Batchelder, *Watching and Waiting on the Border*, 74.

72. Justice, *Little Known History of the Texas Big Bend*, 135; *El Paso Morning Times*, January 4, 1918.

73. Dorothy Messey, Oral History Interview, September 23, 1982, Southwest Collection/Special Collections, Texas Tech University, Lubbock, Texas.

74. Cano and Sochat, *Bandido*, 153.

75. Dorothy Messey, Oral History Interview, September 23, 1982, Southwest Collection/Special Collections, Texas Tech University, Lubbock, Texas.

76. Alice Cummings, interview by Richard Estrada, March 1, 1978, transcript, Institute of Oral History, Special Collections, University of Texas at El Paso, 9.

77. Chico Cano was given a commission of colonel in the Carranza army and was appointed Juez de la Acordada, or judge, with the legal power to sentence a man to death. Cano and Sochat, *Bandido*, 155.

78. Tony Cano, in discussion with the author, March 18, 2008.

79. Ibid.

80. Jane Brite White, oral interview, November 16, 1997, Marfa, Texas, Tony Cano personal collection.

81. "Partial List of Texas Ranger Company and Unit Commanders," http://www.texasranger.org/ReCenter/Captains.pdf, Texas Ranger Research Center, Waco, Texas (accessed June 7, 2007).

82. Big Bend resident and schoolteacher, Harry Warren, recounted the murder of Ranger Jack Howard and the wounding of Joe Sitters in February 1913 and identified Texas Cattle Raisers' Association Field Inspector J. A. Harvick as part of the posse set to arrest Chico Cano. Unpublished essay, Harry Warren Papers, Archives of the Big Bend, Sul Ross State University, Alpine, Texas; "Capturing the Noted Bandit," *The Cattleman*, June 1914, http://www.thecattlemanmagazine.com/earlyDays/earlynotedbandit.asp (accessed May 19, 2009).

83. The village of Porvenir, Texas, is spelled differently by various authors. For the purpose of this study, the spelling and reference to the village are based on the reports by eyewitnesses and those familiar with the village.

84. Testimony given by "Witnesses in U.S." and signed by Capt. Anderson, Co. G. Eighth Cavalry, Camp Evett, Valentine, Texas, and Sgt. Bruin. Files from the Adjutant General, Proceedings of the Joint Committee of the Senate and House Investigation of the Texas State Ranger Force, 1919, 831–62.

85. Justice, *Little Known History of the Texas Big Bend*, 137.

86. Mattie Baca reiterated what the Rangers and local cattlemen thought of Porvenir. She also stated that it was believed that many of Chico Cano's cousins and other family members lived in the village and used the locale to move

goods freely across the river. "Early Day Rangers," El Paso Times, October 27, 1963; Justice, Revolution on the Rio Grande, 36.

87. Harry Warren, "The Porvenir Massacre in Presidio, County, Texas, on January 28, 1918," unpublished essay/testimony, Harry Warren Papers, Archives of the Big Bend, Sul Ross State University, Alpine, Texas (hereafter cited as the Harry Warren Papers of the ABB-SRSU).

88. Justice, Revolution on the Rio Grande, 36–37.

89. Testimony given by "Witnesses in U.S.," Proceedings of the Joint Committee of the Senate and House in the Investigation of the Texas State Ranger Force, 849–53.

90. Letter sent to James M. Day, director of Texas State Archives, by Robert Keil of the Eighth Cavalry on July 11, 1963. Casey Collection, Archives of the Big Bend, Sul Ross State University, Alpine, Texas (hereafter cited as Casey Collection of the ABB-SRSU).

91. Ibid.

92. Harry Warren, "Porvenir Massacre in Presidio County, Texas, On January 28, 1918," unpublished essay, Harry Warren Papers of the ABB-SRSU.

93. According to Porvenir eyewitness Robert Keil, a soldier serving the Eighth Cavalry between 1913 and 1918 in the Big Bend, Captain Anderson "vigorously protested" to Colonel Langhorne that he was sure there weren't any outlaws in the village and was not comfortable with the order. For more on the Eighth Cavalry's role in the Porvenir incident, see Keil, Bosque Bonito, 28; Justice, Little Known History of the Texas Big Bend; and Joyce E. Means, Pancho Villa Days at Pilares: Stories and Sketches of Days-Gone-By from the Valentine Country of West Texas (El Paso: Joyce E. Means, 1976).

94. "Motion on Behalf of the United States to Strike Out Portion of Brief on Behalf of United Mexican States," Special Claims Commission, United States and Mexico, The United States of America on behalf of (17 defendants) v. The United Mexican States, Docket No. 449, "Opinions rendered by the Commission April 26, 1926), folder no. 2: Legal Proceedings, RG 76: Records of Boundary and Claims Commission, Arbitrations, 1923–1937, National Archives at College Park, MD.

95. The sworn testimonies of Librada Montoya Jacquez, Juana Zonilla Flores, Felipa Mendez Castañeda, and Eulalia Gonzales Hernandes gave consistent accounts of how their husbands were taken from their homes and beaten by Rangers and ranchmen in the village. Proceedings of the Joint Committee of the Senate and House in the Investigation of the Texas State Ranger Force, 1919, 838–39.

96. Harry Warren, "Porvenir Massacre in Presidio County, Texas, On January 28, 1918," unpublished essay, Harry Warren Papers of the ABB-SRSU.

97. Letter sent to the adjutant general by Captain J. M. Fox of Company B in Marfa, Texas, on June 30, 1918. Roy W. Aldrich Collection, Folder #71, ABB-SRSU.

98. Letter sent to James M. Day, director of Texas State Archives, by Robert Keil of the Eighth Cavalry on July 11, 1963. Casey Collection of the ABB-SRSU.

99. Justice, Revolution on the Rio Grande, 39.

100. Testimony given by "Witnesses in U.S.," Proceedings of the Joint Committee of the Senate and House in the Investigation of the Texas State Ranger Force, 847.

101. Justice, Revolution on the Rio Grande, 40.

102. Testimony of Juana Zonilla Flores, April 5, 1918, and taken by Patrick Kelly, 1st Lieut., Cavalry, N.A., Summary Cort. Proceedings of the Joint Committee of the Senate and House in the Investigation of the Texas State Ranger Force, 844.

103. Ibid.

104. Harry Warren, "Porvenir Massacre," Harry Warren Papers of the ABB-SRSU; Adjutant General James A. Harley's letter to Texas Ranger Captain J. M. Fox reprinted in the El Paso Times, July 11, 1918, 12.

105. Captain Anderson's letter to Governor Hobby. Joint Committee of the Senate and House in the Investigation of the Texas State Ranger Force, January 1919, 849–51.

106. Ibid.

107. In June 1920, Major Yancey of the Eighth Cavalry, stationed in the Big Bend

region, was court-martialed at Fort Sam Houston in San Antonio, Texas, for ordering the murder of four Mexicans. Several officers and soldiers testified that Major Yancey captured four Mexican males and placed them under guard as the outfit made its way back to headquarters just outside of Carrizo Springs. Sergeant George E. Thomas of Troop A, Fifth Cavalry, testified that the guard with the prisoners left Carrizo probably fifteen to twenty minutes in advance of the main body of troops. Suddenly Major Yancey gave the order to turn the prisoners over to the Rangers, led by John Kerr who had caught up with the guard. Thomas testified that Yancey intended that the prisoners should be murdered. Shortly after the prisoners were released into the custody of the Rangers, shots were heard by several witnesses among the military guard. Colonel George T. Langhorne, commander of the Eighth Cavalry and district commander of the Big Bend District, later testified that commander of the military had authority over all civilians, including the Texas Rangers, and thus Yancey was directly responsible for the killing of the Mexicans. Harry Warren, "Court Martial of Major Yancey, June 12, 1920 in San Antonio, Tex, Fort Sam Houston," Harry Warren Papers of the ABB-SRSU.

108. "José Tomás Canales," Handbook of Texas Online, http://www.tsha.utexas .edu/handbook/online/articles/CC/fcaag.html (accessed June 4, 2007).

109. "El Paso without Rangers for More Than 20 Years," El Paso Herald-Post, March 20, 1935, "Texas Rangers" Vertical File, BHC-EPPL.

110. Webb, Texas Rangers, 514.

111. Evan Anders, Boss Rule in South Texas (Austin: University of Texas Press, 1982), 270.

112. Webb, Texas Rangers, 514.

113. Samora, Bernal, and Peña, Gunpowder Justice, 66.

114. Harris and Sadler, Texas Rangers and the Mexican Revolution, 459.

115. Ibid.

116. Ibid., 461.

117. "Early Day Rangers, Figured Pretty Good," El Paso Times, October 27, 1963.

CHAPTER 2: ¡MUERTE A LOS GRINGOS!
Chapter 2 is based on a revised version of a previously published essay titled "The El Paso Race Riot of 1916," which appears in Arnoldo De León's edited volume War along the Border (College Station: Texas A&M University Press, 2012). The quote in the chapter epigraph is from an interview with Hortencia Villegas by Oscar J. Martínez, February 17, 1976, interview 235, transcript, Institute of Oral History, Special Collections, University of Texas at El Paso.

1. Salvo conducto was an official "safe pass" issued by representatives of the Carranza government to entice foreigners and capitalists back to northern Mexico in 1915. Cusi Mine's general manager Charles Watson met with de facto Chihuahua governor Ignacio Enriquez to negotiate terms for a return to the mines. On January 4, 1916, under the protection of Carranza general Jose Cavazos and one thousand troops, Watson and his men made their way to the Cusi mines. Christopher Lance Habermeyer, Gringo's Curve: Pancho Villa's Massacre of American Miners in Mexico, 1916 (El Paso: Book Publishers of El Paso, 2004), 40–41; Eileen Welsome, The General and the Jaguar: Pershing's Hunt for Pancho Villa: A True Story of Revolution and Revenge (New York: Little, Brown, 2006), 64.

2. "Mining Men Stripped Naked and Ruthlessly Shot Down by Band of Villa Savages," El Paso Morning Times, January 12, 1916, 1.

3. Other similar episodes in West Texas in the nineteenth century included the Alpine race riot of 1886 and the San Elizario Salt War of 1877. The latter episode was not a riot per se, however, the conflict did exhibit strong racial undertones as many lined up along racial lines. For more on the Salt War, see C. L. Sonnichsen, The El Paso Salt War (El Paso: Hertzog, 1961); W. H. Timmons, El Paso: A Borderlands History (El Paso: Texas Western Press, 1990); Walter Prescott Webb, The Texas Rangers: A Century of Frontier Defense (Austin: University of Texas Press, 1935); Paul Cool, Salt Warriors: Insurgency on the Rio

Grande (College Station: Texas A&M University Press, 2008). On the Alpine riot, see Arnoldo De León, *They Called Them Greasers: Anglo Attitudes toward Mexicans in Texas, 1821–1900* (Austin: University of Texas Press, 1983), 92.

4. For readings on the Mexican Revolution and its impact on northern Mexico and the southwestern part of the United States, see Oscar Martínez, *Border Boom Town: Ciudad Juárez since 1848* (Austin: University of Texas Press, 1978); Timmons, *El Paso;* Charles Harris III and Louis R. Sadler, *The Texas Rangers and the Mexican Revolution* (Albuquerque: University of New Mexico Press, 2004); Mario García, *Desert Immigrants: The Mexicans of El Paso, 1880–1920* (New Haven, CT: Yale University Press, 1981).

5. A total of nineteen people were killed in the massacre near Santa Ysabel, January 10, 1916. Seventeen were American citizens, two were British subjects, and fourteen of the American citizens were employees of the Cusi Mining Company, the other three Americans were employees of other mining companies. "Memorial of the Cusi Mining Company to the Secretary of State, Supplemental to the Affidavits and the Brief Heretofore Submitted to the Department of the State for Its Interposition with the Carranza Government of Mexico," Record Group no. 76 (RG 76): Records of Boundary and Claims Commission, Arbitrations, 1923–1937, Records Relating to the Santa Ysabel Cases, 1924–1936, National Archives at College Park, Maryland (NACP).

6. For more on race relations and mob violence in Texas, see William D. Carrigan, *The Making of a Lynching Culture: Violence and Vigilantism in Central Texas, 1836–1916* (Urbana: University of Illinois, 2004); Cynthia Skove Nevels, *Lynching to Belong: Claiming Whiteness through Racial Violence* (College Station: Texas A&M University Press, 2007); Walter L. Buenger, *The Path to a Modern South: Northeast Texas between Reconstruction and the Great Depression* (Austin: University of Texas Press, 2001).

7. David Montejano, ed., *Chicano Politics and Society in the Late Twentieth Century* (Austin: University of Texas Press, 1999), xvi; Elizabeth Benton-Cohen, *Borderline Americans: Racial Divisions and Labor War in the Arizona Borderlands* (Cambridge, MA: Harvard University Press, 2009), 9.

8. James B. Gillett, *Six Years with the Texas Rangers* (Austin: Von Boeckmann-Jones, 1921), 322–23.

9. Timmons, *El Paso,* 170–74, Cleofas Calleros, *El Paso . . . Then and Now* (El Paso: American Printing Company, 1954), 27–37, García, *Desert Immigrants,* 110–11.

10. Martínez, *Border Boom Town,* 20.

11. Ibid., 22–23.

12. Ibid., 28.

13. Mexico eliminated the Free Trade Zone on July 1, 1905. The official explanation stated that improved transportation lines from Mexico City to the northern cities made domestic goods more accessible. Martínez, *Border Boom Town,* 19–37.

14. According to the 1920 Census, El Paso's population had increased approximately 97 percent since 1910. United States Bureau of the Census, *Population of Principal Cities [Texas] from earliest census to 1920,* Bureau of the Census, Washington, DC, 1920.

15. For more on the immigration trends of Mexicans into the United States, see García, *Desert Immigrants;* George J. Sánchez, *Becoming Mexican American: Ethnicity, Culture, and Identity in Chicano Los Angeles, 1900–1945* (New York: Oxford University Press, 1995); Roberto R. Calderón, *Mexican Coal Mining Labor in Texas and Coahuila, 1880–1930* (College Station: Texas A&M University Press, 2000).

16. Racial sentiment toward Mexicans in El Paso began to change when thousands of refugees began to flood the city. The influx led President Woodrow Wilson to order a special census on January 6, 1916, to quantify the number of refugees or persons temporarily residing in El Paso from Mexico. The 1916 Census concluded that the city experienced a 57.6 percent population increase between 1910 and 1916. "Special Census of the Population of El Paso,

Texas, January 15, 1916," Department of Commerce, Bureau of the Census (Washington, DC: GPO, 1916); "Americans and Mexicans to Be Segregated New Federal Census Will List Each Race," El Paso Herald, January 14, 1916, 6. By 1920, some 42,305 of El Paso's population were foreign born. Of these, an overwhelming 91 percent came from Mexico. United States Bureau of the Census, Population of Principal Cities [Texas] from earliest Census to 1920. Bureau of the Census. Washington, DC, 1920; Charles H. Harris III and Louis R. Sadler, "The 'Underside' of the Mexican Revolution, 1912," The Americas (July 1982): 69–83.

17. The Survey 36 (July 8, 1916), 380, Center for American History, University of Texas at Austin.

18. Miguel A. Levario, "Cuando vino la mexicanada: Authority, Race and Conflict in West Texas, 1895–1924" (PhD diss., University of Texas at Austin, 2007), 136.

19. Clarence C. Clendenen, The United States and Pancho Villa: A Study in Unconventional Diplomacy (Ithaca, NY: Cornell University, 1961), 135; Frederick C. Turner, "Anti-Americanism in Mexico, 1910–1913," Hispanic American Historical Review 47 (November 1967): 502–18, "Disorders Continue in Northern Mexico: Anti-American Outbreaks Will Probably Affect Our Reply to Carranza," New York Times, June 10, 1916, 5.

20. David D. Romo, Ringside Seat to a Revolution: An Underground Cultural History of El Paso and Juárez, 1893–1923 (El Paso: Cinco Puntos Press, 2005); T. Lindsay Baker, Ghost Towns of Texas (Norman: University of Oklahoma Press, 1986); and García, Desert Immigrants, 19–20.

21. Levario, "Cuando vino la mexicanada," 22.

22. García, Desert Immigrants, 186–87.

23. Scholars including Rodolfo Rocha argue that the "social banditry" occurring in South Texas was largely a result of revolutionary ideology and the redressing of social conditions and suffering in their locale. Rocha, "The Influence of the Mexican Revolution on the Mexico-Texas Border, 1910–1916" (PhD diss., Texas Tech University, 1981), 256; Levario, "Cuando vino la mexicanada," 57.

24. United States Department of Commerce, Bureau of the Census, Special Census of the Population of El Paso, Tex., prepared under the supervision of Emmons K. Ellsworth, January 15, 1916 (Washington, DC: GPO, 1916).

25. Walter L. Buenger identifies a dramatic shift in racial demography as contributing significantly to racial violence and the lynching of blacks in the town of Paris, Texas. Buenger, The Path to a Modern South, 22–23.

26. García, Desert Immigrants, 102–5.

27. For more on Villa's anti-American rhetoric, see Haldeen Braddy, Pancho Villa at Columbus (El Paso: Texas Western College Press, 1965); John F. Chalkley, Zach Lamar Cobb: El Paso Collector of Customs and Intelligence during the Mexican Revolution, 1913–1918 (El Paso: Texas Western Press, 1998); Don M. Coerver and Linda B. Hall, Texas and the Mexican Revolution: A Study in State and National Border Policy, 1910–1920 (San Antonio: Trinity University Press, 1984).

28. Harris and Sadler, The Border and the Revolution, 103.

29. (Unless otherwise noted, all translations are of the author.) Hortencia Villegas, interview by Oscar J. Martínez, February 17, 1976, interview 235, transcript, Institute of Oral History, Special Collections, University of Texas at El Paso.

30. Timmons, El Paso, 219.

31. General Álvaro Obregón was one of the de facto Mexican president Venustiano Carranza's top generals during the revolution.

32. El Paso Herald, December 31, 1915, 6; Jason T. Darrah, "Anglos, Mexicans, and the San Ysabel Massacre: A Study of Changing Ethnic Relations in El Paso, Texas, 1910–1916," (master's thesis, Texas Tech University, 2003), 70–72.

33. El Paso Morning Times, January 2, 1916, 2, University of Texas at El Paso, Main Library.

34. For more on Villa's anti-American rhetoric, see Braddy, *Pancho Villa at Columbus*; John F. Chalkley, *Zach Lamar Cobb*; Coerver and Hall, *Texas and the Mexican Revolution*.

35. "Tragedy Declared Villa Reply to American Aid to Carranza Cause," *El Paso Morning Times*, January 12, 1916, 1.

36. Ibid.

37. The Cusihuiriáchic Mining Company was often referred to as "Cusi" by newspapers and workers.

38. Two eyewitnesses gave detailed accounts to the *El Paso Morning Times*. Juan Vásquez was identified as a "Mexican mining man." Tom B. Holmes, the lone survivor of the party of Americans who escaped to the border, did not witness the executions of the party, seeing only a few of them shot down. "Eye Witness Brings Tale of Butchery of American Mining Men in Chihuahua," *El Paso Morning Times*, January 13, 1916, 1, hereinafter cited as (EPMT); "Eyewitness Tell of Killing of Eighteen Americans in Mexico," *El Paso Herald*, January 13, 1916, 2, hereinafter cited as (EPH).

39. EPH, January 13, 1916, 2.

40. "Mining Men Stripped Naked and Ruthlessly Shot Down by Band of Villa Savages," EPMT, January 12, 1916, 1.

41. Villista soldier and eyewitness, Adolfo Rivera, would recall several years after the incident that "the Americans [miners] ran and ran." Habermeyer, *Gringos' Curve*, 59.

42. "Eye Witness Brings Tale of Butchery of American Mining Men in Chihuahua," EPMT, January 13, 1916, 1.

43. "In the Matter of the Killing of C. R. Watson, Manager of the Cusi Mining Company, and Others, Near Santa Ysabel, in the State of Chihuahua, Mexico, January 10, 1916," Affidavit of J. O. H. Newby June 27, 1916, "Evidence from Cusi Mining Co.," RG 76, NACP.

44. Richard Estrada, "The Mexican Revolution in Ciudad Juárez–El Paso Area, 1910–1920," *Password* (Summer 1979): 69; Romo, *Ringside Seat to a Revolution*, 220.

45. "Answer to Memorial before the Special Claims Commission Mexico and the United States," The United States of America on behalf of Matilda Symansky Bodine, Administratrix of the Estate of Manuel Bonifacio Romero vs. the United Mexican States, The Santa Ysabel Cases (No. 7), Docket No. 449, Records of Boundary and Claims Commission, 1923–1937, Records Relating to the Santa Ysabel Cases, 1924–1936, RG 76, NACP.

46. Braddy, *Pancho Villa at Columbus*, 26.

47. See note 29 this chapter.

48. In El Paso, Villa's anti-American rhetoric troubled many Anglo residents there and in parts of northern Mexico and it made them fear for their safety. Letter from US consul Edwards to Secretary of State Lansing stating that "distress and fear is evident on every face [in Juárez and El Paso]," December 28, 1915, Records of the Department of State Relating to Internal Affairs of Mexico, 1910–1929, National Archives Microfilm, Microcopy No. 274, Records of the Department of State Relating to Internal Affairs of Mexico, 1910–29, roll 50, 812.00/16776–17150, The National Archives and Records Service, Washington, DC, 1959; Telegram from Z. Cobb to Secretary of State stating that "[El Paso] as a whole is stirred deeply with quiet indignation because of the [Santa Ysabel] murders," January 11, 1916, Records of the Department of State Relating to Internal Affairs of Mexico, 1910–1929, National Archives Microfilm, Microcopy No. 274, Records of the Department of State Relating to Internal Affairs of Mexico, 1910–29, roll 50, 812.00/16776–17150, The National Archives and Records Service, Washington, DC, 1959.

49. "Mutilated Corpses of Murdered Americans Brought to El Paso," EPMT, January 13, 1916, 1.

50. Report received by Commanding General, Eighth Brigade, Fort Bliss, Texas, "Weekly report of general conditions along the Mexican border," January 15, 1916, no. 148, Headquarters Southern Department, Fort Sam Houston,

Texas, Division of Mexican Affairs, National Archives Microfilm, Microcopy No. 274, Records of the Department of State Relating to Internal Affairs of Mexico, 1910–29, roll 51, 812.00/17151–17575, The National Archives and Records Service, Washington, DC, 1959.

51.   "Consul Edwards of Juárez Jeered by American Crowds in El Paso," EPH, January 13, 1916, 3.; "El Pasoans Petition President to Remove Consul T. D. Edwards," EPMT, January 14, 1916, 5.

52.   "Rodríguez Reported Prisoner," EPH, January 13, 1916, 1.

53.   "Mexicans Chased across Border," San Antonio Express, January 14, 1916, 2, hereinafter cited as (SAE)

54.   "Crowd Starts Riot on Broadway; Officers and Soldiers Stop It," EPH, January 14, 1916, 1.

55.   Hortencia Villegas, interview by Oscar J. Martínez, February 17, 1976. Interview 235, transcript, Institute of Oral History, University of Texas at El Paso.

56.   Crowds formed at Overland and Santa Fe Streets, traveled along Santa Fe to Fifth thence to El Paso, back along El Paso to Second, thence to Broadway, along Broadway to Overland, where they encountered still other crowds. "Villistas Vagged and Driven from El Paso, Near Riots and Sporadic Fighting in Downtown Streets Culmination of Day of Excitement Following Funerals of Massacre Victims," EPMT, January 14, 1916, 1.

57.   Report received by Commanding General, Eighth Brigade, Fort Bliss, Texas, "Weekly report of general conditions along the Mexican border," January 15, 1916, no. 148, Headquarters Southern Department, Fort Sam Houston, Texas, Division of Mexican Affairs, National Archives Microfilm, Microcopy No. 274, Records of the Department of State Relating to Internal Affairs of Mexico, 1910–29, roll 51, 812.00/17151–17575, The National Archives and Records Service, Washington, DC, 1959; Texas Tech University Library; "Villistas Vagged and Driven from El Paso," EPMT, January 14, 1916, 1.

58.   El Paso's "Second Ward/Segundo Barrio" was primarily inhabited by Mexicans and Mexican Americans. The area stretches east from the downtown area and along the Rio Grande.

59.   Villegas, interview, February 17, 1976.

60.   "Carranza Orders Assassins Captured Dead or Alive," San Antonio Express, January 14, 1916; "Mexicans Chased across Border," SAE, January 14, 1916.

61.   "Americans Fighting Mexicans in El Paso," New York Times, January 14, 1916; Pershing to Funston, Fort Bliss, Texas, January 17, 1916, Records of the Department of State, Relating to Internal Affairs of Mexico, 1910–1929, roll 51 (NARA 812.00/17158), Texas Tech University Library.

62.   "Carranza Orders Assassins Captured Dead or Alive," SAE, January 14, 1916, 1.

63.   Labor Advocate, front page, January 14, 1916, El Paso, Texas.

64.   Pershing to Funston, January 17, 1916, Records of the Department of State, Relating to Internal Affairs of Mexico, 1910–1929; roll 51 (NARA 812.00/17158), Texas Tech University Library.

65.   "Troops Ready to Prevent Trouble," SAE, January 15, 1916.

66.   "Slain Americans Buried in El Paso," SAE, January 15, 1916.

67.   Villegas, interview, February 17, 1976.

68.   El Paso resident Maurcio Cordero recounted an incident that took place in the aftermath of the Villa Columbus raid (March 1916) where his dark-skinned friend was beaten for violating curfew set forth by the "dead lines" established after the El Paso race riot in January 1916. Mauricio Cordero, Interview by Oscar J. Martínez, February 15, 1974, interview 250, transcript, Institute of Oral History, Special Collections, University of Texas at El Paso.

69.   "Mexicans Chased across Border," SAE, January 14, 1916.

70.   According to the New York Times, the cards read, "Remember the Alamo, Did We Watch and Wait! Remember The Cusi. Shall We Watch and Wait!" "Americans Fighting Mexicans in El Paso," New York Times, January 14, 1916, 2.

71.   Scholars such as William D. Carrigan try to understand mob activity through

the perspective of historical memory, and Texas's culture of violence since 1835 allows the reader to grasp how extralegal activity and brutal acts can be accepted by a progressive society in the early twentieth century. Carrigan, *The Making of Lynching Culture*, 2–3.

72. Nevels, *Lynching to Belong*, 6, 8, 157.

73. Letter from Zach Cobb to Secretary of State Robert Lansing expressing fear that the "Carranza government is slipping backwards," and "if [Carranza is] not more aggressive against bandits, Villa and others may put them on the defensive in the garrisoned towns." February 1, 1916, Records of the Department of State, Relating to Internal Affairs of Mexico, 1910–1929, roll 51 (NARA 812.00/17151–17575), Texas Tech University Library.

74. "Americans and Mexicans to Be Segregated New Federal Census Will List Each Race," *El Paso Herald*, January 14, 1916, 6; "Special Census of the Population of El Paso, Texas," January 15, 1916, Department of Commerce, Bureau of the Census (Washington, DC: Government Printing Office, 1916).

75. Mae Ngai, *Impossible Subjects: Illegal Aliens and the Making of Modern America* (Princeton, NJ: Princeton University Press, 2004), 131–32.

76. Ibid., 132.

77. "Indignation Meeting Is Called Off and Talk of Quick Revenge Subsides: Native Born New Mexicans Ready to Join Volunteers," EPMT, January 15, 1916, 1.

78. Arnoldo De León, *Mexican Americans in Texas: A Brief History*, 3rd ed. (Wheeling, IL: Harlan Davidson, 2009), 42–43, 56–57, 69–70, 104–5, 120–21, 172–73.

CHAPTER 3: "HOW MEXICANS DIE"

1. Weekly report of general conditions along the Mexican border based on weekly reports of January 15, 1916, from the local military commanding officers. Report from commanding General, Eighth Brigade dated January 17, Division of Mexican Affairs, Department of State, roll 51 (NARA 812.00/17152), Texas Tech University Library, hereinafter cited as TTUL.

2. Weekly report of general conditions along the border based on weekly reports of January 22, 1916, from the local military commanding officers and upon information received from all sources to date. Report from Commanding General of Fort Bliss, El Paso, Texas, Eighth Brigade, January 23, 1916, Division of Mexican Affairs, Department of State, Roll 51 (NARA 812.00/17194), TTUL.

3. Letter from Edwards to Secretary of State Lansing, January 14, 1916, Internal Affairs of Mexico, 1910–1929, roll 50 (NARA 812.00/17095), TTUL.

4. Weekly report of general conditions along the Mexican border based on weekly reports of January 15, 1916, from the local military commanding officers. Report from commanding General, Eighth Brigade dated January 17, Division of Mexican Affairs, Department of State, roll 51 (NARA 812.00/17152), TTUL; "Villa Planned to Attack El Paso," *San Antonio Express*, January 14, 1916, 2.

5. The "Rocky Mountain Club of New York" forwarded a resolution by the Board of Governors on behalf of its member killed in Santa Ysabel. The resolution listed several points including a harsh criticism of the Wilson administration and its "weak" and "cowardice" approach to the Mexican problem. In addition, they called for a swift military response by the president for the purpose of restoring order and enforcing "respect for the American flag," Resolution of Board of Governors, Rocky Mountain Club of New York sent to President Woodrow Wilson, January 26, 1916, roll 51 (NARA 812.00/17188), TTUL. The organization was a wealthy outfit of professional men of western nativity in New York with a purpose to "create good fellowship among the members of the Rocky Mountain States." "Rocky Mountain Club Incorporates," *New York Times*, January 20, 1907; "New Club in Times Square," *New York Times*, November 1, 1907.

6. Adolfo Gilly, *The Mexican Revolution* (New York: New Press, 2005), 209.

7. Letter from Cobb to Secretary of State Lansing, December 21, 1915, Internal Affairs of Mexico, 1910–1929, roll 50 (NARA 812.00/16785), TTUL.

8. Letter from Consul Edwards to Secretary of State Lansing, January 14, 1916, Internal Affairs of Mexico, 1910–1929, roll 50 (NARA 812.00/17095), TTUL.

9. Letter from Cobb to Secretary of State Lansing, December 21, 1915, Internal Affairs of Mexico, 1910–1929, roll 50 (NARA 812.00/16785), TTUL; Letter from Consul Edwards to Secretary of State Lansing, January 14, 1916, Internal Affairs of Mexico, 1910–1929, roll 50 (NARA 812.00/17095), TTUL.

10. Letter from Edwards to Lansing, January 14, 1916, Internal Affairs of Mexico, 1910–1929, roll 50 (NARA 812.00/17095), TTUL.

11. Letter to Secretary of State Lansing from Zach Cobb, January 24, 1916, Internal Affairs of Mexico, 1910–1929, roll 51 (NARA 812.00/17193), TTUL.

12. Weekly report of general conditions along the border based on weekly reports of January 22, 1916, from the local military commanding officers and upon information received from all sources to date. Report from Commanding General of Fort Bliss, El Paso, Texas, Eighth Brigade, January 23, 1916, Department of State, Roll 51 (NARA 812.00/17194), TTUL.

13. "Brothers Cursing Americans," *El Paso Morning Times*, January 24, 1916, 1.

14. Ibid.

15. Ibid.

16. Letter to Zach Cobb from Secretary of State Lansing, January 29, 1916, Internal Affairs of Mexico, 1910–1929, roll 51 (NARA 812.00.17193), TTUL.

17. Letter to Secretary of State Lansing from Zach Cobb, January 24, 1916, Internal Affairs of Mexico, 1910–1929, roll 51 (NARA 812.00/17193), TTUL; John F. Chalkley, *Zach Lamar Cobb: El Paso Collector of Customs and Intelligence during the Mexican Revolution, 1913–1918* (El Paso: Texas Western Press, 1998), 56.

18. Chalkley, *Zach Lamar Cobb*, 56.

19. Cobb to Secretary of State Lansing, January 24, 1916, Internal Affairs of Mexico, 1910–1929, roll 51 (NARA 812.00/17193), TTUL, 2; Chalkley, *Zach Lamar Cobb*, 56.

20. Cobb to Secretary of State Lansing, January 24, 1916, Internal Affairs of Mexico, 1910–1929, roll 51 (NARA 812.00/17193), TTUL, 1.

21. Letter from US consul Edwards to Secretary of State Lansing, January 24, 1916, Internal Affairs of Mexico, 1910–1929, roll 50 (NARA 812.00/17145), TTUL.

22. Weekly report of general conditions along the Mexican border, January 22, 1916, Internal Affairs of Mexico, 1910–1929, roll 50 (NARA 812.0017194), TTUL.

23. Ibid.

24. Letter from Cobb to Lansing, January 24, 1916, Internal Affairs of Mexico, 1910–1929, roll 51 (NARA 812.0017193), TTUL.

25. Texas historian Rodolfo Rocha outlines a series of arrests that were believed to be associated with the Plan de San Diego. Rumors surfaced of a Mexican uprising in Kingsville, Corpus Christi, San Antonio, and San Angelo. Rodolfo Rocha, "The Influence of the Mexican Revolution on the Mexico-Texas Border, 1910–1916" (PhD diss., Texas Tech University, 1981), 323–25.

26. Weekly report of general conditions along the Mexican border, January 22, 1916, Internal Affairs of Mexico, 1910–1929, roll 50 (NARA 812.0017194), TTUL.

27. Eileen Welsome, *The General and The Jaguar: Pershing's Hunt for Pancho Villa: A True Story of Revolution and Revenge* (New York: Little, Brown, 2006), 70. In his study of Pancho Villa, Clarence C. Clendenen claims that after the massacre some disorder ensued but that "popular reaction in the United States was horror and indignation but there was no widespread excitement or demand for intervention." Clarence C. Clendenen, *The United States and Pancho Villa: A Study in Unconventional Diplomacy* (Ithaca, NY: Cornell University Press, 1961), 230.

28. Letter from Cobb to Lansing, January 25, 1916, Internal Affairs of Mexico, 1910–1929, roll 50 (NARA 812.00/17178), TTUL, 1.

29. Ibid., 2.

30. Howard Markel, *When Germs Travel: Six Major Epidemics That Have Invaded America since 1900 and the Fears They Have Unleashed* (New York: Pantheon Books, 2004), 126; Carlos Husk, "Typhus Fever," *Bulletin of the El Paso County Medical Society* 78 (1916): 75–79.

31. Natalia Molina, *Fit To Be Citizens?: Public Health and Race in Los Angeles, 1879–1939* (Berkeley: University of California Press, 2006), 63.

32. "Kerosene and Vinegar Only Will Kill Lice; Boston Missionary Expected to See Wild West," EPH, March 8, 1916, 6.

33. "Juarez to Help in Typhus Fight," EPH, March 6, 1916, 4.

34. Markel, *When Germs Travel*, 128.

35. Ibid.

36. "Juarez School Pupils Banned," EPH, March 2, 1916, 13.

37. "1 Case Measles in Chihuahuita," EPH, March 3, 1916, 11.

38. Ibid.

39. Ibid.

40. The southern part of El Paso housed the highest concentration of Mexican residents in the city. "Fumigation for the Louse," EPH, March 6, 1916, 4.

41. "Juarez School Pupils Banned," EPH, March 2, 1916, 13.

42. "Fumigation for the Louse," EPH, March 6, 1916, 4.

43. Ibid.

44. "Gavira Resents U.S. Quarantine," EPH, March 3, 1916, 1.

45. According to public health historian Natalia Molina, a typhus outbreak in Los Angeles, California, infected twenty-six Mexican railroad workers from June to October 1916. Ultimately the disease killed five people, all Mexican. Public health officials at every governmental level began a hygiene, sanitation, and education campaign, all of which were aimed exclusively at Mexicans. As Molina put it, "the stigma of the typhus outbreaks marked all the areas where Mexicans lived, whether railroad camps or 'villages' (temporary housing for Mexicans, located near work site), as locations in need of inspection." Health officials then used the typhus outbreak to justify intruding into the private lives of Mexican residents, regardless of their age, sex, or domicile location. Officials sent out notices to schools that linked typhus with Mexican residents, thus giving the impression that there was already an epidemic when in fact there was none. Efforts made by officials to suppress the spread of typhus succeeded in racializing private and public spaces, as well as stigmatizing the people within those spaces. Molina, *Fit to Be Citizens?*, 61–64; "1 Case Measles in Chihuahuita," EPH, March 3, 1916, 11.

46. "Border Watched for Typhus Cases," EPH, January 18, 1916, 1.

47. Ibid.

48. "Saturday Was Bath Day at the City Jail; Coal Oil and Vinegar Kills Lowly Louse," EPH, weekend edition, March 4–5, 1916, 11.

49. Ibid.

50. Ibid.

51. "Grand Jury Probing Jail Fire; One More Victim Is Identified," EPH, March 8, 1916, 5.

52. "Searching Investigation of Jail Holocaust Ordered," March 8, 1916, EPMT, 1.

53. "Grand Jury Probe," EPH, March 8, 1916, 5.

54. Ibid., 1–2.

55. Ibid., 2.

56. "Grand Jury to Probe Fire," EPH, March 7, 1916, 1.

57. Ibid., 2.

58. Ibid.

59. Ibid.

60. "Searching Investigation of Jail Holocaust Ordered: Grand Jury Instructed to Spare No Effort in Placing Responsibility," EPMT, March 8, 1916, 1.

61. "Grand Jury to Probe Fire," EPH, March 7, 1916, 2.

62. Ibid., 1.

63. Ibid.

64. "23rd Victim of Jail Disaster," EPH, March 13, 1916, 3.

65. "Grand Jury to Probe Fire," EPH, March 7, 1916, 1.

66. Grand Jurors included H. W. Broaddus, A. H. Anderson, R. E. Hines (secretary of the grand jury), A. O. Ridleman, Paul Boland, and C. H. Finlay. "Searching Investigation of Jail Holocaust Ordered," EPMT, March 8, 1916, 1.

67. Ibid.

68. "Grand Jury Probing Jail Fire; One More Victim Is Identified," EPH, March 8, 1916, 5.

69. Ibid.

70. Ibid.

71. "Searching Investigation of Jail Holocaust Ordered," EPMT, March 8, 1916, 1.

72. "Grand Jury to Probe Fire; 16 Prisoners Die from Burns," EPH, March 7, 1916, 2.

73. Several different newspaper accounts listed Ms. Alonzo's name in a variety of spellings (Carmen, Camra, and Cormela). "Grand Jury Instructed to Spare No Effort in Placing Responsibility," EPMT, March 8, 1916, 2.

74. "Grand Jury to Probe Fire; 16 Prisoners Die from Burns," EPH, March 7, 1916, 2.

75. Ibid.

76. Ibid.

77. "Grand Jury Instructed to Spare No Effort in Placing Responsibility," EPMT, March 8, 1916, 2.

78. "Grand Jury Probing Jail Fire," EPH, March 8, 1916, 5.

79. "Grand Jury Instructed to Spare No Effort in Placing Responsibility," EPMT, March 8, 1916, 2.

80. Ibid.

81. "Grand Jury to Probe Fire; 16 Prisoners Die from Burns," EPH, March 7, 1916, 2.

82. Ibid., 1.

83. Telegram from Cobb to Secretary of State Lansing, March 6, 1916, Records of the Department of State Relating to Internal Affairs of Mexico, 1910–1929, roll 51 (NARA 812.00/17357), TTUL; "Searching Investigation of Jail Holocaust Ordered," EPMT, March 8, 1916, 2; "Three Victims of Fire Expected to Die of Injuries," EPMT, March 8, 1916, 2; "American Shot on Juarez Car," EPH, March 7, 1916, 3; Romo, Ringside Seat to a Revolution, 227.

84. Markel, When Germs Travel, 129; San Antonio Express, March 9, 1916, 1.

85. "American Shot on Juarez Car," EPH, March 7, 1916, 3; Romo, Ringside Seat to a Revolution, 227.

86. "American Shot on Juarez Car," EPH, March 7, 1916, 3

87. Ibid.

88. "American Shot on Juarez Car," El Paso Herald, March 7, 1916, 3; Telegram from Cobb to Secretary of State Lansing, March 6, 1916, Records of the Department of State Relating to Internal Affairs of Mexico, 1910–1929, roll 51 (NARA 812.00/17357), TTUL.

89. "Grand Jury to Probe Fire," EPH, March 7, 1916, 1.

90. "Grand Jury Probing Jail Fire; One More Victim Is Identified," EPH, March 8, 1916, 5.

91. A. Margo, Who, Where, and Why is Villa? (New York: Latin-American News Association, 1917), 11.

92. David Starr Jordan, The Days of a Man: Being Memories of a Naturalist, Teacher, and Minor Prophet of Democracy (New York: World Book Company, 1922), 818.

93. "Mexicans Connect Jail Horror with Columbus Outrage," EPMT, March 21, 1916, 2.

94. "Fire in City Jail Ignored," EPH, March 24, 1916, 13.

95. Jordan, *The Days of Man*, 818.
96. "Fire in City Jail Ignored," EPH, March 24, 1916, 13.
97. Markel, *When Germs Travel*, 130.
98. Mario Acevedo, interview by Oscar J. Martínez, May 1, 1975, interview 153.2, transcript, Institute of Oral History, Special Collections, University of Texas at El Paso.
99. Scholars William D. Carrigan and Clive Webb argue that diplomatic hostilities between the United States and Mexico contributed to the spike in anti-Mexican mob violence in Texas and throughout the southwestern United States. They suggest that at least 124 ethnic Mexicans were lynched during the period of the Mexican Revolution 1911–20 (an estimated 597 ethnic Mexicans were lynched between 1848 and 1928). William D. Carrigan and Clive Webb, "The Lynching of Persons of Mexican Origin or Descent in the United States, 1848–1928," *Journal of Social History* 37, no. 2 (2003): 422–23, 425; Friedrich Katz, *The Life and Times of Pancho Villa* (Stanford, CA: Stanford University Press, 1998), 564; Texas Rangers composed a "blacklist" of suspected "bad Mexicans," and any valley Anglo could add a name by denouncing someone he feared or envied. In late September 1915, Texas Rangers and Anglo vigilantes killed dozens of Mexicans "suspected" of banditry or other crimes. James A. Sandos, *Rebellion in the Borderlands: Anarchism and the Plan of San Diego, 1904–1923* (Norman: University of Oklahoma Press, 1992), 98.

CHAPTER 4: ¡VIVA VILLA!

Chapter epigraph quote from "I've Done My Bit on the Border," Benjamin F. Delamater Collection, Archives of Texas Military Forces Museum, Austin, Texas.

1. Letter from Cobb to Secretary of State Lansing, March 3, 1916, Records of the Department of State Relating to Internal Affairs of Mexico, 1910–1929, roll 51 (NARA 812.00/17340), TTUL.
2. Letter from Cobb to Secretary of State Lansing, March 6, 1916, Records of the Department of State Relating to Internal Affairs of Mexico, 1910–1929, roll 51 (NARA 812.00/17355), TTUL; "Villa Reported Close to Border," EPH, March 7, 1916, 1.
3. In regard to vigilante violence and "justice," one must address historian Richard Maxwell Brown's argument that "vigilante violence was used to establish order and stability on the frontier . . . again and again violence has been used as a means to ends that have been widely accepted and applauded." However, William Carrigan and Clive Webb argue that Brown's assessment implies "presumption in the civic virtue of the vigilantes and the criminal guilt of their victims." Carrigan and Webb go further to state that the "popular tribunals" that vilified Mexicans in the Southwest can "seldom be said to have acted in the spirit of the law." Especially, as noted by Carrigan and Webb, only 64 out of 597 Mexican lynchings met their fate at the hands of vigilante committees acting in the absence of a formal judicial system. Therefore, it is imperative to understand why vigilante justice was tolerated along the US-Mexico border when formal legal institutions were already in place in progressive and modern societies in the region. Richard Maxwell Brown, "Violence and Vigilantism in American History," in *American Law and the Constitutional Order: Historical Perspectives*, ed. Lawrence M. Friedman and Harry N. Scheiber (Cambridge, MA: Harvard University Press, 1978), 173–90; William D. Carrigan and Clive Webb, "The Lynching of Persons of Mexican Origin or Descent in the United States, 1848–1928," *Journal of Social History* 37 (Winter 2003): 411–38.
4. Governor Oscar B. Colquitt to Adjutant General Henry Hutchings, April 22, 1914, Records of Oscar B. Colquitt, Texas Office of the Governor, Archives and Information Services Division, Texas State Library and Archives Commission; F. E. Stout to Oscar B. Colquitt, April 23, 1914, Records of Oscar B. Colquitt, Texas Office of the Governor, Archives and Information Services Division, Texas State Library and Archives Commission; J. J. Allen to Oscar B. Colquitt, April 23, 1914, Records of Oscar B. Colquitt, Texas Office of the

Governor, Archives and Information Services Division, Texas State Library and Archives Commission; Oscar B. Colquitt to L. P. Hammonds, April 24, 1914, Records of Oscar B. Colquitt, Texas Office of the Governor, Archives and Information Services Division, Texas State Library and Archives Commission.

5. A South Texas farmer stated, "A Ranger can shoot a poor peon with impunity, and he is scarcely even asked to put in the usual plea of self-defense, which is a general rule an untrue one anyway. No race, however, ignorant or downtrodden, is going to submit to this for long without feeling an overwhelming sentiment, not only against the rangers themselves, but against the race from which they come." James A. Sandos, *Rebellion in the Borderlands: Anarchism and the Plan of San Diego, 1904–1923* (Norman: University of Oklahoma Press, 1992), 92.

6. Letter from Cobb to Secretary of State Lansing, March 27, 1916, Records of the Department of State Relating to Internal Affairs of Mexico, 1910–1929 roll 52 (NARA 812.00/17640), TTUL.

7. Home Guards during the period of the Mexican Revolution were community-based organizations supported by the state and later by the United States Army. Militarized civilian response was renewed in 2005, when Chris Simcox of Tombstone, Arizona, organized the Minutemen, a group of men and women "fed up" with the country being "overrun" by illegal alien invasion and potential terrorists. Tony Payan, *The Three U.S.-Mexico Border Wars: Drugs, Immigration, and Homeland Security* (Westport, CT: Praeger Security International, 2006), 81–83.

8. Carrigan and Webb, "The Lynching of Persons of Mexican Origin or Descent in the United States, 1848–1928," 428; Harvey F. Rice, "The Lynching of Antonio Rodríguez" (master's thesis, University of Texas at Austin, 1990), 31–39, 49–51, 79.

9. William D. Carrigan, *The Making of a Lynching Culture: Violence and Vigilantism in Central Texas, 1836–1916* (Urbana: University of Illinois Press, 2004), 3.

10. "Want S. El Paso Street Opened; Merchants Complain Army 'Dead Line' Works Great Injustice on Them," EPH, June 21, 1917.

11. Customs Agent Cobb wrote a letter to Secretary of State Lansing stating that "we have too many authorities here and need one dominant authority with responsibility in control." Letter from Cobb to Secretary of State Lansing, April 13, 1916, Records of the Department of State Relating to Internal Affairs of Mexico, 1910–1929, roll 52 (NARA 812.00/17837), TTUL.

12. For more on the Mexican War and the Treaty of Guadalupe, see Richard Griswold del Castillo, *The Treaty of Guadalupe Hidalgo: A Legacy of Conflict* (Norman: University of Oklahoma Press, 1990); Paul Foos, *A Short, Offhand, Killing Affair: Soldiers and Social Conflict during the Mexican-American War* (Chapel Hill: University of North Carolina Press, 2002); Richard B. Winders, *Mr. Polk's Army: The American Military Experience in the Mexican War* (College Station: Texas A&M University Press, 1997).

13. Timothy Dunn, *The Militarization of the U.S.-Mexico Border, 1978–1992* (Austin: University of Texas Press, 1996), 6; Carrigan and Webb, "The Lynching of Persons of Mexican Origin or Descent in the United States, 1848 to 1928," 417–18.

14. W. D. Smithers, a soldier and special observer who settled in the El Paso area after military service, called the years from 1916 to the early 1930s as the "border trouble days." Wilfred Dudley Smithers, "Too Rough for Comfort— The Mexico Border," undated, unpublished essay, W. D. Smithers Collection, Dolph Briscoe Center for American History, University of Texas at Austin (hereafter cited as DBCAH).

15. Wilfred Dudley Smithers, "Calling Out the National Guard States Militia," undated manuscript, article, W. D. Smithers Collection, DBCAH.

16. "Maude Wright's Experiences as a Captive of Pancho Villa as Told to Wallace and Verna Crawford," Vertical File "Maude Wright," Columbus Historical Society, Columbus, New Mexico (hereafter cited as CHS-NM).

17. Ibid.

18. Letter from Cobb to Secretary of State Lansing, January 24, 1916, Records of the Department of State Relating to Internal Affairs of Mexico, 1910–1929, roll 51 (NARA 812.00/17193), TTUL; John F. Chalkley, *Zach Lamar Cobb: El Paso Collector of Customs and Intelligence during the Mexican Revolution, 1913–1918* (El Paso: Texas Western Press, 1998), 56.

19. Chalkley, *Zach Lamar Cobb*, 59–60.

20. Ibid., 63.

21. Letter from Cobb to Secretary of State Lansing, March 3, 1916, Records of the Department of State Relating to Internal Affairs of Mexico, 1910–1929, roll 51 (NARA 812.00/17340), TTUL.

22. Letter from Cobb to Secretary of State Lansing, March 6, 1916, Records of the Department of State Relating to Internal Affairs of Mexico, 1910–1929, roll 51 (NARA 812.00/17355), TTUL; Letter from Cobb to Secretary of State Lansing, March 8, 1916, Records of the Department of State Relating to Internal Affairs of Mexico, 1910–1929, roll 51 (NARA 812.00/17368), TTUL.

23. "Villa Captures Palomas Cowboys Including an American Foreman," EPH, March 8, 1916, 1; Bill McGaw, "Columbus Man, Angry for 45 Years, Claims 'Sell-Out' in Villa Raid," February 25, 1961, publisher unknown, Vertical File, "Columbus Raid," CHS-NM; Epitacio Armendaríz, interview by Virgilio H. Sánchez, 1980, *Historia Laboral Fronteriza*, interview 551, transcript, Institute of Oral History, Special Collections, University of Texas at El Paso.

24. James W. Hurst, *Villista Prisoners of 1916–1917* (Las Cruces, NM: Yucca Tree Press, 2000), 19.

25. Marcus M. Marshall, son of the Palomas Land & Cattle Co. president E. J. Marshall, wrote a letter to his father who in turn sent it to General Hugh L. Scott, chief of staff of the United States Army, indicating that Villa had attacked the ranch, abducted and killed two of the ranchers, and ordered his men to run over another who was tied to a horse and dragged. The younger Marshall criticized the troops stationed at Columbus at the time of the raid because of their lack of patrols along the border despite ample warnings from several sources indicating Villa was headed for Columbus. "Says Villa Found Border Unguarded," *New York Times*, March 19, 1916, 1, 3 (hereafter cited as NYT); Bill McGaw, "Columbus Man, Angry for 45 Years, Claims 'Sell-Out' in Villa Raid," February 25, 1961, publisher unknown, Vertical File "Columbus Raid," CHS-NM.

26. "Maude Wright's Experiences as a Captive of Pancho Villa as Told to Wallace and Verna Crawford," Vertical File "Maude Wright," CHS-NM.

27. McGaw, "Columbus Man, Angry for 45 Years, Claims 'Sell-Out' in Villa Raid," February 25, 1961, publisher unknown, Vertical File "Columbus Raid," CHS-NM

28. Ibid.

29. After an investigation conducted by a special inspector on the staff of Brigadier General John J. Pershing and ultimately endorsed by Secretary Barker, on July 31, 1916, Colonel Slocum was exonerated of any blame in connection with the Villa raid on Columbus. "Slocum Blameless for Columbus Raid," NYT, August 1, 1916; "Colonel Slocum Exonerated," NYT, August 2, 1916; McGaw, "Columbus Man, Angry for 45 Years, Claims 'Sell-Out' in Villa Raid," February 25, 1961, publisher unknown, Vertical File "Columbus Raid," CHS-NM.

30. "Five Troops Chase Villa in Mexico," EPH, March 9, 1916, 1.

31. There is some scholarly debate on whether Villa made the speech regarding the jailhouse holocaust; however, Maude Write in her interview was clear that Villa's soldiers were well aware of the events in El Paso. "Maude Wright's Experiences as a Captive of Pancho Villa as Told to Wallace and Verna Crawford," Vertical File "Maude Wright," CHS-NM; Friedrich Katz, *The Life and Times of Pancho Villa* (Stanford, CA: Stanford University Press, 1998), 564.

32. Haldeen Braddy, *Pancho Villa at Columbus* (El Paso: Texas Western College Press, 1965), 32.

33. Letter from Cobb to Secretary of State Lansing, March 9, 1916, Records of the

Department of State Relating to Internal Affairs of Mexico, 1910–1929, roll 51 (NARA 812.00/17385), TTUL; Letter from Cobb to Secretary of State Lansing, March 9, 1916, Records of the Department of State Relating to Internal Affairs of Mexico, 1910–1929, roll 51 (NARA 812.00/17386), TTUL.

34. Braddy, *Pancho Villa at Columbus*, 18.

35. Mrs. Riggs, wife of the customs deputy at Columbus, reached El Paso with her children after the raid and furnished some of the first reports to American officials in El Paso. Her account identified several Americans dead and wounded. She also recounted the property damaged, which included the Lemmon and Romeny General Store, Commercial Hotel, two vacant buildings, Juan Favela's residence, a soldier's home, several vacant houses, warehouse and storeroom. The customs house was spared because the *villistas* believed it would serve well for their "breastworks" (aboveground breastworks). Letter from Cobb to Secretary of State Lansing, March 9, 1916, Records of the Department of State Relating to Internal Affairs of Mexico, 1910–1929, roll 51 (NARA 812.00/17386), TTUL.

36. Bill McGaw, "Columbus Man, Angry for 45 Years, Claims 'Sell-Out' in Villa Raid," February 25, 1961, publisher unknown, Vertical File "Columbus Raid," CHS-NM.

37. Braddy, *Pancho Villa at Columbus*, 18.

38. Letter from Cobb to Secretary of State Lansing, March 9, 1916, Records of the Department of State Relating to Internal Affairs of Mexico, 1910–1929, roll 51 (NARA 812.00/17377), TTUL.

39. "Maude Wright's Experiences as a Captive of Pancho Villa as Told to Wallace and Verna Crawford," Vertical File "Maude Wright," CHS-NM.

40. For more information on the Columbus raid, see Braddy, *Pancho Villa at Columbus*; Friedrich Katz, *Pancho Villa y el ataque a Columbus, Nuevo México* (Chihuahua, Mexico: Sociedad Chihuahuense de Estudios Históricos, 1979); Eileen Welsome, *The General and The Jaguar: Pershing's Hunt for Pancho Villa: A True Story of Revolution and Revenge* (New York: Little, Brown, 2006).

41. "Maude Wright's Experiences as a Captive of Pancho Villa as Told to Wallace and Verna Crawford (June 1960)," Vertical File "Maude Wright," CHS-NM; Letter from Cobb to Secretary of State Lansing, March 9, 1916, Records of the Department of State Relating to Internal Affairs of Mexico, 1910–1929, roll 51 (NARA 812.00/17386), TTUL; Bill McGaw, "Columbus Man, Angry for 45 Years, Claims 'Sell-Out' in Villa Raid," February 25, 1961, publisher unknown, Vertical File "Columbus Raid," CHS-NM.

42. Mary Lee Gaskill, *American Experience: The Hunt for Pancho Villa* (1993), DVD, directed by Hector Galán (Boston: WGBH Educational Foundation, American Experience, 2010).

43. Colonel Slocum immediately went into cover-up mode and knew that if Juan Favela's story got out he would be held responsible for not adequately defending the camp, "there would be a lot of newspaper men coming in here and there will be more. They're coming from all over the world, even Japan, and I don't want you talking to them." Bill McGaw, "Columbus Man, Angry for 45 Years, Claims 'Sell-Out' in Villa Raid," February 25, 1961, publisher unknown, Vertical File "Columbus Raid," CHS-NM.

44. Gaskill, *American Experience: The Hunt for Pancho Villa* (1993), DVD.

45. Epitacio Armendaríz, interviewed by Virgilio H. Sánchez, October 14, 1979, transcript, no. 551, Institute of Oral History, University of Texas at El Paso.

46. Details of Chadborn's experience during the Columbus raid and afterward were "gleaned from Mr. [Jack] Thomas himself," "Buck Chadborn, Foe of Pancho Villa and Border Riffraff, Had Adventerous Career," *The Southwesterner*, May 1966, 10–11, CHS-NM.

47. Several *villistas* were captured, arrested, tried, and hung on June 9, 1916. For more on the *villista* prisoners, see Hurst, *The Villista Prisoners of 1916–1917*; Larry Harris, *Strong Man of the Revolution*, 2nd ed. (Silver City, NM: High Lonesome Press, 1995); Haldeen Braddy, *Cock of the Walk, Qui-Qui-Ri-Quí!: The Legend of Pancho Villa* (Albuquerque: University of New Mexico Press, 1955), 133–34.

159

48. "Buck Chadborn, Foe of Pancho Villa and Border Riffraff, Had Adventurous Career," *The Southwesterner*, May 1966, 10–11, CHS-NM; Letter from Cobb to Secretary of State Lansing, March 9, 1916, Records of the Department of State Relating to Internal Affairs of Mexico, 1910–1929, roll 51 (NARA 812.00/17377), TTUL; Letter from General Funston to Secretary of State Lansing, March 10, 1916, Records of the Department of State Relating to Internal Affairs of Mexico, 1910–1929, roll 51 (NARA 812.00/17396), TTUL.

49. Letter from Cobb to Secretary of State Lansing, March 9, 1916, Records of the Department of State Relating to Internal Affairs of Mexico, 1910–1929, roll 51 (NARA 812.00/17385), TTUL.

50. Letter from Consul Edwards to Secretary of State Lansing, March 9, 1916, Records of the Department of State Relating to Internal Affairs of Mexico, 1910–1929, roll 51 (NARA 812.00/17389), TTUL.

51. Ibid.

52. Letter from Carothers to Secretary of State Lansing, March 10, 1916, Records of the Department of State Relating to Internal Affairs of Mexico, 1910–1929, roll 51 (NARA 812.00/17401), TTUL.

53. Letter from Cobb to Secretary of State Lansing, March 17, 1916, Records of the Department of State Relating to Internal Affairs of Mexico, 1910–1929, roll 51 (NARA 812.00/17503), TTUL.

54. "Twin Cities Are Keeping Cool," EPH, March 13, 1916, 6.

55. Ibid.

56. "El Paso Is Well Protected by Troops; If Trouble Comes, Men Must Stay Home," EPH, March 14, 1916, 1.

57. Letter from Cobb to Secretary of State Lansing, April 14, 1916, Records of the Department of State Relating to Internal Affairs of Mexico, 1910–1929, roll 52 (NARA 812.00/17857), TTUL.

58. Letter from George C. Carothers to Secretary of State Lansing, March 22, 1916, Records of the Department of State Relating to Internal Affairs of Mexico, 1910–1929, roll 51 (NARA 812.00/17583), TTUL.

59. Letter from George C. Carothers to Secretary of State Lansing, March 22, 1916, Records of the Department of State Relating to Internal Affairs of Mexico, 1910–1929, roll 51 (NARA 812.00/17583), TTUL.

60. For more on the Punitive Expedition, see Welsome, *The General and the Jaguar: Pershing's Hunt for Pancho Villa*; Joseph Stout, *Border Conflict: Villistas, Carrancistas, and the Punitive Expedition, 1915–1920* (Ft. Worth: Texas Christian University Press, 1999); James W. Hurst, *Pancho Villa and Black Jack Pershing: The Punitive Expedition in Mexico* (Santa Barbara, CA: Praeger Publishers, 2007).

61. El Paso's civilian training camp was modeled after the national organization American Defense Society, "a national aggressive, non-partisan society having for its sole object the 'adequate national defense of the United States of America.'" Four hundred men needed to sign a petition in order for a camp to be organized and equipped by the government. "Guide to the Records of the American Defense Society, 1915–1942," American Defense Society Records, The New-York Historical Society, http://dlib.nyu.edu/eadapp/transform?source=nyhs/americandefsoc.xml&style=nyhs/nyhs.xsl&part=body (accessed April 29, 2010); "Training Camp for Civilians," EPH, March 16, 1916, 4; "Training Camp at Fort Bliss," EPH, March 17, 1916, 2.

62. For more information on the history of state militias and the National Guard, see Miguel A. Levario, "Cuando vino la mexicanada: Authority, Race and Conflict in West Texas, 1895–1924" (PhD diss., University of Texas at Austin, 2007); Emily Tessier Zillich, "History of the National Guard in El Paso" (master's thesis, Texas Western College [University of Texas at El Paso], 1958); Allan R. Purcell, "The History of the Texas Militia, 1835–1903" (PhD diss., University of Texas at Austin, 1981); Clarence C. Clendenen, *Blood on the Border: The United States Army and the Mexican Irregulars* (London: Macmillan, 1969); "Constitutional Charter of the Guard," *Army National Guard*, http://www.arng.army.mil/aboutus/history/Pages/ConstitutionalCharteroftheGuard.aspx (accessed July 3, 2007).

63. Zillich, "History of the National Guard in El Paso," 26.

64. Ibid., 36.

65. Don M. Coerver and Linda B. Hall, *Texas and the Mexican Revolution: A Study in State and National Border Policy, 1910–1920* (San Antonio: Trinity University Press, 1984), 21.

66. Shawn Lay, *War, Revolution, and the Ku Klux Klan: A Study of Intolerance in a Border City* (El Paso: Texas Western Press, 1985), 20.

67. Letter from Sheriff John F. Robinson of Val Verde County to Governor Oscar B. Colquitt, April 30, 1914, Adjutant General's Department, July 1, 1914–April 1, 1915, Records, Texas Governor O. B. Colquitt. Archives and Information Services Division, Texas State Library and Archives Commission, Austin, Texas (hereafter cited as TSLAC).

68. Dr. W. E. Ashton complained that "drunken Mexicans" were discharging their weapons and causing a disturbance. His letter emphasized that the American population was a small minority among "1500 or 200 Mexicans." The quote by Dr. Ashton was an exaggeration in of itself. Presidio County claimed only 5,218 inhabitants in the 1910 US Census and 12,202 in 1920. United States Census Bureau, Texas, Population of Counties by Decennial Census: 1900–1990, compiled by Richard L. Forstall, Population Division, US Bureau of the Census, March 27, 1995, http://www.census.gov/population/cencounts/tx190090.txt (accessed April 29, 2010).

69. In a telegram to Governor Colquitt, J. J. Allen of Sanderson, Texas, asked to send the adjutant general to "swear in home guard" in the town. Letter from J. J. Allen to Governor Oscar B. Colquitt, April 23, 1914, Adjutant General's Department, July 1, 1914–April 1, 1915, Records, Texas Governor O. B. Colquitt. Archives and Information Services Division, TSLAC; Lay, *War, Revolution and the Ku Klux Klan*, 22.

70. Letter from Lynton Garrett to Governor Oscar B. Colquitt, April 24, 1914, Adjutant General's Department, July 1, 1914–April 1, 1915, Records, Texas Governor O. B. Colquitt. Archives and Information Services Division, TSLAC.

71. Letter from Charles O. Adains to Governor Oscar B. Colquitt, April 24, 1914, Adjutant General's Department, April 23–24, 1914, Records, Texas Governor O. B. Colquitt. Archives and Information Services Division, TSLAC.

72. Letter from J. O. Jones to Governor Oscar B. Colquitt, May 9, 1914, Adjutant General's Department, May 8–15, 1914, Records, Texas Governor O. B. Colquitt. Archives and Information Services Division, TSLAC.

73. Letter from Governor Colquitt to Adjutant General Henry Hutchings, April 24, 1914, Records, Texas Governor O. B. Colquitt. Archives and Information Services Division, TSLAC.

74. Lay, *War, Revolution, and the Ku Klux Klan*, 22–24.

75. Charles H. Harris III and Louis R. Sadler, *The Texas Rangers and the Mexican Revolution: The Bloodiest Decade, 1910–1920* (Albuquerque: University of New Mexico Press, 2004), 181.

76. Coerver and Hall, *Texas and the Mexican Revolution*, 77.

77. Lay, *War, Revolution, and the Ku Klux Klan*, 23.

78. "Mayor Prepares for Contingency," EPH, April 21, 1914, 1; "No Trouble Anticipated by Officials: El Pasoans Do Not Think There Will Be Any Difficulty in This City," EPH, April 22, 1914, 2.

79. "No Trouble Anticipated by Officials: El Pasoans Do Not think There Will Be Any Difficulty in This City," EPH, April 22, 1914, 2.

80. "Colquitt Asks That All Border Towns Be Taken," EPH, April 22, 1914, 2.

81. "Citizens Offer to Serve as Policemen," EPH, April 24, 1914, 1.

82. "Soldiers Cover City at Night," EPH, April 25, 1914, 2.

83. Ibid., 2.

84. "Home Guards in El Paso Not Needed," EPH—*Weekend Edition*, April 25–26, 1914, 5-A; Fort Bliss Post Return 1915, Fort Bliss Archives and Museum, El Paso, Texas, data compiled by Angie Chávez and Jennifer Nielsen.

85. "Troops in City," *El Paso Times*, May 13, 1915.

86. "Units Patrol Streets," *El Paso Times*, August 30, 1915.

87. Coerver and Hall, *Texas and the Mexican Revolution*, 85–86.

88. Ibid., 89.

89. Lay, *War, Revolution, and the Ku Klux Klan*, 24.

90. Ibid.

91. Alice Cummings, interview by Richard Estrada, March 1, 1978, transcript, Institute of Oral History, University of Texas at El Paso.

92. Telegram from Secretary of War, Newton D. Baker to Texas Governor, James E. Ferguson. May 1, 1916, Governor James E. Ferguson Papers, TSLAC.

93. "Constitutional Charter of the Guard," Army National Guard, http://www .arng.army.mil/aboutus/history/Pages/ConstitutionalCharteroftheGuard .aspx (accessed September 6, 2006).

94. Smithers, "Calling Out the National Guard States Militia," undated manuscript, unpublished essay, W. D. Smithers Collection, DBCAH.

95. "Two Regiments at Fort Bliss to Go on Border Patrol," EPMT, January 27, 1917.

96. Roger Batchelder, *Watching and Waiting on the Border* (Boston: Houghton Mifflin, 1917), 64.

97. Ibid., 65.

98. Letter from George C. Carothers to Secretary of State Lansing, March 22, 1916, Records of the Department of State Relating to Internal Affairs of Mexico, 1910–1929, roll 51 (NARA 812.00/17583), TTUL.

99. Smithers, "Calling Out the National Guard," 8, DBCAH.

100. Ibid., 12.

101. "Constitutional Charter of the Guard," *Army National Guard*, http://www .arng.army.mil/aboutus/history/Pages/ConstitutionalCharteroftheGuard .aspx (accessed July 3, 2007).

102. "Our Unpreparedness Revealed by Villa," *The Literary Digest*, New York, April 1, 1916, 884.

103. Ibid.

104. Wilfred Dudley Smithers, undated, unpublished essay, "Ranching and Fighting Bandits," W. D. Smithers Collection, DBCAH.

105. Brigadier General Parker, General Orders, No. 4, Headquarters Brownsville District, Brownsville, Texas, May 27, 1916, Benjamin F. Delamater Collection, Archives of Texas Military Forces Museum, Austin, Texas (hereafter cited as BFDC-ATMFM).

106. Circular Letter addressed to all commanding officers from Brigadier General Parker regarding "neutrality," Brigadier General James Parker, Circular Letter, Headquarters Brownsville District, Brownsville, Texas, January 8, 1917, BFDC-ATMFM.

107. "2 Arrested on Arson Charge," EPH, March 25, 1916, 2.

108. Cummings, interview, March 1, 1978.

109. General Orders Number 4, May 27, 1916, Headquarters Brownsville District, Brownsville, Texas, BFDC-ATMFM.

110. Bulletin No. 12, May 30, 1917, Headquarters, First Brigade, Reinforced, First Provisional Infantry Division, Brownsville, Texas, BFDC-ATMFM.

111. General Orders Number 7, June 10, 1916, Headquarters Brownsville District, Brownsville, BFDC-ATMFM.

112. General Orders Number 26, August 17, 1916, Headquarters Brownsville District, Brownsville, Texas, BFDC-ATMFM.

113. General Orders Number 7, June 10, 1916, Headquarters Brownsville District, Brownsville, Texas, BFDC-ATMFM.

114. Smithers, "Calling Out the Guard," DBCAH.

115. General Orders Number 4, May 27, 1916. Headquarters Brownsville District, Brownsville, Texas, BFDC-ATMFM.

116. "Baker Puts Ban upon Social Evil," EPMT, June 3, 1917.

117. "Ill-Fame Houses Throughout City Also Will Close," EPMT, June 8, 1916.

118. General Orders, No. 22, War Department, Washington, February 10, 1917, BFDC-ATMFM.

119. Bulletin No. 11, Copy of Sections 12, 13 and 14 of "Emergency Army Bill against Liquor and Disorderly Resorts," Headquarters First Brigade, First Provisional Infantry Division, Brownsville, Texas, May 28, 1917, BFDC-ATMFM.

120. General Orders Number 22, February 10, 1917, War Department, Washington, DC, BFDC-ATMFM.

121. Some church leaders, members of the Salvation Army, and the city council suggested "wholesome diversions" for soldiers stationed at Ft. Bliss that were not near the Chihuahuita sector of the city. "Recreation for Soldiers Here," EPH, June 11, 1917.

122. "Give Opinions on 'Redlight,'" EPH, June 20, 1917.

123. "Want S. El Paso Street Opened," EPH, June 21, 1917.

CHAPTER 5: "AGENTS UNDER FIRE"

1. Alexandra Minna Stern, Eugenic Nation: Faults and Frontiers of Better Breeding in Modern America (Berkeley: University of California Press, 2005), 57; Telegram, Secretariat of Foreign Relations to Jesus Acuña, March 6, 1916, 17–9-204, Historical Archive of the Secretariat of Foreign Relations, Mexico City.

2. "Juarez to Help in Typhus Fight," EPH, March 6, 1916, 4.

3. Stern, Eugenic Nation, 61.

4. Mae M. Ngai, Impossible Subjects: Illegal Aliens and the Making of Modern America (Princeton, NJ: Princeton University Press, 2004), 23.

5. "Border Patrolmen Must Be Versatile and Courageous," El Paso Times, March 26, 1934, Southwest Vertical File, "Border Patrol," BHC-EPPL.

6. Frank Tompkins, Chasing Villa: The Last Campaign of the U.S. Cavalry (Silver City, NM: High-Lonesome Books, 1934, 1996), 228.

7. "Baker Announces Pershing Recall," NYT, January 29, 1917.

8. Tompkins, Chasing Villa, 230.

9. "Baker Announces Pershing Recall," NYT, January 29, 1917; "Villa Expected to Take Possession of District Evacuated by Americans," EPMT, January 29, 1917, 1.

10. Stern, Eugenic Nation, 58–59.

11. "Border Patrolmen Must Be Versatile and Courageous," El Paso Times, March 26, 1934, Southwest Vertical File, "Border Patrol," BHC-EPPL.

12. Much of the history of the United States Border Patrol is drawn from the following works: Alvin Edward Moore, Border Patrol (Santa Fe: Sunstone Press, 1988); Clifford Allan Perkins, Border Patrol: With the U.S. Immigration Service on the Mexican Boundary, 1910–1954 (El Paso: Texas Western Press, 1978); Mary Rak, Border Patrol (Boston: Houghton Mifflin, 1938); Kelly Lytle Hernández, Migra!: A History of the U.S. Border Patrol (Berkeley: University of California Press, 2010); Ngai, Impossible Subjects.

13. El Paso historian W. H. Timmons, stated that "others living on the borders of the United States . . . could perceive the enormous profits to be made in smuggling illegal liquor from Mexico into the United States. Opportunists could envision the El Paso–Juárez area as a major oasis for thirst-stricken Americans—an oasis that would bring in tourist dollars from all over the bone-dry United States." W. H. Timmons, El Paso: A Borderlands History (El Paso: Texas Western Press, 1990), 226–27; E. W. Rheinheimer was a doctor in El Paso who serviced Mexican residents in South El Paso. In an interview with Professor Oscar J. Martínez, Dr. Rheinheimer recalled an incident in South El Paso where he tended to a rumrunner who suffered some knife wounds and was paid handsomely for his services by one of the smugglers. The smuggler "pulled out a wad of bills that would choke an ox" and gave the good doctor some cash and two bottles of tequila for tending to his wounded friend. E. W. Rheinheimer, interview by Oscar J. Martínez, February 4, 1977, Interview 427, transcript, Institute of Oral History, Special Collections, University of Texas at El Paso.

14. Alexandra Minna Stern, "Buildings, Boundaries, and Blood: Medicalization and Nation-Building on the U.S.-Mexico Border, 1910–1930," *Hispanic American Historical Review* 79, no. 1 (1999): 64; EPH, November 25, 1905, 2.

15. Howard Markel, *When Germs Travel: Six Major Epidemics That Have Invaded America since 1900 and the Fears They Have Unleashed* (New York: Pantheon Books, 2004), 113.

16. Alexandra Minna Stern used USPHS's case records over an approximately four-month period of the typhus quarantine in 1917. Stern, *Eugenic Nation*, 62–63.

17. "Order to Bathe Starts Near Riot among Juarez Women," EPMT, January 29, 1917, 1.

18. "Gavira Resents U.S. Quarantine," EPH, March 3, 1916, 1.

19. "Order to Bathe Starts Near Riot among Juarez Women," EPMT, January 29, 1917, 1.

20. "Bath Rioting Renewed at Santa Fe Bridge," EPMT, January 30, 1917, 1.

21. "Order to Bathe Starts Near Riot among Juarez Women," EPMT, January 29, 1917, 1.

22. Ibid.

23. Borderlands scholar David D. Romo states that American officials found the "rumors" of soldiers and immigration agents photographing women in the nude and circulating them publicly credible enough for these same officials to hire a detective agency to investigate the matter. David Dorado Romo, *Ringside Seat to a Revolution: An Underground Cultural History of El Paso and Juárez: 1893–1923* (El Paso: Cinco Puntos Press, 2005), 226; "Baker Announces Pershing Recall: Quarantine Riot in Juarez," NYT, January 29, 1917.

24. "Baker Announces Pershing Recall: Quarantine Riot in Juarez," NYT, January 29, 1917; Stern, *Eugenic Nation*, 62.

25. "Baker Announces Pershing Recall: Quarantine Riot in Juarez," NYT, January 1917.

26. Ibid.

27. "Bath Rioting Renewed at Santa Fe Bridge," EPMT, January 30, 1917, 1.

28. Ibid., 2.

29. Ibid., 1.

30. Romo, *Ringside Seat to a Revolution*, 237–38; Raul Delgado File. Proyecto Bracero Archives, Centro de Trabajadores Agrícolas Fronterizos, El Paso; for more on immigration inspection policy, see Stern, *Eugenic Nation*; Markel, *When Germs Travel*; Eithne Luibheid, *Entry Denied: Controlling Sexuality on the Border* (Minneapolis: University of Minnesota Press, 2002).

31. Stern, *Eugenic Nation*, 59.

32. Ibid., 66–67.

33. David Montejano, *Anglos and Mexicans in the Making of Texas, 1836–1986* (Austin: University of Texas Press, 1987), 131.

34. Letter from vice consul William P. Blocker to Secretary of State Lansing, July 6, 1916, Records of the Department of State Relating to the Internal Affairs of Mexico, roll 54 (NARA 812.00/18662), TTUL.

35. Ibid.

36. Letter from Zach Cobb to Secretary of State Lansing, June 25, 1916, Records of the Department of State Relating to the Internal Affairs of Mexico, roll 54 (NARA 812.00/18564), TTUL.

37. Letter from Zach Cobb to Secretary of State Lansing, June 27, 1916, Records of the Department of State Relating to the Internal Affairs of Mexico, roll 54 (NARA 812.00/18588 [1/2]), TTUL.

38. Letter from Zach Cobb to Secretary of State Lansing, June 29, 1916, Records of the Department of State Relating to the Internal Affairs of Mexico, roll 54 (NARA 812.00/18612), TTUL.

39. Ibid.

40. "Carranzistas Seize Arms of Americans," *New York Times*, June 29, 1916.

41. United States vice consul William P. Blocker of Piedras Negras, Coahuila, Mexico, stated in a letter to Secretary of State Lansing that the Mexican press continued its promotion of armed resistance against American forces in Chihuahua. In addition, American refugees claimed that war between the two countries was inevitable. Letter from vice consul William P. Blocker to Secretary of State Lansing, June 22, 1916, Records of the Department of State Relating to the Internal Affairs of Mexico, roll 54 (NARA 812.00/18538), TTUL.

42. Letter from John R. Silliman to Secretary of State Lansing, June 22, 1916, Records of the Department of State Relating to the Internal Affairs of Mexico, roll 54 (NARA 812.00/18540), TTUL.

43. The Chinese Exclusion Act of 1882 saw at least three major amendments that expanded the number of Chinese who were prohibited from entering the United States. First, the act was intended to prohibit laborers. The second amendment prohibited all immigrants from China except for diplomats, teachers, students, and tourists. Finally, in 1902 immigration from China was completely prohibited. For more information on the changing nature of Chinese immigration policy, see Ngai, *Impossible Subjects*; Erika Lee, *At America's Gates: Chinese Immigration during the Exclusion Era, 1882–1943* (Chapel Hill: University of North Carolina Press, 2007); Estelle T. Lau, *Paper Families: Identity, Immigration Administration, and Chinese Exclusion* (Durham, NC: Duke University Press, 2007).

44. Perkins, *Border Patrol*, 7.

45. Ibid., 9.

46. "The United States Border Patrol, 1924–1999, El Paso Sector: Where the Legend Began," pamphlet published by the El Paso Border Patrol Office, Special Collections, University of Texas at El Paso.

47. "Border Patrol Growth, History Told," *El Paso Times*, July 27, 1951, "Border Patrol" Vertical File, BHC-EPPL.

48. Dr. E. W. Rheniheimer, interview by Robert H. Novak, April 3, 1974, Interview 124, transcript, Institute of Oral History, Special Collections, University of Texas at El Paso.

49. Mark Reisler, "Always the Laborer, Never the Citizen: Anglo Perceptions of the Mexican Immigrant during the 1920s," *Pacific Historical Review* 45, no. 2 (1976): 233.

50. For more on increased Mexican labor at the turn of the century, see Mario García, *Desert Immigrants: The Mexicans of El Paso, 1880–1920* (New Haven, CT: Yale University Press, 1981); Rudolfo Acuña, *Occupied America: A History of Chicanos*, 2nd ed. (New York: Harper and Row, 1981); Emilio Zamora, *The World of the Mexican Worker in Texas* (College Station: Texas A&M University Press, 1993); Gilbert Gonzalez, *Guest Workers or Colonized Labor?: Mexican Labor Migration to the United States* (Boulder, CO: Paradigm Publishers, 2007).

51. Perkins, *Border Patrol*, 9.

52. Ibid.

53. Sucheng Chan, ed., *Entry Denied: Exclusion and the Chinese Community in America, 1882–1943* (Philadelphia: Temple University Press, 1991), 62.

54. Chester Chope, interview by Wilma Cleveland, July 27, 1968, Interview 27, transcript, Institute of Oral History, Special Collections, University of Texas at El Paso.

55. Perkins, *Border Patrol*, 13.

56. Ibid., 33.

57. García, *Desert Immigrants*, 41

58. Ngai, *Impossible Subjects*, 129.

59. William Edward Garnett, "Immediate and Pressing Race Problems of Texas," *Proceedings of the Sixth Annual Convention of the Southwestern Political and Social Science Association*, ed. Caleb Perry Patterson (Austin: The Southwestern Political and Social Science Association, 1925), 32.

60. The Immigration Act of 1917 (a.k.a. Asiatic Barred Zone Act) was passed by Congress on February 5, 1917 and restricted the immigration of "undesir-

ables" from other countries, including "idiots, imbeciles, epileptics, alcoholics, poor, criminals, beggars, any person suffering attacks of insanity, those with tuberculosis, and those who have any form of dangerous contagious disease, aliens who have a physical disability that will restrict them from earning a living in the United States . . . polygamists and anarchists, those who were against the organized government or those who advocated the unlawful destruction of property and those who advocated the unlawful assault of killing of any officer." A tax of $8 a head was imposed on immigrants, except children under sixteen accompanying a parent, and those over sixteen who had not paid for their own ticket were prohibited from entering the country. Another important provision of the Immigration Act was the literacy test imposed on immigrants entering the country. Those who were over the age of sixteen and could read some language must read thirty to forty words to show they are capable of reading. Those who were entering the United States to avoid religious persecution from their country of origin did not have to pass this test. Immigration Act of 1917, H.R. 10384, 64th Cong., 2nd sess., Pub. L. 301, 39 Stat. 874 (February 5, 1917), *U.S. Immigration Legislation Online*, University of Washington–Bothell, http://library.uwb.edu/guides/ USimmigration/1917_immigration_act.html (accessed March 29, 2011).

61. The Immigration Act of 1924 quotas that limited annual emigration from European countries. Immigrants were subject to annual numerical limitations. Until July 1, 1927, allowable annual quotas for each nationality would be 2 percent of the total population of that nationality as recorded in the 1890 Census. The minimum quota was one hundred. After July 1, 1927, allowable annual quotas for each nationality would be based on the national origins— "by birth or ancestry"—of the total US population as recorded in 1920. The overall quota of 150,000 immigrants would be divided between countries in proportion to the ancestry of the 1920 population, with a minimum quota of one hundred. Immigration Act of 1924, H.R. 7995, 68th Cong., 1st sess., Pub. L. 68–139; 43 Stat. 153 (May 26, 1924), *U.S. Immigration Legislation Online*, University of Washington–Bothell, http://library.uwb.edu/guides/US immigration/1924_immigration_act.html (accessed March 29, 2011).

62. "Uncle Sam's Border Patrol," *National Republic*, March 1930, vol. 17, no. 11, "Border Patrol" Vertical File, BHC-EPPL.

63. Leon C. Metz, "A Brief History of the United States Border Patrol," unpublished article, Dale Swancutt Papers, The National Border Patrol Museum, El Paso, Texas.

64. Perkins, *Border Patrol*, 89.

65. "Uncle Sam's Border Patrol," *National Republic*, March 1930, vol. 17, no. 11, "Border Patrol" Vertical File, BHC-EPPL.

66. "United States Border Patrol—Protecting Our Sovereign Borders," http:// www.cbp.gov/xp/cgov/border_security/border_patrol/history.xml (accessed April 11, 2007).

67. Ibid.

68. Wesley E. Stiles, interview by Wesley C. Shaw, January 1986, Interview 756, transcript, Institute of Oral History, Special Collections, University of Texas at El Paso.

69. Ibid.

70. Ibid.

71. The Quota Act of 1921 is also known as the Emergency Quota Act. The Immigration Act of 1924 is also known as the Johnson-Reed Act. Both acts outlined quota restrictions for foreign immigration into the United States.

72. Act of May 19, 1921: The Quota Act of 1921, 42 Stat. 5; 8 U.S.C. 229.

73. *Papers Read at the Meeting of Grand Dragons, Knights of the Ku Klux Klan* (New York: Arno Press, 1977), 69–74.

74. Ngai, *Impossible Subjects*, 21.

75. Statements of Hon. Robe Carl White, Hon. E. Hull, Mr. W. H. Wagner, U.S. Congress, Hearings before the Committee on Immigration and Naturalization, Sixty-Ninth Congress, 1st Session, January 12, 1926, 23–55.

76. Michael Lemay and Elliot Robert Barkan, eds., U.S. Immigration and Natural-ization Laws and Issues: A Documentary History (Westport, CT: Greenwood Press, 1999), 129, 140–45.

77. John M. Myers, Border Wardens (Englewood Cliffs, NJ: Prentice-Hall, 1971), 35.

78. Brigadier General S. L. A. Marshall recalled that in the early 1920s the Ku Klux Klan in El Paso "permeated the community. It was in control, for in-stance, of the American Legion in [El Paso]. It was in control of the Masonic Lodge. It was in control of the National Guard. I had been an officer in the National Guard and practically every other member of the Guard was in the Klan." Brigadier General S. L. A. Marshall, interview by Richard Estrada, July 5, 7, 9, 11, and 19, 1975, Interview No. 181, transcript, Institute of Oral History, Special Collections, University of Texas at El Paso.

79. Myers, Border Wardens, 209.

80. Commissioner of Immigration Harry E. Hull in a 1930 report identified the "Mexican border, where easily ninety-five per cent of the smuggling frater-nity is alien." "Uncle Sam's Border Patrol," National Republic, March 1930, vol. 17, no. 11, 6, "Border Patrol" Vertical File, BHC-EPPL.

81. "United States Border Patrol—Protecting Our Sovereign Borders," http://www.cbp.gov/xp/cgov/about/history/legacy/bp_historcut.xml (accessed June 9, 2010).

82. "United States Border Patrol—Protecting Our Sovereign Borders," http://www.cbp.gov/xp/cgov/toolbox/about/hitsory/ins_history.xml (accessed April 17, 2007).

83. "The History of the United States Border Patrol," unpublished essay, United States Border Patrol, 1924–99, "Border Patrol" Vertical File, Special Collec-tions, University of Texas at El Paso.

84. "Border Here to Be Guarded by Air Patrol," El Paso Times, May 5, 1937, 5, "Border Patrol" Vertical File, BHC-EPPL.

85. Ngai, Impossible Subjects, 70.

86. Abraham Hoffman, Unwanted Mexican Americans in the Great Depression: Repatria-tion Pressures, 1929–1939 (Tucson: University of Arizona Press, 1974), 54.

87. Ngai, Impossible Subjects, 70.

88. Hoffman, Unwanted Mexican Americans in the Great Depression, 54–55.

89. Abraham Hoffman, "Stimulus to Repatriation: The 1931 Federal Deportation Drive and the Los Angeles Mexican Community," Pacific Historical Review 42, no. 2 (1973): 206.

90. The recruitment of local and state authorities was also used to provide what was called a "psychological gesture." Los Angeles Citizens' Relief Committee coordinator Charles P. Visel believed that adding more Border Patrol agents to the Los Angeles area would provide a hostile environment for immigrants, prompting them to leave their jobs and homes voluntarily. Hoffman, "Stimu-lus to Repatriation," 208.

91. Ibid., 209.

92. The Immigration Act of 1917 regulated the admission of aliens that included classes of aliens that should be excluded from admission into the United States. Among the excluded classes were Asian Indians and all other native inhabitants of a "Barred Asiatic Zone" that ran from Afghanistan to the Pa-cific. For more information, see "Act of February 5, 1917: Immigration Act of 1917, 39 Stat. 874; 8 U.S.C; Ngai, Impossible Subjects; LeMay and Barkan, U.S. Immigration and Naturalization Laws and Issues.

93. Hoffman, "Stimulus to Repatriation," 206.

94. Ibid.

95. Abraham Hoffman, "Mexican Repatriation Statistics: Some Suggested Al-ternatives to Carey McWilliams," Western Historical Quarterly 3, no. 4 (1972): 391–404.

96. Reisler, "Always the Laborer, Never the Citizen," 233.

97. Oscar J. Martínez, Mexican-Origin People in the United States: A Topical History (Tucson: University of Arizona Press, 2001), 28.

98. Perkins, *Border Patrol*, 54.

99. "Mexican Laborers," U.S. *Immigration Service Bulletin* 1, no. 7 (1918): 2.

100. For more information on the "series" of amendments regarding temporary work status for Mexican and Canadian laborers, see "Amended Revised Rules for the Admission of Agricultural and Other Laborers," U.S. *Immigration Service Bulletin*. 1, no. 3 (1918): 1; "Mexican Farm Laborers," U.S. *Immigration Service Bulletin*1, no. 5 (1918): 7; "Laborers from Mexico for Sugar-Beet Production," U.S. *Immigration Service Bulletin* 1, no. 10 (1919): 1.

101. Kelly Lytle Hernández, "Entangled Bodies and Borders: Racial Profiling and the U.S. Border Patrol, 1924–1955" (PhD diss., University of California at Los Angeles, 2002), 174; E. A. Wright, interviewed by Jim Cullen, June 14, 1983, interview No. 86, Archives of the Big Bend, Bryan Wildenthal Memorial Library, Sul Ross State University, Alpine, Texas.

102. Montejano, *Anglos and Mexicans in the Making of Texas, 1836–1986*, 188–89.

103. Chester Chope, interview by Wilma Cleveland, July 27, 1968, Interview 27, transcript, Institute of Oral History, Special Collections, University of Texas at El Paso.

104. "Patrol Chief to Retire," *El Paso Times*, June 14, 1940, 11, "Border Patrol" Vertical File, BHC-EPPL.

105. Lewis L. Gould, *Progressives and Prohibitionists: Texas Democrats in the Wilson Era* (Austin: University of Texas Press, 1973), 50–51.

106. "Uncle Sam's Border Patrol," *National Republic*, March 1930, vol. 17, no. 11, "Border Patrol" Vertical File, BHC-EPPL.

107. Chester Chope, interview by Wilma Cleveland, July 27, 1968, Interview 27, transcript, Institute of Oral History, Special Collections, University of Texas at El Paso.

108. The document describes the circumstances of border patrolmen Robert Caldwell's kidnapping by Mexican smugglers near Ciudad Juárez. "Statement of Robert Caldwell made on February 15, 1930," anonymous manuscript, E. A. "Dogie" Wright Papers, DBCAH.

109. Brigadier General S. L. A. Marshall recalled an "era of good feelings" between middle-class Mexicans and Americans. However, he drew a clear class distinction and reiterated that hostility still resonated on the Mexican side at the "lower levels" of society. Brigadier General S. L. A. Marshall, interview by Richard Estrada, July 5, 7, 9, 11, and 19, 1975, Interview No. 181, transcript, Institute of Oral History, Special Collections, University of Texas at El Paso.

110. "Border Patrol Shoot-Outs Plagued City," EPT, June 5, 1981.

111. "Border Patrolmen Recall Early Gun Fights," EPH, May 21, 1974.

112. US Congress, "Immigration Border Patrol," Hearings before the Committee on Immigration and Naturalization House of Representatives, Seventieth Congress, 1st Session, March 5, 1928, 3–4.

113. Brigadier General S. L. A. Marshall, interview by Richard Estrada, July 5, 7, 9, 11, and 19, 1975, Interview No. 181, transcript, Institute of Oral History, Special Collections, University of Texas at El Paso.

114. Timmons, *El Paso: A Borderlands History*, 229–30.

115. Brigadier General S. L. A. Marshall, interview by Richard Estrada, July 5, 7, 9, 11, and 19, 1975, Interview No. 181, transcript, Institute of Oral History, Special Collections, University of Texas at El Paso.

116. "Border Patrolmen Recall Early Gun Fights," *El Paso Herald Post*, May 21, 1974. The newspaper article is the first of two stories on the Border Patrol during its 50th Anniversary celebration in El Paso. Bob Ybarra of the *El Paso Herald Post* interviewed several "old-timers," including Edwin Reeves, E. A. "Dogie" Wright, and others at the Border Patrol headquarters in El Paso.

117. Dr. E. W. Rheinheimer, interview by Robert H. Novak, April 3, 1974, Interview 124, transcript, Institute of Oral History, Special Collections, University of Texas at El Paso.

118. During Prohibition, chief inspector H. C. Horsley identified three "hotspots" for smuggling. They were Cordova Island, the Smelter District, and the

standpipes above the Santa Fe Bridge. "Patrol Chief to Retire," *EPT*, June 14, 1940, 11, "Border Patrol" Vertical File, BHC-EPPL.

119. Rak, *Border Patrol*, 76.

120. Cordoba Island was a plot of Mexican land created by the changing course of the Rio Grande/Río Bravo that extended into United States territory. "'No Man's Land' Cordova Island, Smuggler Hotbed," *EPT*, December 8, 1930.

121. Perkins, *Border Patrol*, 69.

122. Dr. E. W. Rheinheimer, interview by Robert H. Novak, April 3, 1974, Interview 124, transcript, Institute of Oral History, Special Collections, University of Texas at El Paso.

123. Armando A. Sanchez and his family lived in the eastern part of the city in the early 1930s. His home was located near a popular crossing point for immigrants and contraband. Armando A. Sanchez, interview by Rosa Morales, November 30, 1976, Interview 270, transcript, Institute of Oral History, Special Collections, University of Texas at El Paso; Estella Duran Vega, interview by Alfredo Antonio Vega, November 18, 1977, Interview 308, transcript, Institute of Oral History, Special Collections, University of Texas at El Paso.

124. Armando A. Sanchez served as an infantryman during World War II and taught infantry tactics to members of various levels of the United States and foreign armies. Armando A. Sanchez, interview by Rosa Morales, November 30, 1976, Interview 270, transcript, Institute of Oral History, Special Collections, University of Texas at El Paso; "'No Man's Land' Cordova Island, Smuggler Hotbed," *El Paso Times*, December 8, 1930, "Border Patrol" Vertical File, BHC-EPPL.

125. "'No Man's Land' Cordova Island, Smuggler Hotbed," *El Paso Times*, December 8, 1930, "Border Patrol" Vertical File, BHC-EPPL.

126. Brigadier General S. L. A. Marshall, interview by Richard Estrada, July 5, 7, 9, 11, and 19, 1975, Interview No. 181, transcript, Institute of Oral History, Special Collections, University of Texas at El Paso.

127. "'No Man's Land' Cordova Island, Smuggler Hotbed," *El Paso Times*, December 8, 1930, "Border Patrol" Vertical File, BHC-EPPL.

128. Ibid.

129. Edwin Reeves, interview by Richard Novak, June 24, 1974, Interview No. 135, transcript, Institute of Oral History, Special Collections, University of Texas at El Paso.

130. Leon Metz, "A Brief History of the United States Border Patrol," unpublished essay, The National Border Patrol Museum, El Paso, Texas.

131. "Border Patrolmen Recall Early Gun Fights," *El Paso Herald*, May 21, 1974.

132. George E. Barnhart, interview by Carlos Tapia, December 1976, interview No. 282, transcript, Institute of Oral History, Special Collections, University of Texas at El Paso.

133. Mauricio Cordero, interview by Oscar Martínez, February 15, 1974, interview No. 142, transcript, Institute of Oral History, Special Collections, University of Texas at El Paso.

134. Perkins, *Border Patrol*, 83.

135. "Border Patrolmen Recall Early Gun Fights," *El Paso Herald Post*, May 21, 1974.

136. This document describes various encounters by border patrolmen with Mexican smugglers. "Case XII. October 21, 1930," anonymous manuscript, E. A. "Dogie" Wright Papers, the Center for American History, University of Texas at Austin.

137. Chester Chope, interview by Wilma Cleveland, July 27, 1968, Interview 27, transcript, Institute of Oral History, Special Collections, University of Texas at El Paso.

138. "Statement of Enrique Duenas made at the El Paso's Border Patrol Headquarters to Chief Inspector H. C. Horsley on July 29, 1929," E. A. "Dogie" Wright Papers, DBCAH.

139. "Cordova Island Fenced to Shut Smugglers Out," *El Paso Herald Post*, May 13, 1940, 14, "Border Patrol" Vertical File, BHC-EPPL.

140. "Minute Signs Loom Large across Trail of 'Dawn Patrol,'" *El Paso World News*, May 19, 1935, "Border Patrol" Vertical File, BHC-EPPL.

141. "Buildings, Terrain Aid Smugglers to Enter United States," *El Paso World News*, May 26, 1935, "Border Patrol" Vertical File, BHC-EPPL.

142. Hugh E. Williams, Deputy Regional Chief of the Southwest Region of the US Border Patrol, outlined the history of the modern Border Patrol in a column published in the *El Paso Times*. "Border Patrol Strengthens Ranks with Influx of Illegal Alien Cargo," *El Paso Times*, May 30, 1974, "Border Patrol" Vertical File, BHC-EPPL.

143. In the 1918 "U.S. Immigration Service Bulletin," updates on laws and amendments are published to inform immigration officers of their duties. In various months throughout 1918, notices are given to the officers to allow Mexicans into a variety of low-wage jobs under the supervision of the employer and immigration office. Surveillance of the workers was utilized to prevent them from seeking higher-paying jobs. *U.S. Immigration Service Bulletin*, published monthly under the direction of the Commissioner General of Immigration, US Department of Labor, April 1, 1918–August 1, 1919.

144. "Border Patrolmen Recall Early Gun Fights," *El Paso Herald Post*, May 21, 1974.

CONCLUSION

1. David Montejano, *Anglos and Mexicans in the Making of Texas, 1836–1986* (Austin: University of Texas Press, 1987), 179–96.

2. Ibid.

EPILOGUE: "WHERE THE BAD GUYS ARE"

The title for the epilogue is taken from "Texas Rangers' Deployment to Mexico Border a Military-Style Effort," *Ft. Worth Star-Telegram*, September 15, 2009, Governor Rick Perry Homepage, http://www.rickperry.org/media -articles/texas-rangers-deployment-mexico-border-military-style-effort (accessed June 21, 2010).

1. In 1989, General Colin Powell was the commanding general of the US Army's Forces Command. After September 28, 2004, Joint Task Force 6 became known as Joint Task Force North. "History of Joint Task Force North: Joint Task Force Originally Established in 1989," Joint Task Force North homepage, http://www.jtfn.northcom.mil/subpages/history.html (accessed June 18, 2010).

2. Ibid.

3. Ibid.

4. "Family Doubts Marines' Account," *El Paso Times*, May 23, 1997, 2A, "Border Patrol" Vertical File, BHC-EPPL.

5. Ibid., 1A. For more on America's "War on Drugs," see Dan Baum, *Smoke and Mirrors: The War on Drugs and the Politics of Failure* (New York: Back Bay Books, 1997); Mike Gray, *Drug Crazy: How We Got into This Mess and How We Can Get Out* (New York: Routledge, 2000); Tony Payan, *The Three U.S.-Mexico Border Wars: Drugs, Immigration, and Homeland Security* (Westport, CT: Praeger Security International, 2006); Douglas Valentine, *The Strength of the Wolf: The Secret History of America's War on Drugs* (London: Verso, 2006).

6. "Border Patrol Brings in Marines," *El Paso Times*, August 8, 1992, "Border Patrol" Vertical File, BHC-EPPL.

7. Ibid.

8. Julia Prodis, "Fatal Shooting of Goat Herder by Marines Enrages Border Town," Associated Press, June 29, 1997, http://www.dpft.org/hernandez/ ap_062997.html (accessed June 22, 2010).

9. "Family Doubts Marines' Account," *El Paso Times*, May 23, 1997, "Border Patrol" Vertical File, BHC-EPPL.

10. Prodis, "Fatal Shooting of Goat Herder by Marines Enrages Border Town," Associated Press, June 29, 1997, http://www.dpft.org/hernandez/ap_062997 .html (accessed June 18, 2010).

11. "Family Doubts Marines' Account," *El Paso Times*, May 23, 1997, 1A–2A, "Border Patrol" Vertical File, BHC-EPPL.

12. Many law enforcement officials including Texas Ranger Captain Barry Caver speculated that Hernández "might have thought he was shooting at a wild animal rustling in the brush." Julia Prodis, "Fatal Shooting of Goat Herder by Marines Enrages Border Town," Associated Press, June 29, 1997, http://www.dpft.org/hernandez/ap_062997.html (accessed June 18, 2010).

13. "Family Doubts Marines' Account," *El Paso Times*, May 23, 1997, 2A, "Border Patrol" Vertical File, BHC-EPPL.

14. "Border Patrol Cuts Military's Drug Fight Role," *El Paso Times*, July 11, 1997, 1A, "Border Patrol" Vertical File, BHC-EPPL; "Troops Pulled from Anti-Drug Patrols," *Washington Post*, July 30, 1997, http://www.dpft.org/hernandez/wp_073097.html (accessed June 18, 2010).

15. The grand jury believed that Corporal Banuelos and the other Marines were following the rules of engagement when they pursued Hernández; the grand jury believed that Esequiel fired first but did not conclude that he shot at the Marines intentionally. "Marine Avoids Indictment," *Dallas Morning News*, August 15, 1997, http://www.dpft.org/hernandez/dmn_081597.html (accessed June 28, 2010).

16. Representative James Traficant, sponsor of the bill, clarified that the bill only authorized the deployment of the military and did not require it. "Military Authorized to Return to Border Patrol Duty," Associated Press, May 22, 1998, http://www.dpft.org/articles/militaryokd.htm (accessed June 18, 2010).

17. Jack Zimmerman, *The Ballad of Esequiel Hernández* (2008), DVD, directed by Kieran Fitzgerald (Taos, NM: Heyoka Pictures, LLC, 2008).

18. Joseph Nevins, *Operation Gatekeeper and Beyond: The War on "Illegals" and the Remaking of the U.S.-Mexico Boundary*, 2nd ed. (New York: Routledge, 2010), 171; Enrique Madrid, *The Ballad of Esequiel Hernández* (2008), DVD, directed by Kieran Fitzgerald (Taos, NM: Heyoka Pictures, LLC, 2008).

19. Nevins, *Operation Gatekeeper and Beyond*, 172.

20. "9/11" is a popular reference to the terrorist attacks on September 11, 2001, in New York City, Washington, DC, and Pennsylvania.

21. "Texas Rangers' Deployment to Mexico Border a Military-Style Effort," *Ft. Worth Star-Telegram*, September 15, 2009, Governor Rick Perry Homepage, http://www.rickperry.org/media-articles/texas-rangers-deployment-mexico -border-military-style-effort (accessed June 21, 2010).

22. Ibid.

23. Ibid.

24. "Perry Sending Rangers, Guard to the Border," *Texas Tribune*, September 10, 2009, http://www.texastribune.org/texas-mexico-border-news/texas-mexico -border/perry-sending-rangers-guard-to-the-border/ (accessed June 21, 2010).

25. "Texas Governor Sends Rangers to Mexico Border," Associated Press, September 11, 2009, http://www.msnbc.msn.com/id/32793136/ns/us_news -security (accessed June 21, 2010).

26. One of the comments listed below the article announcing Perry's deployment of Rangers stated: "Rangers were overtly lynching Mexicans until just a few decades ago. It is very dangerous to be Mexican American around one. Ten cuidado! (Be Careful!)." "Texas Rangers to Get Border Duty," MySanAntonio .com (San Antonio Express News), September 10, 2009, http://www.mysan antonio.com/news/local_news/Texas_Rangers_to_get_border_duty.html? c=y&viewAllComments=y (accessed June 21, 2010).

27. Press Release from the Office of the Governor Rick Perry, "Gov. Perry Announces Highly Skilled Ranger Recon Teams as Texas' Latest Efforts to Enhance Border Security," Office of the Governor Rick Perry, http://www .governor.state.tx.us/news/press-release/13577 (accessed June 23, 2010).

28. "About Us," Jim Gilchrist's Minutemen Project Website, http://www.minute manproject.com/organization/about_us.asp (accessed June 22, 2010); "The

Angry Patriot," Salon.com, May 11, 2005, http://dir.salon.com/news/feature/2005/05/11/minuteman/index.html (accessed June 22, 2010).

29. "Minuteman's goal: To Shame Feds Into Action," USAToday.com, May 25, 2006, http://www.usatoday.com/news/nation/2006-05-24-minuteman-goals_x.htm (accessed June 22, 2010).

30. "Bush Ordering Up to 6,000 in Guard to Border," MSNBC.com, May 15, 2006, http://www.msnbc.msn.com/id/12796688/ (accessed June 22,2010).

31. The "Secure Fence Act of 2006 (H.R. 6061)" authorized the Department of Homeland Security to spend $1.2 billion for the construction of a 700-mile fence along the US-Mexico border. 109th Congress, 2nd sess., H.R. 6061, United States Congress, September 14, 2006; "Operation Jump Start Jumps into Gear along Southwest Border," American Forces Press Service (Department of Defense), June 15 2006, http://www.defense.gov/news/newsarticle.aspx?id=16033 (accessed June 23, 2010).

32. "Operation Jump Start Officially Ends," ABQNews.com (Albuquerque Journal), July 16, 2008, http://www.abqjournal.com/abqnews/index.php?option=com_content&task=view&id=7954&Itemid=2 (accessed June 23, 2010); "Operation Jump Start Ends on Quiet Note," The Monitor Online (McAllen, Texas), July 12, 2008, http://www.themonitor.com/articles/border-14503-set-patrol.html (accessed June 23, 2010).

33. Timothy Dunn, *Blockading the Border and Human Rights: The El Paso Operation That Remade Immigration Enforcement* (Austin: University of Texas Press, 2009), 226–27.

34. Ibid.

35. "Obama to Send up to 1,200 Troops to Border," *New York Times*, May 25, 2010, http://www.nytimes.com/2010/05/26/us/26border.html (accessed June 23, 2010); "Obama Relents, Send National Guard to Arizona Border," *The Examiner* (Washington, DC), May 26, 2010, http://www.washingtonexaminer.com/politics/white-house/Obama-relents_-sends-National-Guard-to-Arizona-border-94877654.html (accessed June 23, 2010); "Mexico under Siege," Los Angeles Times Online, News series, http://projects.latimes.com/mexico-drug-war/#/its-a-war (accessed June 23, 2010).

36. Governor Jan Brewer signed Senate Bill 1070 into law on April 23, 2010. State of Arizona, Senate, Forty-Ninth Legislature, Second Regular Session, 2010, http://www.azleg.gov/legtext/49leg/2r/bills/sb1070s.pdf; "Arizona Enacts Stringent Law on Immigration," *New York Times*, April 23, 2010, http://www.nytimes.com/2010/04/24/us/politics/24immig.html (accessed June 21, 2010).

37. State of Arizona, Senate, Forty-Ninth Legislature, Second Regular Session, 2010, http://www.azleg.gov/legtext/49leg/2r/bills/sb1070s.pdf (accessed June 21, 2010).

38. "Arizona Enacts Stringent Law on Immigration," *New York Times*, April 23, 2010, http://www.nytimes.com/2010/04/24/us/politics/24immig.html (accessed June 21, 2010).

39. "Official Statement by Governor Jan Brewer: SB 1070," *Sonoran Weekly Review*, April 23, 2010, http://sonoranweeklyreview.com/statement-by-governor-jan-brewer-sb1070/ (accessed June 21, 2010).

40. "Crime in the United States," *Preliminary Annual Uniform Crime Report, January–December 2009, Report* issued by Robert S. Mueller III, Director, Federal Bureau of Investigation, United States Department of Justice, Washington, DC, May 24, 2010, http://www.fbi.gov/ucr/prelimsem2009/index.html (accessed June 23, 2010); Christopher Dickey, "Reading, Ranting, and Arithmetic," *Newsweek*, May 27, 2010, http://www.newsweek.com/2010/05/27/reading-ranting-and-arithmetic.html (accessed June 22, 2010).

41. Attributed to Porfirio Díaz (b. 1830 Oaxaca; d. 1915 Paris), president of the Republic of Mexico (1877–80; 1884–1911).

42. Nevins, *Operation Gatekeeper and Beyond*, 172.

43. Ibid.

44. Payan, *The Three U.S.-Mexico Border Wars*, 87–111; Monica Miller, "La Raza,

Mexican Terrorist Organization," *Canada Free Press* (canadafreepress.com), August 3, 2009, http://www.canadafreepress.com/index.php/article/13357 (accessed June 25, 2010); Malcolm Beith, "Are Mexico's Drug Cartels Terrorists Groups?" Slate (slate.com), April 15, 2010, http://www.slate.com/id/2250990 (accessed June 25, 2010).

45. "Arizona to birther the entire world, starting with this truck driver," Rachel Maddow Show, April 26, 2010, http://maddowblog.msnbc.msn.com/_news/2010/04/26/4206306-arizona-to-birther-entire-world-starting-with-this-truck-driver (accessed June 25, 2010).

46. Peter Andreas, *Border Games: Policing the U.S.-Mexico Divide* (Ithaca, NY: Cornell University Press, 2000), 10.

47. Ibid., 8–10.

48. General Motors' "This Is Our Country" television ad featuring the Chevrolet Silverado 2006, http://www.youtube.com/watch?v=QVVT-wumaLk (accessed July 17, 2010); General Motors' "This is my truck" television ad featuring the Chevrolet Silverado, http://www.youtube.com/watch?v=qriNbVCIsow&feature=related (accessed July 17, 2010).

49. William D. Carrigan, *The Making of a Lynching Culture: Violence and Vigilantism in Central Texas, 1836–1916* (Urbana: University of Illinois Press, 2004), 28.

Bibliography

GOVERNMENT PUBLICATIONS

"Crime in the United States." *Preliminary Annual Uniform Crime Report, January–December 2009*. Federal Bureau of Investigation. Report issued by Robert S. Mueller III, Director.

Records of Boundary and Claims Commission, Arbitrations, 1923–1937. "Motion on Behalf of the United States to Strike Out Portion of Brief on Behalf of United Mexican States," Special Claims Commission, United States and Mexico, The United States of America on behalf of (17 defendants) v. The United States of Mexico, Docket No. 449, Record Group 76, National Archives and Records Administration, Washington, DC.

———. "Memorial of the Cusi Mining Company to the Secretary of State, Supplemental to the Affidavits and the Brief Heretofore Submitted to the Department of the State for its Interposition with the Carranza Government of Mexico." Records Relating to the Santa Ysabel Cases, 1924–1936, Record Group 76, National Archives and Records Administration, College Park, MD.

———. "In the Matter of the Killing of C. R. Watson, Manager of the Cusi Mining Company, and Others, Near Santa Ysabel, in the State of Chihuahua, Mexico, January 10, 1916," Affidavit of J. O. H. Newby, June 27, 1916.

———. "Answer to Memorial Before the Special Claims Commission Mexico and the United States," The United States of America on behalf of Matilda Symansky Bodine Administration of the Estate of Manuel Bonifacio Romero vs. the United Mexican States, The Santa Ysabel Cases, no. 7.

Records of the Department of State Relating to Internal Affairs of Mexico, 1910–1929. National Archives Microfilm, National Archives and Records Service, Washington, D.C.

State of Arizona Legislature. Senate. *Support Our Law Enforcement and Safe Neighborhoods Act of 2010*. SB 1070. 49th Legis., 2nd regular session. (April 23, 2010).

Sworn Testimonies. *Proceedings of the Joint Committee of the Senate and House Investigation of the Texas State Ranger Force*, 36th Legislature, Regular Session, 1919, Legislative Papers, Texas State Library and Archives Commission, Austin, Texas.

Texas Adjutant General Department. *Adjutant General Thomas Scurry, General Order No 62, July 3, 1901*. Archives and Information Services Division, Texas State Library and Archives Commission. Austin, Texas.

———. *General's Report, June 1870–December 1870*. Austin, Texas, 1870.

———. *General's Report, 1903–1904*. Austin, Texas, 1904.

———. *Company 'D,' Monthly Returns, November 30, 1908*. Ranger records, Texas Adjutant General's Department. Archives and Information Services Division, Texas State Library and Archives Commission, Austin, Texas, 1908.

———. *Ranger Force Correspondence, 1917*. Ranger records, Texas Adjutant General's Department. Archives and Information Services Division, Texas State Library and Archives Commission, Austin, Texas, 1917.

Texas Governor James Edward Ferguson. *Telegram from Secretary of State, Newton D. Baker to Texas Governor, James E. Ferguson, May 1, 1916*, Records, Archives and Information Services Division, Texas State Library and Archives Commission, Austin, Texas.

Texas Governor O. B. Colquitt. *Correspondence*, Records, Archives and Information Services Division, Texas State Library and Archives Commission, Austin, Texas.

Texas State Legislature. *Proceedings of the Joint Committee of the Senate and House Investigation of the Texas State Ranger Force*, 36th Legislature, Regular Session, 1919,

Legislative Papers, Texas State Library and Archives Commission, Austin, Texas.

US Army. Post Returns, 1910–1916. Fort Bliss, Texas (El Paso, Texas).

US Bureau of the Census. *Population of Principal Cities [Texas] from earliest Census to 1920*, Bureau of the Census. Washington, DC, 1920.

———. *Special Census of the Population of El Paso, Texas, January 15, 1916*, Bureau of the Census. Washington, DC, 1916.

———. United States Department of the Interior. *Statistics of the Population of the United States, 1880*, Census Office. Washington, DC, 1882.

———. United States Department of the Interior, *Report on Population of the United States, 1890*, Census Office. Washington, DC, 1895.

———. United States Department of the Interior. *Census Reports, Volume I: Population of the United States, 1900.* Prepared under the supervision of William C. Hunt, Census Office. Washington, DC, 1901.

———. United States Department of Commerce. *Population 1910: General Report and Analysis.* Prepared under the supervision of William C. Hunt, Bureau of the Census. Washington, DC, 1913.

———. United States Department of Commerce. *Population of the United States, Volume I & III, 1920.* Prepared under the supervision of William C. Hunt, Bureau of the Census. Washington, DC, 1921, 1922.

———. United States Department of Commerce. *Population of the United States 1930, Volume I & III.* Prepared under the supervision of Leon E. Truesdell, Bureau of the Census. Washington, DC, 1931, 1932.

US Congress. *Emergency Quota Act of 1921*, 57th Cong., 1st sess., 42 Stat. 5; 8 U.S.C. 22.

———. *Immigration Act of 1917*, 39 Stat. 874; 8 U.S.C.

US Congress. Hearings before the Committee on Immigration and Naturalization. 69th Cong., 1st sess., January 12, 1926.

US Congress. *The Secure Fence Act of 2006*, 109th Cong., 2nd sess., September 14, 2006.

US Congress. House. Committee on Immigration and Naturalization. *Restriction of Immigration.* 69th Cong., 1st sess., January 12, 1926.

———. *Immigration Border Patrol.* 70th Cong., 1st sess., March 5, 1928.

———. *El Paso Troubles in Texas.* 45th Cong., 2nd Sess., March 1877–1879.

US Congress. Senate. Subcommittee of the Committee on Foreign Relations. *Investigation of Mexican Affairs.* 66th Cong., 2nd sess., December 6, 1919.

US Congress. Senate. Subcommittee of the Committee on Foreign Relations. "Investigation of Mexican Affairs, 1920: Partial Report of Committee, Abstracts of Testimony, and Index." 66th Cong, 2nd sess., 1920. Committee Print.

US Department of Labor. *U.S. Immigration Service Bulletin.* Commissioner General of Immigration. Washington, GPO, April 1, 1918–August 1, 1919.

US First Brigade. First Provisional Infantry Division. *Circular Letter Regarding Neutrality, January 8, 1917*, Headquarters, Brownsville District, Benjamin F. Delamater Collection, Archives of Texas Military Forces Museum, Austin, Texas.

———. *Bulletin Number 11, copy of sections 12, 13 and 14 of 'Emergency Army Bill Against Liquor and Disorderly Resorts, May 28, 1917*, Headquarters, Brownsville District. Brownsville, Texas.

———. *Bulletin Number 12, May 30, 1917*, Headquarters, Brownsville District. Brownsville, Texas.

———. *General Orders Number 4, May 27, 1916*, Headquarters, Brownsville District. Brownsville, Texas.

———. *General Orders Number 7, June 10, 1916*, Headquarters, Brownsville District. Brownsville, Texas.

———. *General Orders Number 22, February 10, 1917.* War Department, Washington, D.C.

———. *General Orders Number 26, August 17, 1916*, Headquarters, Brownsville District. Brownsville, Texas.

ARCHIVAL AND OTHER PRIMARY SOURCES

Adjutant General Papers. Texas State Library and Archives Commission, Austin, Texas.

American Defense Society Records. The New York Historical Society, New York University Digital Library, http://dlib.nyu.edu/eadapp/transform?source=nyhs/americandefsoc.xml&style=nyhs/nyhs.xsl&part=body (accessed April 29, 2010).

Border Heritage Center, Southwest Collection, El Paso Public Library, El Paso, Texas.

Border Patrol Vertical Files. Border Heritage Center, Southwest Collection, El Paso Public Library, El Paso, Texas.

Cano, Tony. Papers. Personal Notes and Archives, Canutillo, Texas.

Casey Collection. Archives of the Big Bend, Bryan Wildenthal Memorial Library, Sul Ross State University, Alpine, Texas.

C. L. Sonnichsen Special Collections Department, University of Texas at El Paso.

"Columbus Raid" Vertical File. Columbus Historical Society, Columbus, New Mexico.

El Paso Historical Society.

Institute of Oral History, University of Texas at El Paso.

"Maude Wright" Vertical File. Columbus Historical Society, Columbus, New Mexico.

National Archives and Records Administration, College Park, Maryland and Washington, DC.

"National Guard in Texas" Vertical File. Benjamin F. Delamater Collection, Archives of Texas Military Forces Museum, Austin, Texas.

Otis A. Aultman Photo Collection Online. Border Heritage Center, El Paso Public Library, El Paso, Texas.

Papers Read at the Meeting of Grand Dragons, Knights of the Ku Klux Klan. New York: Arno Press, 1977.

Roy W. Aldrick Collection. Archives of the Big Bend, Bryan Wildenthal Memorial Library, Sul Ross State University, Alpine, Texas.

Smithers (W. D.) Collection. Dolph Briscoe Center for American History, University of Texas at Austin.

Southwest Collections/Special Collections, Texas Tech University.

Swancutt, Dale. Papers. National Border Patrol Museum, El Paso Texas.

Texas Governor James E. Ferguson Papers. Texas State Library and Archives Commission, Austin, Texas.

Texas Governor Oscar B. Colquitt Papers. Texas State Library and Archives Commission, Austin, Texas.

Texas Ranger Research Center, Texas Ranger Hall of Fame and Museum, Waco, Texas.

Texas Ranger Vertical Files. Border Heritage Center, Southwest Collection, El Paso Public Library, El Paso, Texas.

Warren, Harry. Papers. Archives of the Big Bend, Bryan Wildenthal Memorial Library, Sul Ross State University, Alpine, Texas.

Wright, E. A. "Dogie." Papers. Dolph Briscoe Center for American History, University of Texas at Austin.

ORAL HISTORIES
Archives of the Big Bend, Bryan Wildenthal Memorial Library, Sul Ross State University, Alpine, Texas.
E. A. Wright oral history, interview no. 86

Institute of Oral History, University of Texas at El Paso
Mario Acevedo, interview 153.2
Epitacio Armendaríz, interview no. 551
George E. Barnhart, interview no. 282

Chester Chope, interview no. 27
Mauricio Cordero, interview no. 250
Alice B. Cummings, interview no. 426
Brigadier General S. L. A. Marshall, interview no. 181
Edwin Reeves, interview no. 135
E. W. Rheinheimer, interview no. 427
Armando A. Sanchez, interview no. 270
Wesley E. Stiles, interview no. 756
Estella Duran Vega, interview no. 308
Hortencia Villegas, interview no. 235

Southwest Collection/Special Collections, Texas Tech University
Dorothy Massey, September 23, 1982

With Author
Tony Cano
Jane Brite White (with Tony Cano)

PERIODICALS
Albuquerque Journal
Armed Services Press Service
Associated Press
Canada Free Press
Dallas Morning News
El Paso Herald Post
El Paso Morning Times
El Paso Times
El Paso World News
Fort Worth Star-Telegram
Houston Chronicle
Labor Advocate
Los Angeles Times
Mesilla Valley Independent
National Republic
Newsweek
New York Times
Pioneer News Observer
Salon.com
San Antonio Express
Slate.com
Sonoran Weekly Review
Texas Tribune
The Cattleman
The Examiner
The Literary Digest
The Monitor Online
The Southwesterner
USAToday
U.S. Immigration Service Bulletin
Washington Post

FILMS AND DOCUMENTARIES
The Ballad of Esequiel Hernández. Taos, NM: Heyoka Pictures, LLC, 2008.
The Hunt for Pancho Villa. Boston: WGBH Educational Foundation, American Experience, 1993.

ELECTRONIC SOURCES
"Arizona to Birther the Entire World, Starting with This Truck Driver." Rachel Maddow Show, April 26, 2010. At http://maddowblog.msnbc.com/_news/2010/04/26/4206306-arizona-to-birther-entire-world-starting-with-this-truck-driver (accessed June 25, 2010).
General Motors. "This Is Our Country." Television ad featuring the Chevrolet Silverado 2006. At http://www.youtube.com/watch?v=QVVT-wumaLk (accessed July 17, 2010).
———. "This is my truck." Television ad featuring the Chevrolet Silverado. At http://www.youtube.com/watch?v=qriNbVCIsow&feature=related (accessed July 17, 2010).
"Governor Perry Announces Highly Skilled Ranger Recon Teams as Texas' Latest

Efforts to Enhance Border Security." Office of the Governor Rick Perry. At http://www.governor.state.tx.us/ (accessed June 21, 2010).

Tuck, Jim. "The Mexican Revolution: A Nation in Flux, pt. 1 and pt. 2." *mexconnect .com*, October 9, 2008. At http://www.mexconnect.com/articles/296-the -revolution-a-nation-in-flux-part-1-1910-20 (accessed April 5, 2011).

US Customs and Border Protection. "United States Border Patrol—Protecting Our Sovereign Borders." At http://www.cbp.gov/xp/cgov/border_security/ border_patrol/history.xml (accessed April 11, 2007).

Articles, Books, and Dissertations

Acuña, Rodolfo. *Occupied America: A History of Chicanos*. San Francisco: Canfield Press, 1972.

Army Historical Series. "American Military History." Center of Military History, US Army, Washington, DC, 1989.

Alonso, Ana Maria. *Thread of Blood: Colonialism, Revolution, and Gender on Mexico's Northern Frontier*. Tucson: University of Arizona Press, 1995.

Anders, Evan. *Boss Rule in South Texas: The Progressive Era*. Austin: University of Texas Press, 1982.

Anderson, Gary Clayton. *The Conquest of Texas: Ethnic Cleansing in the Promised Land, 1820–1875*. Norman: University of Oklahoma Press, 2005.

Andreas, Peter. *Border Games: Policing the U.S.-Mexico Divide*. Ithaca, NY: Cornell University Press, 2000.

Baker, T. Lindsay. *Ghost Towns of Texas*. Norman: University of Oklahoma Press, 1986.

Batchelder, Roger. *Watching and Waiting on the Border*. Boston: Houghton Mifflin, 1917.

Baum, Dan. *Smoke and Mirrors: The War on Drugs and the Politics of Failure*. New York: Back Bay Books, 1997.

Beezley, William H. *Insurgent Governor: Abraham González and the Mexican Revolution in Chihuahua*. Lincoln: University of Nebraska Press, 1973.

Beezley, William H., and Colin M. MacLachlan. *Mexicans in Revolution, 1910–1946: An Introduction (The Mexican Experience)*. Lincoln: University of Nebraska Press, 2009.

Benton-Cohen, Elizabeth. *Borderline Americans: Racial Divisions and Labor War in the Arizona Borderlands*. Cambridge, MA: Harvard University Press, 2009.

Braddy, Haldeen. *Cock of the Walk, Qui-Qui-Ri-Quí: The Legend of Pancho Villa*. Albuquerque: University of New Mexico Press, 1955.

———. *Pancho Villa at Columbus*. El Paso: Texas Western College Press, 1965.

Brenner, Anita. *The Wind That Swept Mexico: The History of the Mexican Revolution, 1910– 1942*. Austin: University of Texas Press, 1984.

Brown, Richard Maxwell. "Violence and Vigilantism in American History." In *American Law and the Constitutional Order: Historical Perspectives*, edited by Lawrence M. Friedman and Harry N. Scheiber, 173–90. Cambridge, MA: Harvard University Press, 1978.

Buenger, Walter L. *The Path to a Modern South: Northeast Texas between Reconstruction and the Great Depression*. Austin: University of Texas Press, 2001.

Bush, Ira Jefferson. *Gringo Doctor*. Caldwell, ID: Caxton Printers, 1939.

Calderón, Roberto R. *Mexican Coal Mining Labor in Texas and Coahuila, 1880–1930*. College Station: Texas A&M University Press, 2000.

Callahan, Manuel. "Mexican Border Troubles: Social War, Settler Colonialism, and the Production of Frontier Discourses, 1848–1880." PhD diss., University of Texas at Austin, 2003.

Calleros, Cleofas. *El Paso . . . Then and Now*. El Paso: American Printing Company, 1954.

Calvert, Peter. *The Mexican Revolution, 1910–1914: The Diplomacy of Anglo-American Conflict*. Cambridge: Cambridge University Press, 1968.

Camarillo, Albert. *Chicanos in a Changing Society: From Mexican Pueblos to American Bar-*

rios in Santa Barbara and Southern California, 1848–1930. Cambridge, MA: Harvard University Press, 1979.

Cano, Tony, and Ann Sochat. Bandido: The True Story of Chico Cano, the Last Western Bandit. Canutillo, TX: Reata Publishing, 1997.

Carrigan, William D. The Making of a Lynching Culture: Violence and Vigilantism in Central Texas, 1836–1916. Urbana: University of Illinois Press, 2004.

Carrigan, William D., and Clive Webb. "The Lynching of Persons of Mexican Origin or Descent in the United States, 1848–1928." Journal of Social History 37 (Winter 2003): 411–38.

Castillo, Pedro, and Albert Camarillo, eds. Furia y muerte: Los bandidos Chicanos. Los Angeles: Aztlán Publications, 1973.

Chalkley, John F. Zach Lamar Cobb: El Paso Collector of Customs and Intelligence during the Mexican Revolution, 1913–1918. El Paso: Texas Western Press, 1998.

Chan, Sucheng, ed. Entry Denied: Exclusion and the Chinese Community in America, 1882–1943. Philadelphia: Temple University Press, 1991.

Clendenen, Clarence C. Blood on the Border: The United States Army and the Mexican Irregulars. London: Macmillan, 1969.

———. The United States and Pancho Villa: A Study in Unconventional Diplomacy. Ithaca, NY: Cornell University Press, 1961.

Coerver, Don M., and Linda B. Hall. Texas and the Mexican Revolution: A Study in State and National Policy, 1910–1920. San Antonio: Trinity University Press, 1984.

Collins, Michael L. Texas Devils: Rangers and Regulars on the Lower Rio Grande, 1846–1861. Norman: University of Oklahoma Press, 2008.

Cool, Paul. "El Paso's First Real Lawman, Texas Ranger Mark (Marcus) Ludwick." Quarterly of the National Association for Outlaw and Lawman History (October–December 2001): 1–9.

———. Salt Warriors: Insurgency in the Rio Grande. College Station: Texas A&M University Press, 2008.

Coolidge, Dane. Fighting Men of the West. New York: E. P. Dutton, 1932.

Cunningham, Eugene. Triggernometry: A Gallery of Gunfighters. Caldwell, ID: Caxton Printers, 1958.

Darrah, Jason T. "Anglos, Mexicans, and the San Ysabel Massacre: A Study of Changing Ethnic Relations in El Paso, Texas, 1910–1916." Master's thesis, Texas Tech University, 2003.

De Grazia, Sebastian. "What Authority Is Not." American Political Science Review (June 1959): 321–31.

De León, Arnoldo. Mexican Americans in Texas: A Brief History. 3rd ed. Wheeling, IL: Harlan Davidson, 2009.

———. They Called Them Greasers: Anglo Attitudes toward Mexicans in Texas, 1821–1900. Austin: University of Texas Press, 1983.

———. War Along the Border. College Station: Texas A&M University Press, 2012.

Diener, Alexander C., and Joshua Hagen. Borderlines and Borderlands: Political Oddities at the Edge of the Nation-State. Lanham, MD: Rowman and Littlefield, 2010.

Douglas, Claude Leroy. The Gentlemen in the White Hats: Dramatic Episodes in the History of the Texas Rangers. Dallas: Southwest Press, 1934.

Dunn, Timothy. Blockading the Border and Human Rights: The El Paso Operation That Remade Immigration Enforcement. Austin: University of Texas Press, 2009.

———. The Militarization of the U.S.-Mexico Border, 1978–1992. Austin: University of Texas Press, 1996.

Estrada, Richard. "The Mexican Revolution in Ciudad Juárez–El Paso Area, 1910–1920." Password (Spring 1979): 69.

Foos, Paul. A Short, Offhand, Killing Affair: Soldiers and Social Conflict during the Mexican-American War. Chapel Hill: University of North Carolina Press, 2002.

Fregoso, Rosa Linda. MeXicana Encounters: The Making of Social Identities on the Borderlands. Berkeley: University of California Press, 2003.

Frost, H. Gordon. The Gentlemen's Club: The Story of Prostitution in El Paso. El Paso: Mangan Books, 1983.

Ganster, Paul, and David E. Lorey, eds. *Borders and Border Politics in a Globalizing World.* Lanham, MD: SR Books, 2005.

García, Mario. *Desert Immigrants: The Mexicans of El Paso, 1880–1920.* New Haven, CT: Yale University Press, 1981.

Garnett, William Edward. "Immediate and Pressing Race Problems of Texas." In *Proceedings of the Sixth Annual Convention of the Southwestern Political and Social Science Association,* edited by Caleb Perry. Austin: Southwestern Political and Social Science Association, 1925.

Gillett, James B. *Six Years with the Texas Rangers, 1875–1881.* New Haven, CT: Yale University Press, 1925.

Gilly, Adolfo. *The Mexican Revolution: A People's History.* New York: New Press, 2006.

Gómez-Quiñones, Juan. "Plan de San Diego Reviewed." *Aztlán: Chicano Journal of the Social Sciences and Arts* 1 (Spring 1970): 125.

———. "Toward a Perspective on Chicano History." *Aztlán: Chicano Journal of the Social Sciences and Arts* (Fall 1971): 1–51.

Gonzalez, Gilbert. *Guest Workers or Colonized Labor?: Mexican Labor Migration to the United States.* Boulder, CO: Paradigm Publishers, 2007.

Gould, Lewis. *Progressives and Prohibitionists: Texas Democrats in the Wilson Era.* Austin: University of Texas Press, 1973.

Gray, Mike. *Drug Crazy: How We Got into This Mess and How We Can Get Out.* New York: Routledge, 2000.

Griswold del Castillo, Richard. *The Treaty of Guadalupe Hidalgo: A Legacy of Conflict.* Norman: University of Oklahoma Press, 1990.

Gutiérrez, David. *Walls and Mirrors: Mexican Americans, Mexican Immigrants, and the Politics of Ethnicity.* Berkeley: University of California Press, 1995.

Habermeyer, Christopher Lance. *Gringo's Curve: Pancho Villa's Massacre of American Miners in Mexico, 1916.* El Paso: Book Publishers of El Paso, 2004.

Harris, Charles H., III, and Louis R. Sadler. *The Border and the Revolution: Clandestine Activities of the Mexican Revolution: 1910–1920.* Silver City, NM: High-Lonesome Books, 1988.

———. "Pancho Villa and the Columbus Raid: The Missing Documents." *New Mexico Historical Review* (October 1975): 335–46.

———. *The Secret War in El Paso: Mexican Revolutionary Intrigue, 1906–1920.* Albuquerque: University of New Mexico Press, 2009.

———. *The Texas Rangers and the Mexican Revolution: The Bloodiest Decade, 1910–1920.* Albuquerque: University of New Mexico Press, 2004.

———. "The 'Underside' of the Mexican Revolution, 1912." *The Americas* (July 1982): 69–83.

Harris, Larry. *Pancho Villa: Strong Man of the Revolution.* Silver City, NM: High-Lonesome Books, 1955.

Hart, John Mason. *Revolutionary Mexico: The Coming and Process of the Mexican Revolution.* 10th ed. Chapel Hill, NC: University of North Carolina Press, 1997.

Hernández, Kelly Lytle. "Entangled Bodies and Borders: Racial Profiling and the U.S. Border Patrol, 1924–1955." PhD diss., University of California at Los Angeles, 2002.

———. *Migra!: A History of the U.S. Border Patrol.* Berkeley: University of California Press, 2010.

Hobsbawm, Eric J. *Bandits.* London: Weidenfeld and Nicolson, 1969.

Hoffman, Abraham. "Mexican Repatriation Statistics: Some Suggested Alternatives to Carey McWilliams." *Western Historical Quarterly* (October 1972): 391–404.

———. "Stimulus to Repatriation: The 1931 Federal Deportation Drive and the Los Angeles Mexican Community." *Pacific Historical Review* (May 1973): 205–19.

———. *Unwanted Mexican Americans in the Great Depression: Repatriation Pressures, 1929–1939.* Tucson: University of Arizona Press, 1974.

Hurst, James W. *Pancho Villa and Black Jack Pershing: The Punitive Expedition in Mexico.* Santa Barbara, CA: Praeger Publishers, 2007

———. *Villista Prisoners of 1916–1917.* Las Cruces, NM: Yucca Tree Press, 2000.

Husk, Carlos. "Typhus Fever." *Bulletin of the El Paso County Medical Society* (1916): 75–79.

Johnson, Benjamin Heber. *Revolution in Texas: How a Forgotten Rebellion and Its Bloody Suppression Turned Mexicans into Americans.* New Haven, CT: Yale University Press, 2005.

Joint Task Force North. "History of Joint Task Force North: Joint Task Force Originally Established in 1989." At http//:www.jtfn.northcom.mil/subpages/history.html (accessed June 18, 2010).

Jordan, David Starr. *The Days of a Man: Being Memories of a Naturalist, Teacher, and Minor Prophet of Democracy.* New York: World Book, 1922.

Judson, Pieter M. *Guardians of the Nation: Activists on the Language Frontier of Imperial Austria.* Cambridge, MA: Harvard University Press, 2006.

Justice, Glenn. *Little Known History of the Texas Big Bend: Documented Chronicles from Cabeza de Vaca to the Era of Pancho Villa.* Odessa, TX: Rimrock Press, 2001.

———. *Revolution on the Rio Grande.* El Paso: Texas Western Press, 1992.

Katz, Friedrich. *The Life and Times of Pancho Villa.* Stanford, CA: Stanford University Press, 1998.

———. *Pancho Villa y el ataque a Columbus, Nuevo México.* Chihuahua, Mexico: Sociedad Chihuahuense de Estudios Históricos, 1979.

Keil, Robert. *Bosque Bonito: Violent Times along the Borderland during the Mexican Revolution.* Alpine, TX: Sul Ross State University Press, 2002.

Ku Klux Klan. *Papers Read at the Meeting of the Grand Dragons, Knights of the Ku Klux Klan: Together with Other Articles of Interest to Klansmen.* 2nd ed. New York: Arno Press, 1977.

Lau, Estelle T. *Paper Families: Identity, Immigration Administration, and Chinese Exclusion.* Durham, NC: Duke University Press, 2007.

Lay, Shawn. *War, Revolution, and the Ku Klux Klan: A Study of Intolerance in a Border City.* El Paso: Texas Western Press, 1985.

Lee, Erika. *At America's Gates: Chinese Immigration during the Exclusion Era, 1882–1943.* Chapel Hill: University of North Carolina Press, 2003.

Lemay, Michael, and Elliot Robert Barkan, eds. *U.S. Immigration and Naturalization Laws and Issues: A Documentary History.* Westport, CT: Greenwood Press, 1999.

Levario, Miguel Antonio. "Cuando vino la mexicanada: Authority, Race, and Conflict in West Texas, 1895–1924." PhD diss., University of Texas at Austin, 2007.

———. "The El Paso Race Riot of 1916." In *War along the Border,* edited by Arnoldo De León. College Station: Texas A&M University Press, 2012.

López, Ian Haney. "Race and Colorblindness after *Hernández* and *Brown.*" In *"Colored Men" and "Hombres Aquí,"* edited by Michael A. Olivas, 41–52. Houston: Arte Público Press, 2006.

Luibheid, Eithne. *Entry Denied: Controlling Sexuality on the Border.* Minneapolis: University of Minnesota Press, 2002.

Margo, A. *Who, Where, and Why Is Villa?.* New York: Latin-American News Association, 1917.

Markel, Howard. *When Germs Travel: Six Major Epidemics That Have Invaded America since 1900 and the Fears They Have Unleashed.* New York: Pantheon Books, 2004.

Martin, Jack. *Border Boss: Captain John R. Hughes, Texas Ranger.* Austin: State House Press, 1990.

Martin, John L. "Can We Control the Border? A Look at Recent Efforts in San Diego, El Paso, and Nogales." Washington DC: Center for Immigration Studies, May 1995. At http://www.cis.org/articles/1995/border/index.html (accessed April 12, 2007).

Martínez, Oscar J. *Border Boom Town: Ciudad Juárez since 1848.* Austin: University of Texas Press, 1975.

———. *Mexican-Origin People in the United States: A Topical History.* Tucson: University of Arizona Press, 2001.

———. *Troublesome Border.* Tucson: University of Arizona Press, 1988.

Mayhall, Mildred P. *Indian Wars of Texas*. Waco: Texian Press, 1965.

McElhaney, Jacquelyn Masur. *Pauline Periwinkle and Progressive Reform in Dallas*. College Station: Texas A&M University Press, 1998.

McWilliams, Carey. *North from Mexico: The Spanish-Speaking People of the United States*. New York: Greenwood Press, 1948.

Means, Joyce E. *Pancho Villa Days at Pilares: Stories and Sketches of Days-Gone-By from the Valentine Country of West Texas*. El Paso: Joyce E. Means, 1976.

Metz, Leon Claire. *Border: The U.S.-Mexico Line*. El Paso: Mangan Books, 1989.

———. *Desert Army: Fort Bliss on the Texas Border*. El Paso: Mangan Books, 1988.

———. *El Paso Chronicles: A Record of Historical Events in El Paso, Texas*. El Paso: Mangan Books, 1993.

Meyer, Marshall W. "Two Authority Structures of Bureaucratic Organization." *Administrative Science Quarterly* (September 1968): 211–28.

Molina, Natalia. *Fit to Be Citizens?: Public Health and Race in Los Angeles, 1879–1939*. Berkeley: University of California Press, 2006.

Montejano, David. *Anglos and Mexicans in the Making of Texas, 1836–1986*. Austin: University of Texas Press, 1987.

Montejano, David, ed. *Chicano Politics and Society in the Late Twentieth Century*. Austin: University of Texas Press, 1999.

Moore, Alvin Edward. *Border Patrol*. Santa Fe: Sunstone Press, 1988.

Myers, John M. *Border Wardens*. Englewood Cliffs, NJ: Prentice-Hall, 1971.

Nevels, Cynthia Skove. *Lynching to Belong: Claiming Whiteness through Racial Violence*. College Station: Texas A&M University Press, 2007.

Nevins, Joseph. *Operation Gatekeeper and Beyond: The War on "Illegals" and the Remaking of the U.S.-Mexico Boundary*. 2nd ed. New York: Routledge, 2010.

Ngai, Mae M. *Impossible Subjects: Illegal Aliens and the Making of Modern America*. Princeton, NJ: Princeton University Press, 2004.

Nunnally, Michael. *American Indian Wars: A Chronology of Confrontations between Native Peoples and Settlers and the United States Military, 1500s–1901*. Jefferson, NC: McFarland, 2007.

Omi, Michael, and Howard Winant. *Racial Formation in the United States: From the 1960s to the 1990s*. 2nd ed. New York: Routledge, 1994.

Paredes, Américo. *With His Pistol In His Hand: A Border Ballad and Its Hero*. Austin: University of Texas, 1958.

Payan, Tony. *The Three U.S.-Mexico Border Wars: Drugs, Immigration, and Homeland Security*. Westport, CT: Praeger Security International, 2006.

Perkins, Clifford Allan. *Border Patrol: With the U.S. Immigration Service on the Mexican Boundary, 1910–1954*. El Paso: Texas Western Press, 1978.

Prodis, Julia. "Fatal Shooting of Goat Herder by Marines Enrages Border Town." *Associated Press*, June 29, 1997, http://www.dpft.org/hernandez/ap_062997.html.

Purcell, Allan R. "The History of the Texas Militia, 1835–1903." PhD diss., University of Texas at Austin, 1981.

Raht, Carlysle Graham. *The Romance of Davis Mountains and Big Bend Country: A History*. Odessa, TX: Rahtbooks, 1963.

Rak, Mary. *Border Patrol*. Boston: Houghton Mifflin, 1938.

Reisler, Mark. "Always the Laborer, Never the Citizen: Anglo Perceptions of the Mexican Immigrant during the 1920s." *Pacific Historical Review* (May 1976): 231–54.

Reséndez, Andrés. *Changing National Identities at the Frontier: Texas and New Mexico, 1800–1850*. Cambridge: Cambridge University Press, 2004.

Rice, Harvey F. "The Lynching of Antonio Rodríguez." Master's thesis, University of Texas at Austin, 1990.

Rocha, Rodolfo. "The Influence of the Mexican Revolution on the Mexico-Texas Border, 1910–1916." PhD diss., Texas Tech University, 1981.

Rodriguez, Jaime E. *Common Border, Uncommon Paths: Race, Culture, and National Identity in U.S.-Mexican Relations*. Wilmington, DE: Scholarly Resources, 1993.

Romo, David Dorado. *Ringside Seat to a Revolution: An Underground Cultural History of El Paso and Juárez, 1893–1923*. El Paso: Cinco Puntos Press, 2005.

Samora, Julian, Joe Bernal, and Albert Peña. *Gunpowder Justice: A Reassessment of the Texas Rangers*. Notre Dame, IN: University of Notre Dame Press, 1979.

Sánchez, George J. *Becoming Mexican American: Ethnicity, Culture, and Identity in Chicano Los Angeles, 1900–1945*. New York: Oxford University Press, 1995.

Sandos, James A. *Rebellion in the Borderlands: Anarchism and the Plan of San Diego, 1904–1923*. Norman: University of Oklahoma Press, 1992.

Schrag, Peter. *Not Fit for Our Society: Nativism and Immigration*. Berkeley: University of California Press, 2010.

Shipman, Jack. "Texas Rangers." Photocopy, Border Heritage Center, Southwest Collection, El Paso Public Library, El Paso, Texas.

Smedley, Audrey. *Race in North America: Origins and Evolution of a Worldview*. 3rd ed. Boulder, CO: Westview Press, 2007.

Sonnichsen, Charles Leland. *The El Paso Salt War of 1877*. El Paso: Hertzog, 1961.

———. *Pass of the North*. El Paso: Texas Western Press, 1968.

St. Clair, Robert, Guadalupe Valdés, and Jacob Ornstein-Galicia, eds. *Social and Eduational Issues in Bilingualism and Biculturalism*. Washington, DC: University Press of America, 1981.

Stern, Alexandra Minna. "Buildings, Boundaries, and Blood: Medicalization and Nation-Building on the U.S.-Mexico Border, 1910–1930." *Hispanic American Historical Review* (February 1999): 64.

———. *Eugenic Nation: Faults and Frontiers of Better Breeding in Modern America*. Berkeley: University of California Press, 2005.

Stopka, Christina. "Partial List of Texas Ranger Company and Unit Commanders," At http://www.texasranger.org/ReCenter/Captains.pdf. Publication date unknown (accessed June 7, 2007). Texas Ranger Research Center, Waco, Texas.

Stout, Joseph. *Border Conflict: Villistas, Carrancistas, and the Punitive Expedition, 1915–1920*. Fort Worth: Texas Christian University Press, 1999.

Timmons, Wilbert H. *El Paso: A Borderlands History*. El Paso: Texas Western Press, 1990.

Tompkins, Frank. *Chasing Villa: The Last Campaign of the U.S. Cavalry*. Silver City, NM: High-Lonesome Books, 1934.

Turner, Frederick C. "Anti-Americanism in Mexico, 1910–1913." *Hispanic American Historical Review* (November 1967): 502–18.

Tyler, Ronnie C. *The Big Bend: A History of the Last Texas Frontier*. Washington, DC: Office of Publications, 1975.

Utley, Robert M. *Lone Star Justice: The First Century of the Texas Rangers*. New York: Oxford University Press, 2002.

———. *Lone Star Lawmen: The Second Century of the Texas Rangers*. New York: Oxford University Press, 2007.

Valdés, Guadalupe, ed. *Social and Educational Issues in Bilingualism and Biculturalism*. Washington, DC: University Press of America, 1981.

Valentine, Douglas. *The Strength of the Wolf: The Secret History of America's War on Drugs*. London: Verso, 2006.

Vanderwood, Paul J. *Disorder and Progress: Bandits, Police, and Mexican Development*. Wilmington, DE: Scholarly Resources, 1992.

Vila, Pablo. *Crossing Borders, Reinforcing Borders*. Austin: University of Texas Press, 2000.

———. "Everyday Life, Culture, and Identity on the Mexican-American Border: The Ciudad Juárez–El Paso case." PhD diss., University of Texas at Austin, 1994.

Webb, Walter Prescott. *The Texas Rangers: A Century of Frontier Defense*. Austin: University of Texas Press, 1935.

Weber, C. Edward. "The Nature of Authority: Comment." *Journal of the Academy of Management* (April 1961): 62–63.

Welsome, Eileen. *The General and The Jaguar: Pershing's Hunt for Pancho Villa: A True Story of Revolution and Revenge*. New York: Little, Brown, 2006.

Wilson, Thomas M., and Hastings Donnan, eds. *Border Identities: Nation and State at International Frontiers*. Cambridge: Cambridge University Press, 1998.

Winders, Richard B. *Mr. Polk's Army: The American Military Experience in the Mexican War*. College Station: Texas A&M University Press, 1997.

Zamora, Emilio. *Claiming Rights and Righting Wrongs in Texas: Mexican Workers and Job Politics during World War II*. College Station: Texas A&M University Press, 2009.

———. *The World of the Mexican Worker in Texas*. College Station: Texas A&M University Press, 1993.

Zillich, Emily Tessier. "History of the National Guard in El Paso." Master's thesis, Texas Western College (University of Texas at El Paso), 1958.

Index

Acebes, Diego, 63–64, 65
African Americans: abduction of
  Buck Spencer, 71; American
  identity of, 126; lynchings, 10,
  68; and Plan de San Diego, 80
"Africanization" of northeast Texas,
  4, 42
agriculture and demand for
  Mexican labor, 8, 90, 97–98,
  101–103, 117–18
Aguas Calientes, Mexico, 57
Aguirre, Ben, 74
air patrols, border, 100
airplanes and smuggling, 104
Akers, Bert L., 54
Alcohol: consumption and
  violence/disorder, 48–49, 85;
  smuggling of, 6–7, 13, 90, 94,
  95, 100, 103–108, 112, 116; US
  demand for, 90, 103, 116; See also
  Prohibition
"alien citizens" and American
  national constructs, 2
alliances; fluidity of, 31; ranchers
  and Mexican revolutionaries,
  7–8; with revolutionary factions,
  25, 27, 36, 143n 41; Villa and
  Anglos, 29, 36, 114, 143n 41,
  144n 65
Alonso, Ana María, 10, 11
Alonzo, Carmela, 62
Alpine race riot, 147–48n 3
American citizens/investments in
  Mexico, danger to, 41, 43–44,
  48, 70–72
American Defense Society, 160n 61
American Federation of Labor
  (AFL), 99
Americanization of border, 17
American National Livestock
  Association, 56
American Smelting and Refining
  Company, 57
ammunition, smuggling of, 25,
  104, 107
Anderson, Henry H., 32–34
Anderson, Maurice, 45, 46
Andreas, Peter, 125
Anglo cultural homogeneity,
  preservation of, 88–89, 118; See
  also nationalism, race-based;
  restrictionist sentiments
anti-Americanism; and Mexican
  Revolution, 41, 43–44; of Villa,

42–43, 43–44, 45, 75, 77, 82,
  115
Aoy, Olivas V., 40
Argudin, Raul, 59
Arizona; border security and racial
  identity in, 2; and Joint Task
  Force 6, 120; The Minuteman
  Project, 123, 157n 7; and
  National Guard deployment, 82;
  Senate Bill 1070, 123–24
arms, smuggling of, 25, 104, 107
arms embargo, 70
army, Mexican; and ineffectivity of
  forces, 70–71, 75, 76–77, 90;
  and retribution for jailhouse fire,
  64; and smugglers, 107–108;
  and tensions in Ciudad Juárez,
  53–54
Army, US, 113; and Brite Ranch
  raid, 29, 31; Operation Block
  It, 120; and Porvenir massacre,
  32–33; See also Cavalry, US; Fort
  Bliss, Texas; National Guard;
  Pershing, John J. "Blackjack"
Asian immigrants, 116; See also
  Chinese immigration
Asiatic Barred Zone Act (1917),
  97, 100, 101; See also Chinese
  immigration
assimilation issues, 3–4, 101, 122
attack (Mexican), fear of, 53, 71, 81,
  93, 94
"audience-directed" border
  enforcement, 125
authority structure in West Texas;
  development of, xix–xxi,
  xxii–xxiii, 110–113; and social
  economy, 8–12
Avila, Antonio, 30

Bagby, R. H., 59–60, 62–63
Bagley, R. H. See Bagby, R. H.
Bailey, John J., 32
Baker, Newton, 69, 80–81
bandits; and carrancista soldiers,
  56; definitions, 140n 44; raids
  on ranchers, 25, 26–27, 36–37,
  41, 71–72, 115; and Sitters–Cano
  feud, 27–29; stereotyping of,
  115; and vengeance, cycle of,
  18–19
Banuelos, Clemente, 120–21
baths, disinfecting, 57–59, 59–66,
  90–92

Battle of Celaya, 8, 43
Bell, George, Jr., 92
Benton-Cohen, Elizabeth, 2
Big Bend region, 28, 29–32, 32–34, 85
binational identity, 5, 11
biological/racial inferiority of Mexicans, imagined, 52, 93
"Black School," 40
Blaine Act (1933), 108
Bledsoe, William H., 35
Blocker, William P., 93
Boca Grande Ranch, 71
Bonner, H. F., 27
bootleggers, 104; See also alcohol
Borah, William E., 83
Border Patrol, US; and control of imported labor, 101–103; establishment of, 88, 89–90; and Great Depression, 100–101; historical perspective, 95–100; overview of roles and influence, 108–109, 116–117
borders, characterization of, 5–7, 9, 139n 19
border security; air patrols, 100; contemporary efforts, 120–26; early challenges, 83–84; National Guard, 80–83; See also Border Patrol, US; immigration policy; National Guard
"border trouble days," 3, 7–8, 20, 38, 69
boxing incident, 18, 23–24, 114
Bracero Program, 92–93, 108
"branding" of Mexicans, 88
Braun, Marcus, 90
Breen, Jack, 73
Brewer, Jan, 123–24
Brite, Lucas C., 29, 31–32
Brite Ranch raid, 29–32
Brownsville, Texas, 52, 56
Bryant, R. E., 24
Buenger, Walter L., 138n 15
buffalo soldiers, 22
Bush, George H. W., 120
Bush, George W., 123

Caldwell, Robert, 168n 108
California; Border Patrol sweeps in, 101; and Joint Task Force 6, 120; and Mexican labor, 97; and The Minuteman Project, 123; National Guard in, 82; typhus in, 154n 45
Calnan, George B., 57, 59–60, 61–62, 63, 65
cameras, border, 123
Campbell, Bob, 23
Camp Chigas, 100, 108
Camp Evetts, 32

Canadian border, 98
Canales, José T., 34–35
Candelaria Rim, 29
Cano, Chico, 17, 18, 27–29, 31–33
"Cano Gang," 28
Cardis, Louis, 21–22
Carothers, George C., 76–77, 82
carrancistas, 43, 53, 56
Carranza, Venustiano; ineffectivity of forces, 70–71, 75, 76–77, 90; and post-riot relations with US, 53–54; recognition as leader of Mexico by US, viii, 8, 42–43, 43–44, 79–80, 82; and Villa's movements, 70–71
Carrigan, William D., 10, 11
Casas Grandes River, 71
cattle industry. See ranchers
Cavalry, US, 22, 72, 73; See also Fort Bliss, Texas
Celaya, Battle of, 8, 43
census, 4, 99, 136
centralized control, challenges to, 5–6, 9, 11, 18, 23
Chadborn, Daniel J. "Buck," 74–75
Chamberlain, George E., 83
chemical baths, 57–59
Chevrolet commercials, 125
Chihuahua, Mexico (state); Free Trade Zone in, 40; and Mexican Revolution, 7–8; and Santa Ysabel massacre, 38, 43–45, 46, 47, 50–51, 54–55; Villa in, 70–71, 71–72, 76–77
Chihuahuita district; and "dead lines" policy, 50, 51, 68, 86, 113, 115–116, 117; and El Paso race riot, 48–50; National Guard in, 78–80, 82, 115; support for Villa in, 45; and typhus scare, 57–58, 66; vice industry in, 85–86
Chinese immigration
Chinese Consolidated Benevolent Association, 96
Chinese Division, Immigration Service, 95, 96
Chinese Exclusion Act (1882), 90, 95, 102
Chinese Inspectors, 97
Chinese Six Companies, 96
Chope, Chester, 104
citizen mobilization; contemporary, 122–23; and creation of "enemy other," 2; deputizations, 78; in El Paso, 77; Home Guards, 67–68, 70, 75–76, 79, 84, 116
citizenship status and "foreignness," 2, 45, 52, 122
Ciudad Chihuahua, 44
Ciudad Juárez; bath riots, 91–92; and El Paso race riot, 49, 53;

historical perspective, 12–13, 39–41; prizefight incident in, 22; and revolutionary activities, 8; "clean-up" of El Paso, post-riot, 49–50

Clint, Texas, 26

Coahuila, Mexico (state), 93

coal oil in delousing baths, 57, 58, 59, 60, 91–92

Coast Guard, US, 100

Cobb, Zachary Lamar; on disarming Mexicans in El Paso, 94; on hostilities in El Paso/Ciudad Juárez, 54, 55, 56; on instability in Mexico, 71; and Santa Ysabel massacre, 44; on Villa's movements, 67, 71, 75

Coke, Richard, 19–20

Colonia Morelos, Sonora, 42–43

Colquitt, Oscar, 67–68, 78–79

Columbus, New Mexico raid, 8, 67, 69, 70–72, 72–77, 80–81, 116

Comanches, 20

combat training for Border Patrol, 100; community division, racial, 3–4

Company B (Texas Rangers), 32

Company C (Texas Rangers), 22

Company D (Texas Rangers), 24–26, 114

containment policies; and El Paso race riot, 50, 51

contraband. See smuggling

contrabandistas, 105

Cordova (Cordoba) Island, 105–106, 108

Cortez, Gregorio, 52

courts martial, 85, 146–47n 107

criminalization of ethnic Mexicans, 7, 12–13, 25, 27, 66, 94, 115, 122, 125

Cross, H. M., 60, 61, 63

Culberson, Charles A., 23, 111, 114

cultural attachments of Mexicans, 51

cultural homogeneity (Anglo), preservation of, 88–89, 118; See also nationalism, race-based; restrictionist sentiments

Cusihuiriáchic Mining Company, 38, 44

Cusi Mines, 38, 44

Customs Service, US, 95, 100

Davidson, James, 19

DDT (insecticide), 93

"dead lines," 50, 51, 68, 86, 113, 115–116, 117

Deaver, James, M., 61, 62

Defense Department, US, 120–21

de Grazia, Sebastian, 10, 11

Delgado, Raul, 92–93

delousing baths, 57–59, 59–66, 90–92

Deming, New Mexico, 73–74

Department of Homeland Security, 172n 31

deportations, 99, 101

Detroit, Michigan, 100

Díaz, Porfirio, 7

discriminatory policies, modern, 123–24

disease, typhus scare, 57–59

Disease Act (1891), 90

disinfecting baths, 57–59, 59–66, 90–92

Doak, William, 100–101

docility of Mexicans, perception of, 21

Donnan, Hastings, 5–6

Downs, Douglas, 55

drugs, illegal, 103, 120, 123–24

Dunaway, J. D., 25

Dunn, Timothy, 2, 123

Durán, Bernardo, 54–55

Durán, Federico, 54–55

economic instability of Mexico (revolutionary), 26–27, 40–41, 56, 97

Edwards, Payton, 79

Edwards, Thomas D., 48, 53, 56, 75

Eighteenth Amendment, 94

Ellis Island, 96

El Paso, Texas; Border Patrol in, 90, 98, 100; citizen mobilization in, 78–79; economic consequences of quarantines, 92; immigration enforcement in, 95–97; jailhouse fire incident, 59–66, 72–73; race riot of 1916, 38–39, 45, 48–52; Santa Ysabel massacre, 38, 43–45; and smuggling, 104, 105–106

El Paso/Ciudad Juárez; historical perspective, 6–7, 39–41; pre-revolution immigration practices, 96; and Prohibition Era, 104–105; as reflection of transnational relations, 4–7, 41, 51, 110; tension, increase in, 1916, 54–56

El Paso del Norte, 40; See also Ciudad Juárez

El Paso Herald, 64, 65

El Paso Morning Times, 30

El Paso Times, 34

"El Segundo Barrio," 49

Emergency Army Bill 1917, 85–86

Emergency Quota Act (1921), 88–89, 99

"enemy other," creation of; and El Paso race riot, 50–52; and

"enemy other" (continued)
Mexican Revolution, 42–43; and militarization of border, 2–5, 67–69, 122–26; overview and perspective, 118–19; state's role in, 3; Texas Rangers' role in, 18
Enriquez, Ignacio, 38
ethnic cleansing, 17, 93
ethnic Mexican, definition, 137n 3
eugenic philosophy and immigration policy, 93, 97
European immigration, 96, 99, 116
exclusionary policies, 2
exemption of Mexican from immigration quotas, 98, 100
extortion of smugglers, 107–108

Fall, Albert B., 53
Favela, Juan, 72, 73–74
federal response to border unrest, 67–70, 77–80
federal troops. See army, US
fences on border, 105, 108, 123
Ferguson, James, 67–68, 80–81
Feuille, Frank, Jr., 61, 63
Fierro, Manuel, 32
fiscales, corruption of, 90, 107–108
Fitzgerald, Raymond, 33
Fitzsimmons, Bob, 18, 23
Florida coastline, 98
"foreignness" concept, 52
Fort Bliss, Texas; and El Paso race riot, 48–50; Joint Task Force 6, 120–21; manpower shortage and civilian vigilantism, 67–68; Pershing's diplomacy, 43; and San Elizario Salt War, 22; timeline records 1910–1916, 127–33; and violence in El Paso/Ciudad Juárez, 55–56
Fort Davis, Texas, 22
Fourteenth Amendment rights, 137n 6
Fourth Texas Infantry, 81
Fox, Jim M., 28–29, 32, 33–34, 143n 41
Fraere, Hilario, 72
Free Trade Zone, 40
Frontier Battalion (Rangers), 19–20, 21–22
frontier nature of West Texas, 5, 9, 18, 83
fumigation of Mexicans, 92–93; See also disinfecting baths
Funston, Frederick, 89

gambling, 18, 23–24, 85, 114
Gándara, Mecedonio, 21
García, Andrés G., 43, 44
García, Gregorio, 21
García, Héctor P., 52
Garner, Jolly, 74

Garnett, William Edward, 97
Garza, Catarino, 52
Gaskill, Mary Lee, 73
gasoline in delousing baths, 57
gassing (fumigation) of Mexicans, 92–93
Gavira, Gabriel; on inhumane disinfecting baths, 91; and jailhouse fire, 64; and tension in Ciudad Juárez, 53–54, 55–56; and typhus scare, 57, 58; on Villas movements, 67
General Motors commercials, 125
geography of region, challenges of, 29, 83, 85, 86, 116
German influence, fears of, 71, 89
Gibson Line Ranch, 72
GI Forum, 52
Gilchrist, James, 123
Gonzales, Eutimio, 32
good vs. evil dichotomy, 27
governors; of Arizona, 123–24; of Mexican states, 38, 93; of Texas; Charles Culberson, 23, 111, 114; James Ferguson, 67–68, 80–81; Oscar Colquitt, 67–68, 78–79; Richard Coke, 19–20; Rick Perry, 122–23
grand jury investigations, 61–63, 65, 121
Great Depression, 100–101
"great migration," 40–41
Griffin, Fred, 73
guest worker program, 102

Hall, Lee, 84
Hamer, Frank, 35
Hamilton, H. J., 88
Harley, James A., 26, 33–34
Harris, Charles H. III, 18
Harvis, J. A., 28
Hatfield, C. A. P., 79
Hayden, Frank, 71
"head tax," 97
health issues, 57–59, 59–66, 88, 90–92
Hernández, Esequiel, Jr., 120–21, 122
Hernández v. State of Texas, 137n 6
hijackings, 38, 43–45, 91
historical memory, 10, 24, 51
Holguin gang, 24
holocaust, jailhouse, 59–66, 72–73, 92
Home Guards, 67–68, 70, 75–76, 79, 84, 116
horses, theft of, 28–29, 73
Horsley, Hubert C., 98, 103, 106
Houghton, Susanna, 65
Howard, Charles, 21–22
Howard, Jack, 28
Hudspeth, Claude, 98
Huerta, Victoriano, 7–8, 79

Hughes, John R., 24, 25–26, 36, 114
human trafficking, 96, 104
Husk, Carlos, 57
Hutchison, Kay Bailey, 122

Immigrant Inspectors, 97
Immigration Act (1903), 90
Immigration Act (1917), 97, 100, 102
Immigration Act (1924), 88–89, 98, 99, 102, 116
Immigration Bureau, 98
immigration policy; Chinese immigration, 90, 95, 96, 97, 102; labor importation programs, 101–103; and Mexican labor, need for, 89, 90, 94, 97–98, 112; and militarization of border, 92–95; Quota Act (1921), 88–89, 99
Immigration Service, US, 90, 95–96, 102–103
Indians (America) and Texas Rangers, 17, 19–20
insecticide "baths," 93; See also delousing baths
integration. See assimilation issues
International Boundary Commission, 24
Internet and border security, 123
interventionist sentiments, 56, 79
invasion (Mexican), fear of, 53, 71, 80, 81, 93, 94
irredentist movement, 13, 80
isolation of West Texas, 5, 9, 18, 23, 96

Jackson, Dan M., 61
jailhouse fire incident, 59–66, 72–73, 92
Jim Crow practices, 137n 6
Johnson, Dewey, 59, 62
Johnson, Don, 64, 84
Johnson-Reed Act (1924), 98
Joint Task Force 6 (JTF6), 120
Jones, Frank, 24–25
Jones, John B., 20, 21–22
juntas, guarding against, 69–70, 77, 81
Justice Department, US, 108

Kelly, C. E., 79
Kelly, Thomas, 121
Kerber, Charles, 21, 22
kerosene in delousing baths, 57, 58, 59, 60, 91–92
kidnapping, 168n 108
Kiowas, 20
Ku Klux Klan, 99–100

Labor Advocate, 49–50, 51
Labor Department, US, 95, 98, 99, 102

labor force, Mexican; agricultural demand for, 8, 90, 97–98, 101–103, 117–18; and Chinese immigration, restriction of, 95, 96; and Great Depression, 100–101; growth of in El Paso, 40, 42; need for vs. immigration policy, 8, 97–98, 117–18
labor importation programs, 102–103
Langhorne, George T., 32
Lansing, Robert, 55, 67, 71, 82, 94
L.C. Brite Ranch, 29–32
Lea, Tom, 43, 64–65, 66
Lee, Erika, 3
lice, head and body, 57–59; See also delousing baths
"line riders," 95, 96
liquor. See alcohol
literacy requirement for immigration, 97
livestock, theft of, 25, 27, 28–29, 71–72
local vs. state government and vice industry, 23–24
Longoria, Félix, 52
López, Pablo, 38, 43, 44–45
Los Angeles, California, 101
Los Colorados, 70
low-intensity conflict doctrine, 2
Lucas, Edwin, 72, 73
lynchings, 10, 66, 68, 138n 15

machine guns, 73
Madero, Francisco, 7–8
Magoffin, Joseph, 21
Maher, Peter, 18, 22
marginalization of ethnic Mexicans, 2, 36, 66–67, 117–18, 124
María Juárez, José, 21
marijuana, 103
Marines, US, 120–21
Marshall, S. L. A., 168n 109
martial arts training for Border Patrol, 100
martial law in El Paso, 49–50, 51, 81
Martínez, Félix, 43
Martínez, Oscar, 9
mass migrations from Mexico, 2, 4, 8, 11, 38, 40–41, 90–91
matches and jailhouse fire. See jailhouse fire incident
mayors; Ciudad Juárez, 64; El Paso, 23, 43, 64–65, 66, 68, 79; McGowan, Edward, 60, 61, 63; McKenzie, Sam, 25; McKinney, Arthur, 72; McNelly, L. H., 20
media attention; Hernández shooting, 121; jailhouse fire, 61, 63–64; of militarization, 79; on post-Columbus raid mobilization, 76; smuggling,

media attention (*continued*)
103, 104; South Texas, tension in, 80; television ads, Mexicans in, 125–26; typhus scare, 58; on vice industry, 104
Medina Vieta, Manuel F., 53
mercenaries, 31
Mesa, Rosendo, 32
Messey, Dorothy, 30–31
Mexican, definition, 137n 3
Mexican Central Railroad Company, 40
"Mexican invasion," 97
"Mexicanization" of El Paso, 4, 42
Mexican Northwestern Railroad, 38
Mexican Revolution; and border conflicts, influence on, 5, 7–8, 38, 51, 69, 77, 111, 113–116; and mass migrations from Mexico, 2, 4, 8, 11, 38, 40–41, 88, 90–91; and mobilization of state militia, 77–78; and racial identity, 110–111; *See also* alliances
Meyers, Marshall W., 8–9
Michigan, Border Patrol in, 100
migrations from Mexico (mass), 2, 4, 8, 11, 38, 40–41
migratory identity, 3–4, 101–102
militarization, definition, 2
militarization of border; contemporary, 120–26; and "enemy other," creation of, 2–5, 67–69, 122–26; and Home Guards, 67–68, 70, 75–76, 79, 84, 116; and immigration policy, 92–95; and Mexican Revolution, 38–39; overview and perspective, 110–119; and typhus scare, 58; *See also* authority structure in West Texas; Border Patrol, US; National Guard
military doctrine, US, 2
Miller, Jeff, 95
mining industry, 25–26, 38, 40, 43–45
Minuteman Project, The, 123, 157n 7
Molina, Ernesto, 61, 63
Molina, Natalia, 154n 45
Montejano, David, 119
Moore, J. K., 73
Morris, Harry, 59, 60, 62–63
"mounted guard," 95
Murguía, Francisco, 92
mutilations, 33
"My Truck" ad campaign, 125–26

narcotics, 103
National Defense Act of 1916, 69–70, 81
National Guard; border emplacement, 81–83; contemporary border activities, 123; difficulties of West Texas duty, 83–86; dispersal of, wartime, 82–83; mobilization of, 68–69, 77–80, 116; overview of impact, 86–87
nationalism, race-based, 49–50, 51, 88–89, 93–94
nationalism and immigration policy, 99–100
nationalism of Mexicans, 93–94
National Prohibition Act (1919), 90; *See also* Prohibition
Native Americans and Texas Rangers, 17, 19–20
nativist sentiments, 89, 111–112; *See also* nationalism, race-based; restrictionist sentiments
Neill, Sam, 27, 30
Neill, Van, 29, 31
Nevins, Joseph, 122, 124–25
Newby, J. O. H., 44–45
New Mexico; Columbus raid by Villa, 8, 67, 69, 70–72, 80–81, 116; and Joint Task Force 6, 120; vigilantism in, 73–75
Ngai, Mae, 2, 52
Nieves, Román, 32
9/11, influence of, 122, 125

Obama, Barack, 123, 124
Obregón, Álvaro, 7, 43–44
O'Connor, J. P., 64
Operation Blockade, 1
Operation Block It, 120
Operation Hold the Line, 1
Operation Jump Start, 123
Orozco, Pascual, 7–8, 70, 80
Orozquistas, 93
Ortiz, Alfredo, 55

Palomas Land & Cattle Company, 71–72
Pancho Villa. *See* Villa, Francisco "Pancho"
"Patrol Inspectors," 98
Pearson, Chihuahua, Mexico, 70
pecan shellers' strike, 52
Perkins, Clifford Alan, 96
Perry, A. B., 59, 60, 63
Perry, Rick, 122–23
Pershing, John J. "Blackjack"; diplomacy at Fort Bliss, 43; and El Paso race riot, 49–50, 115; presence in Mexico, 93–94; Punitive Expedition, 8, 38, 68, 89, 94; recall of, 82, 89
Phelps, C. A., 64
photographing of women in baths, 90, 91
Pierce, Claude C., 57–58, 88, 91
Pilares, Mexico, 30, 31
Pino Suárez, José, 8

Pirate Island, 24–25
Plan de San Diego, 13, 56, 80, 82
politicization of border, contemporary, 122–25
Pool, John and Buck, 33
population growth; demographic 1880–1930, 134–35; of El Paso, 39–40, 81–82, 97; and mass migrations from Mexico, 2, 4, 8, 11, 38, 40–41, 90–91; and race relations, 4–5, 42, 51
Porvenir massacre, 18, 32–34
posse comitatus, 120
Powell, Colin, 120
Prieto, Manuel M., 64
prisoners, delousing of, 58, 59–66
prisoners, killing in custody, 22, 28, 35, 37, 115
privatization of lands, 21
prizefight incident, 18, 23–24, 114
"profiling" of Mexicans, 121, 123–24
Prohibition; and border issues, 103–108, 109, 112, 116; Eighteenth Amendment, passing of, 95; National Prohibition Act of 1919, 90; repeal of, 108; See also smuggling
prostitution, 85–86, 104
public health issues, 57–59, 59–66, 88, 90–92
Public Health Service, US (USPHS), 88
publicity stunts of Border Patrol, 101
public services and immigrants, 100–101
Puerto Rico, 120
Punitive Expedition, 8, 38, 68, 89, 94

quarantine regulations, 88, 91
Quota Act (1921), 88–89, 99

racial identity; and American national constructs, 2, 38–39, 40–41, 51; binational, 5, 11; contemporary issues, 124–26; marginalization of ethnic Mexicans, 2, 36, 66–67, 117–18, 124; and Mexican Revolution, 110–111
racialization of border; and immigration policy, 92–95; and Mexican Revolution, 38–39; San Elizario Salt War, 20–23; Texas Rangers' role in, overview, 35–37
railroads; closure of (Mexican), 56; and immigration enforcement, 96; Mexican Central Railroad Company, 40; Mexican Northwestern Railroad, 38; recruiting of Mexican labor, 102;

Santa Fe Railroad, 48; Southern Pacific Railroad, 20, 39; Texas Pacific Railroad, 20
Rak, Mary, 105
ranchers; bandit raids on, 25, 26–27, 36–37, 41, 71–72, 115; Brite Ranch raid, 29–32; and Mexican labor, need for, 98; and Mexican revolutionaries, alliances with, 7–8; and Sitters–Cano feud, 28–29; and Texas Ranger protection, 19–20
Rangers, Texas. See Texas Rangers
Recon Rangers, 122–23
Reconstruction (post Civil War), 19–20
recruiting of Mexican labor, 102–103, 109, 117
Red Flaggers, 70, 93
Redford, Texas, 120, 122
"Red Light" district, 86
reform of Texas Rangers, 35
refugees, revolutionary, 41–42, 81, 97
Renteria, Jesus "Pegleg," 31
restrictionist sentiments, 88, 93, 97, 99–100, 100–101, 112, 125
retaliatory actions. See vengeance/violence, cycle of
retributive acts. See vengeance/violence, cycle of
Revel's Commercial Hotel, 73
revenge actions. See vengeance/violence, cycle of
Reyes, Silvestre, 1
Riggs, Lee, 72
Rio Grande City, 52
Rio Grande Valley, 34–35, 52, 56; See also South Texas
riots; Alpine race riot, 147–48n 3; disinfecting baths, riots against, 90–92; El Paso, Texas race riot, 38–39, 45, 48–52
"Rocky Mountain Club of New York," 152n 5
Rodriguez, Juan, 84
Rodriguez, Samuel, 84
Romero, Manual Bonifacio, 45
Ross, Alex, 25
rules of military engagement, 121
rumrunners, 104–105, 106–107; See also alcohol

Sadler, Louis R., 18
safe conduct passes, 38, 44
Salt War, San Elizario, 18, 20–23, 24, 36
salvos conductos, 38, 44
Samora, Julian, 17, 19
San Antonio, Texas, 52
San Antonio Canyon, 25–26
San Antonio Express, 64

Sanchez, Armando A., 169nn 123–24
San Diego revolt, 27
San Elizario Salt War, 18, 20–23, 24, 36
sanitation baths, 57–59, 59–66, 89, 90–92
Santa Fe Bridge, 91
Santa Fe Railroad, 48
Santa Ysabel massacre, 38, 43–45, 46, 47, 50–51, 54–55
schools, 40, 58
Scotten, Frank, 59–60, 61, 63
Secure Fence Act (2006), 172n 31
segregation, racial, 3, 38, 50, 51, 68, 113, 117
Senate Bill 1070, 123–24
September 11, 2001 attacks, influence of, 122, 125
Shafter Mines incident, 25–26
Shutz, Solomon, 21
Silliman, John Reid, 94
Simcox, Chris, 123, 157n 7
Simmons, R. H., 45
Simpson, Bill, 107
Sitters, Joe, 18, 27–29
Slocum, Herbert, 72, 73
smallpox, 91
smelting industry, 40, 92
Smoot, Reed, 83
smuggling; alcohol, 6–7, 13, 90, 94, 95, 100, 103–108, 112, 116; arms/ammunition, 25, 104, 107; and Border Patrol enforcement, 103–108; and Customs Service enforcement, 95; drugs, 103, 120–22; duty-free goods, 40; illegal immigrants, 96, 104, 105; livestock, 29; Pirate Island, 24–25
Snyder, Tom, 33
social economy of border; and authority structure development, 8–12; historical perspective, 3–5, 6, 39–41, 117–19; Texas Rangers' influence on, 17–19
Soto, Ocario, 61, 63
Southern Pacific Railroad, 20, 39
South Texas; Plan de San Diego revolt, 13, 27, 56, 80, 82; Ranger violence in, 34–35; Tejano retaliatory activities in, 52
Southwest Texas State Normal School, 78
special census (1916), 4, 52, 136, 148–49n 16
Special Ranger force, 20, 35
Spencer, Buck "Babb," 71
"stamping" of Mexican, 88
stash houses, 105–106
state militia, 69; See also National Guard, mobilization of

state police forces. See Texas Rangers
state's role in creation of "enemy other," 3
steam-shower-disinfecting facilities, 57
stereotyping of Mexicans, 59, 68, 82, 115, 121, 125–26
Stern, Alexandra Minna, 91, 93
Stewart, Dan, 23
stigmatization and typhus scare, 58–59, 66
Stiles, Wesley, 98–99
streetcar incidents, 64, 91
"Support Our Law Enforcement and Safe Neighborhoods Act," 123–24
surveillance, border, 122–23
sweeps, Border Patrol, 101

Tampico, Tamaulipas, Mexico, 76, 79
Tappan, John W., 57, 59, 92
tariffs on trade zone goods, 40
Tays, John B., 21–22
technology and border security, 123
temperance laws, 90, 94; See also Prohibition
Temporary Admissions Program, 102
Tenayuca, Emma, 52
terrain of region, challenges of, 29, 83, 85, 86, 116
Texas Cattle Raisers Association, 28
Texas Department of Public Safety (DPS), 122
Texas Pacific Railroad, 20
Texas Rangers; and Chico Cano, feud with, 27–29, 31–32; contemporary activities, 122–23; and criminal activity, local, 24–25; and Hernández shooting, 121; historical perspective, 19–20; investigation and reform of, 34–35; overview and impacts of, 17–19, 35–37, 114–115, 117; Porvenir massacre, 32–34; and San Elizario Salt War, 20–23; as troublemakers, 26
Texian, 78
"This Is Our Country" ad campaign, 125–26
Thomas, G. N., 58
Thomas, J. F. "Jack," 74
Thompson, Herbert H., 65
Tompkins, Frank, 74
Torreon, Chihuahua, Mexico, 76–77
Torres, Carmelita, 91
training, Border Patrol, 100
Treaty of Guadalupe Hidalgo, 137n 6
typhus fever scare, 57–59, 90–92

unemployment, 40, 100–101
US–Mexico relations and Mexican Revolution, 41–42, 93–94

Valentine, Texas, 28, 29
Van Horn, Texas, 84
Vaughn, Jeff, 26
Vázquez, Juan, 44
Vedder, Simon, 22
vengeance/violence, cycle of, 18–19; Brite Ranch raid, 29–32; Columbus, New Mexico raid, 8, 67, 69, 70–72, 72–77, 80–81, 116; El Paso race riot of 1916, 38–39, 45, 48–52; and frontier culture, 10; and murder of Frank Jones, 24–25; overview, 112–114; Porvenir massacre, 32–34; and ranch raids, 26–27; San Elizario Salt War, 18, 20–23, 24, 36; Santa Ysabel massacre, 38, 43–45, 46, 47, 50–51, 54–55; Sitters–Cano feud, 27–29
Veracruz, American occupation of, 78
vice industry; in Chihuahuita, 85–86; in Ciudad Juárez, 104; local vs. state government, 23–24; prostitution, 85–86, 104; and temperance laws, 94
vigilantism; Columbus, New Mexico, 73–75; and Home Guards, 67–68, 70, 75–76, 79, 84, 116; Shafter Mine incident, 25–26; See also vengeance/violence, cycle of
Villa, Francisco "Pancho"; alliances with Anglos, 29, 36, 114, 143n 41, 144n 65; anti-Americanism of, 42–43, 43–44, 45, 75, 77, 82, 115; and Chico Cano, relationship with, 30–31; as hero to Mexicans, 43, 45; on jailhouse fire incident, 65–66; Madero, opposition to, 8; raid on Columbus, New Mexico, 67, 69, 70–72, 72–77; revolutionary encounters, 8; Santa Ysabel massacre, 38, 43–45, 46, 47, 50–51, 54–55
Villanueva, Placido, 31
Villegas, Hortencia, 38, 48, 49, 50
villistas, 38, 43
vinegar in delousing baths, 57, 58, 60

violence. See vengeance/violence, cycle of
Virgin Islands, US, 120
Virtual Border Watch Program, 123 "voluntary return" option, 99
"Volunteers to Defend Nation," 93

Waco, Texas, 10
wages of laborers, 102, 103
"War on Drugs," 120–22
Warren, Harry, 32, 33
Washington, Jesse, 10
Watson, C. R., 44
Weber, C. Edward, 9–10
Wells, Homer, 26
West Texas; Border Patrol in, 98; definition, 137n 2; historical perspective, 110–119; isolation of, 5, 9, 18, 23, 96; National Guard in, 67; as reflection of transnational relations, 3–4, 110; terrain of region, challenges of, 29, 83, 85, 86, 116; Texas Rangers' presence in, 23–24
Whalen, W. A., 99
white/black racial tension, 38
"whiteness"; and American national constructs, 2, 38–39, 40–41, 51; definition, 137n 6; and Mexicans as enemy other, 68
Wilmuth, Grover C., 104
Wilson, Thomas, 5–6
Wilson, William B., 102
Wilson, Woodrow; criticism of by whites, 152n 5; on invasion possibility, 79; and militarization of border, 79; recognition of Carranza as leader of Mexico, viii, 8, 42–43, 43–44, 79–80, 82
women (Mexican), activism of, 91–92
World War I, 82–83, 97, 102
Wray, John W., 61
Wright, E. A. "Dogie," 103, 106–107
Wright, Ed, 70, 71
Wright, Maude, 70–71, 72, 73
Wright, S. A., 25–26

xenophobia and policy, 124

Yrias, Daniel, 63
Ysleta, Texas, 21–22

Zapata, Emiliano, 7
Zimmerman, Jack, 121, 122